Road to Mach 10: Lessons Learned from the X-43A Flight Research Program

John J. Spravka

Road to Mach 10: Lessons Learned from the X-43A Flight Research Program

Curtis Peebles
Analytical Services and Materials, Inc.
History Office, NASA Dryden Flight Research Center
Edwards, California

LIBRARY
OF FLIGHT

Ned Allen, Editor-in-Chief
Lockheed Martin Corporation
Palmdale, California

Published by
American Institute of Aeronautics and Astronautics, Inc.
1801 Alexander Bell Drive, Reston, VA 20191-4344

Quotations that open each chapter were taken from *Great Aviation Quotes*,
http://www.skygod.com/quotes/index.html.

American Institute of Aeronautics and Astronautics, Inc., Reston, Virginia

1 2 3 4 5

Library of Congress Cataloging-in-Publication Data

Peebles, Curtis.
  Road to Mach 10 : lessons learned from the X-43A flight research program / Curtis Peebles.
    p. cm.
  Includes bibliographical references.
  ISBN 978-1-56347-932-8 (alk. paper)
  1. X-43A (Hypersonic plane) [proposed] 2. Dryden Flight Research Facility--History.
3. United States. National Aeronautics and Space Administration--Research. 4. Hypersonic
planes--Research--United States. I. Title.

  TL567.R47P435 2008
  629.133'349--dc22   2007050605

Cover design by Virginia Kozlowski

For I dipped into the future, far as human eye could see,
Saw the Vision of the world, and all the wonder that would be;
Saw the heavens fill with commerce, argosies of magic sails,
Pilots of the purple twilight, dropping down with costly bales.

Alfred, Lord Tennyson, "Locksley Hall," 1842

FOREWORD

The Library of Flight is part of the growing portfolio of information services from the American Institute of Aeronautics and Astronautics. It augments the two established book series of the Institute—the Progress in Astronautics and Aeronautics Series and the AIAA Education Series—with the best of a growing variety of other topics in aerospace from aviation policy, to case studies, to studies of aerospace law, management, and beyond. Curtis Peebles' fine recounting of the X-43 story, beginning with the roots of its technology development and extending through to the milestone flight tests, is a prime example of the intent of the Library of Flight Series. The X-43 program remains an important milestone along the way to realization of the dreams of hypersonic flight and low cost access to space.

The Library of Flight seeks to document the crucial role of aerospace in enabling, facilitating, and accelerating global commerce, communication, and defense. Distinct from the Institute's other series, the lively Library of Flight authors often express opinions on matters of policy and controversy. As new aerospace programs grow and change around the world, we plan for the Library to host a wide array of international authors, expressing their own points of view on aerospace visions, events, and issues. As the demands on the world's aerospace systems grow to support new capabilities like unmanned vehicles, international relief, agricultural management, environmental monitoring, and others, the series will seek to document the landmark events, emerging trends, and new views.

Curtis Peebles is an experienced and widely respected author, and he is a very welcome contributor to the series.

Ned Allen
Editor-in-Chief
Library of Flight

TABLE OF CONTENTS

PREFACE: THE HISTORIAN AS PARTICIPANT

This book is the result of an opportunity rarely available to an historian. In the late summer of 2004, as the third and final X-43A flight neared, I was assigned to be the project historian. The goal was to produce a lessons-learned history of the X-43 project. The planned audience was aerospace undergraduates, to give them an understanding of the difficulties they will face working on an advanced project. Many histories of aeronautical and space projects have been written, but typically these were done years or even decades after the project ended.

With the X-43 history, I was a participant in the events as they unfolded. I received e-mail updates and documents, I attended the engineering meetings, I witnessed the emergency procedure training of the flight controllers, I was at the flight readiness review and the preflight briefings, and I watched the third flight from one of the control rooms. Finally, I had access to the project engineers and personnel. After the third flight, I interviewed many of the X-43A engineers and managers at the NASA Dryden Flight Research Center about their still-fresh experiences and recollections.

This gives the account an immediacy often lacking in traditional history. The story is told in the words of those who lived it. It was often a difficult experience. The history of hypersonics is marked with high hopes and repeated disappointments. The engineers working on the X-43A experienced both difficulties and success. The development took longer than expected. When launch day finally came, the first flight ended within seconds of the launch. This was followed by the mishap investigation, then a three-year return-to-flight effort, when the project underwent a detailed technical review. In 2004, the second and third X-43A flights were made, reaching speeds of nearly Mach 7 and 10 and providing the first data from a scramjet engine in flight.

Finally, the book would not have been possible without the assistance of the X-43A project personnel. They welcomed a stranger into their midst, answering my many questions regarding the physics and technology involved in the flight. Because of them, I was able to be part of this extraordinary experience. They have my thanks.

Curtis Peebles
November 2007

Chapter 1

INTRODUCTION

> A single lifetime, even though entirely devoted to the sky, would not be enough for the study of so vast a subject. A time will come when our descendants will be amazed that we did not know things that are so plain to them.
>
> *Seneca, Book 7, First Century A.D.*

During an aerospace engineer's undergraduate studies, he or she will attend classes in aerodynamics, thermodynamics, structures, stability and control, dynamics, design, propulsion, and computer science, along with the related courses in mathematics, physics, statistics, and chemistry required to understand the material. Upon graduation, the new engineer will have acquired a basic knowledge of how to build an aerospace vehicle.

What only comes through experience, however, is the understanding of the inevitable imperfect process through which an aerospace vehicle *is* built. This is the adventure of turning a basic concept into functional hardware. Engineers working on a project must often deal with ambiguous situations. They are routinely asked by management to provide risk assessments of a project, yet even after careful analysis uncertainties remain. The project must be accomplished within finite limits of time and money. The question an engineer answers is whether the solution to a potential problem is worth the cost and schedule delay, or if the solution might actually be worse than the problem it is meant to solve. Review protocols are established to ensure that an unknown has not been overlooked. But these cannot protect against an unknown that has not been recognized.

Examples of these situations can be found in the history of the X-43A Hyper-X (Hypersonic Experiment) program. In this NASA project, a supersonic combustion ramjet (scramjet) engine was flight tested on a subscale vehicle. The X-43A Hyper-X Research Vehicle (HXRV) was launched from a B-52B mothership and then boosted to the test speed by a modified Pegasus rocket first stage, called the Hyper-X Launch Vehicle (HXLV). Once at the proper speed and altitude, the X-43A separated from the booster, stabilized itself, and then the engine test began.

The focus of this book is on the X-43A flight activities at the NASA Dryden Flight Research Center. It documents the experiences of the personnel working on flight preparation, integration, and flights of the project, and the lessons they learned in the process. It is not intended as a formal history of the complete X-43A Hyper-X Program, and as such it does not give an overall perspective.

Although wind-tunnel scramjet engine tests had begun in the late 1950s, before the Hyper-X program there had never been an actual in-flight test of such an engine integrated with an appropriate airframe. Thus, although the scramjet had successfully operated in the artificial airflow of wind tunnels, the concept had yet to be proven in "real air." These conditions meant changes in density and temperature, as well as changes in angle of attack and sideslip of a free-flying vehicle. A wind tunnel is limited in its ability to simulate these subtle factures, which have a major impact on almost any vehicle, but especially that of a scramjet's performance.

The Hyper-X project was to provide a real-world benchmark of the ground-test data. The full-scale X-43A engine would be operated in the wind tunnel, and then flown, and the data from its operation would then be compared with projections. If these matched, the wind-tunnel data would be considered a reliable design tool for future scramjet. If there were significant differences, the reasons for these would have to be identified. Until such information were available, scramjets would lack the technological maturity to be considered for future space launch or high-speed atmospheric flight vehicles.

DEVELOPMENT OF THE SCRAMJET

The basic concept of airbreathing jet propulsion began with the ramjet. This was the result of theoretical studies by René Lorin in France during the years prior to the outbreak of World War I. The ramjet is the simplest form of an airbreathing engine. A cone-shaped spike in the inlet creates a shock wave that slows incoming air to subsonic velocity. As a result, the kinetic energy of the mass of high-speed air entering the engine is converted into pressure in the combustion chamber. (This is referred to as "pressure recovery.") Fuel is then injected into the combustion chamber from a set of spray bars. The fuel mixes with the compressed air, and the air/fuel mixture is ignited, with a flame holder providing stable combustion. The hot exhaust gases produced expand out through a convergent/divergent nozzle to produce thrust. The engine is a simple tube, with no turbine blades or other moving parts.

Despite development efforts between the 1930s and the 1950s, the ramjet had only niche roles, such as target drones or surface-to-air missiles. This was caused by a basic limitation of the design. A ramjet could not be started unless air was already flowing through the engine. The vehicle must have a separate propulsion system, such as a rocket booster, to accelerate it to a speed where the ignition sequence would occur. The added weight and complexity of a separate propulsion system was a major limiting factor. A ramjet-powered fighter, for example, proved to be impractical, as it still required a turbojet engine for takeoff. Any performance gains would be reduced or eliminated by the weight of the secondary propulsion system.

Additionally, the top speed of a ramjet vehicle was limited to about Mach 6. This was because, as the incoming air was slowed to subsonic speed and compressed, it also heated up. Eventually, the internal heating would reach a point at which it damaged the vehicle's structure.[1]

The solution to the heating problem was for the combustion to occur in a supersonic airflow. By the mid-1950s, some tests had been done with supersonic combustion in the base of artillery shells and with external combustion on a wing's surface to improve performance. National Advisory Committee for Aeronautics (NACA) researchers at the Lewis Flight Propulsion Laboratory attempted to test the idea's feasibility by burning aluminum borohydride in a supersonic wind tunnel. During these tests, sustained burning was believed to have been observed at Mach 1.5, Mach 2, and Mach 3, and for as long as 2 seconds.[2]

This study on *external* supersonic combustion in a wind tunnel's airflow inspired Richard J. Weber and John B. MacKay, who were researchers at Lewis, to consider sustained *internal* supersonic combustion within a supersonic airflow. If this were possible, they concluded, the engine's performance could be improved and internal heating reduced. Weber and MacKay were encouraged by these positive results and undertook a theoretical analysis of scramjet engine design elements in the mid-1950s.

Weber and MacKay were the first researchers to identify the design requirements needed to build a successful scramjet engine. These included an inlet design that would maximize pressure recovery, the effects of combustion temperature, the nozzle velocity and expansion ratio, combustion area and cooling loads, wall friction, the need to minimize nozzle pressure losses, and the advantages of using hydrogen as the fuel. Their report indicated that a scramjet was more efficient at speeds above Mach 5 than were conventional ramjets.[3]

Ironically, the study was a low-priority effort that Weber and MacKay thought would spark little interest and that would have few practical applications. It was not published until September 1958, only a month before the NACA became NASA, and Weber and MacKay's study came at a time of growing interest in hypersonic propulsion technology.

The same year their report was published, the first ground test of a scramjet was made, by Fred Billig and G. L. Dugger of Johns Hopkins University's Applied Physics Laboratory (APL). Billig and Dugger successfully achieved positive thrust with a small scramjet model, burning aluminum alkyl fuel, in a Mach 5 airflow, and the two researchers were subsequently awarded the first scramjet patent. APL followed up on this initial effort with, in the early 1960s, work on inlets, fuel injectors, and combustor designs. Antonio Ferri also conducted wind-tunnel scramjet tests at the General Applied Sciences Laboratory (GASL), a private engineering firm. He was best known, however, for his passionate advocacy of scramjets as a hypersonic propulsion system for a reusable orbital launch vehicle.[4]

A scramjet uses oxygen from the atmosphere. A rocket, in contrast, carries its own supply of both fuel and oxidizer. Although this means a rocket can operate in a vacuum, having to carry both propellants also means greatly increased vehicle size and weight. In contrast, a scramjet-powered vehicle carries only its fuel, as the oxygen come from the atmosphere. This translated into several important advantages. Not only is a scramjet-powered vehicle smaller and lighter than a rocket, but the engine's efficiency, called the "specific impulse," is greatly increased. The specific impulse of a rocket using oxygen and hydrogen is just over 400 seconds, while a hydrogen-fueled scramjet has, in theory, a specific impulse of over 3000 seconds at Mach 7, and over 2000 seconds at Mach 10 speeds.

The idea of an orbital vehicle powered by an airbreathing propulsion system fit well with existing concepts of how human spaceflight would be accomplished. During the 1950s, aeronautical engineers had assumed that spaceflight would come about through a series of experimental aircraft. Each experimental aircraft would fly faster and higher than the previous one, until one would eventually reach orbit. This aircraft paradigm, and the emergence of the scramjet, came at a time of technological optimism. Between the 1940s and the early 1960s, flight had gone from piston-engine aircraft to manned orbital spacecraft. During the next decade, the United States planned to land a man on the moon. There was a firm belief that such technological advances would continue to be made, and that all things were possible.[5]

The first attempt to build a scramjet-powered vehicle was the U.S. Air Force's Aerospaceplane program of the late 1950s and early 1960s. Republic Aircraft enlisted Ferri and GASL engineers to assist with design of the orbital vehicle. Ferri proposed a scramjet propulsion system that operated from Mach 8 to orbital speeds of Mach 25. General Dynamics, Lockheed, Douglas, Boeing, Goodyear, and North American Aviation all undertook studies of different designs and operational concepts. The appeal of the Aerospaceplane concept was that it promised routine and lower-cost access to space. Proposed missions for an operational vehicle included orbital resupply, space rescue, orbital strike missions, and low-cost launch of satellites.

But the Aerospaceplane had a number of basic problems. Its single-stage-to-orbit design, for example, required a highly speculative lightweight structural design. The massive scramjets that would propel these huge vehicles to near-orbital speeds existed only as small-scale wind-tunnel test models. In 1962 the

Model of the proposed delta wing X-15 vehicle. The aircraft could have been used for tests of various airbreathing propulsion systems had it been approved. (NASA photo E65-13857.)

Air Force shifted the Aerospaceplane program toward a two-stage-to-orbit vehicle. Despite the change in focus, however, problems continued, and the program ended when Congress eliminated fiscal year 1964 funding.[6]

This did not mean the end of work on scramjet development efforts in the 1960s and 1970s. NASA's Hypersonic Research Engine (HRE) emerged as the Aerospaceplane program was ending in the early 1960s. The original HRE concept called for the engine to be flight tested on the NASA/Air Force X-15A-2 rocket plane. The aircraft had been rebuilt following a crash landing in November 1962 and now carried two large external tanks to increase the vehicle's top speed to about Mach 8, while an ablative heat shield covered the aircraft to protect it from thermal damage at the higher velocity. The fuselage also was stretched to accommodate a small liquid hydrogen tank and plumbing for the scramjet. The HRE would be attached to the X-15A-2's lower fin.

The X-15A-2 with its ablative heat-shield coating. This was to provide additional protection from the higher heat load the vehicle would experience at speeds near Mach 8 at altitudes of about 100,000 feet. (NASA photo E67-17336.)

The dummy Hypersonic Research Engine (HRE) attached to the lower fin of the X-15A-2. The dummy engine had no working parts and was intended to check the aerodynamic effects on the X-15's flight characteristics. (NASA photo E67-17493.)

In the spring of 1967, the X-15A-2 was ready to begin research flights with a dummy HRE on its lower fin. On October 3, 1967, it reached a maximum speed of Mach 6.7. Because of unexpected heating problems caused by shock waves from the dummy HRE, the lower fin burned through, and the X-15A-2 was badly damaged. The X-15A-2 never flew again, and the X-15 program ended in December 1968, after 199 flights. Without a hypersonic vehicle to carry the engine, the HRE flight-test program was cancelled, and the effort was reduced to a wind-tunnel test effort.

HRE engines were ground tested between 1971 and 1973, with disappointing results. The engine's design shortcomings included a shallow annular duct, large drag-producing surfaces, and high internal friction and heating. In ground tests, the HRE inlet design resulted in huge total-pressure losses within the combustor. Tests of the airflow through the HRE, without combustion, showed a 75% inlet pressure recovery loss. When fuel was burned, the loss was greater still. To compound the problem, only 48% of the fuel was burned in the combustor. The HRE's thrust was so low that it was cancelled out by the engine's own external drag.[7]

In retrospect, the failure of the HRE program was inevitable. Its fatal flaw lay in the fact that the actual state of scramjet technology did not match the

Fin damage to the X-15-A2 after the October 3, 1967, flight to Mach 6.7. The shock waves from the HRE inlet spike caused shock-on-shock heating, which burned through the heat shield and the steel skin of the lower fin. (NASA photos E67-17526 and -17527.)

The dummy HRE after being found in the desert. The heat damaged its attachment to the lower fin, and it fell off the X-15A-2 during the landing approach. (NASA photo E67-17537.)

overly optimistic claims being made about it. Ferri said in a 1964 lecture that supersonic combustion flow, which was critical to scramjet design, had reached the stage of "complete understanding." In response to a question at the end of the lecture, Ferri qualified this, explaining that the "complete understanding" remark applied only to simplified flow models. Actual supersonic combustion, Ferri added, was "too complex to be calculated."

He was not alone in his optimism. An Air Force–sponsored study, Project Forecast, recommended in 1964 that a high-priority national scramjet development effort be undertaken. In support of this recommendation, a number of sweeping claims were made. The study text flatly stated that, "Supersonic combustion can be mix-controlled to Mach 25," yet added that, "successful future research is forecast to provide a sufficiently large body of information for actual combustor design."

The planning and development of the HRE were influenced by this optimism. The NASA proposal for the Phase I work on the HRE stated that scramjet design had advanced to the point that "gaps" in component technology "had been filled." This, the proposal continued, left uncertainties "which can be discovered and resolved only by design and construction of a truly practical research engine."

Institutional issues and political factors also shaped the history of the HRE program. Some believed that the correct approach to developing scramjet technology was through ground testing. K. F. Rubert, who was NASA Langley Research Center's leading expert on scramjet technology, said in a 1963 memo that engine research and development "is better done on the ground," and that "there is no genuine need [for flight tests]."

Engineers in Langley's Aero Physics Division disagreed with his assessment, however. For many years, the Aero Physics Division had worked on propulsion-related fluid dynamics and hypersonic inlet/diffuser design, but their efforts lacked real-world applications. Having the division involved in development of a real scramjet for the X-15 flight tests would revitalize their efforts. Additionally, there were no existing scramjet ground-test facilities that could provide realistic simulations at speeds above Mach 5. Higher-speed simulations, such those of Mach 7 or 8, could only be done at that time with combustion-heated air. This process contaminated the air with large amounts of water vapor. Several methods had been proposed for simulating these high Mach numbers with "clean air" (i.e., not contaminated by water vapor), but all had shortcomings.

Flight testing of the HRE with the X-15 would eliminate all of these issues. Thus the aircraft represented a unique engine-test opportunity otherwise not available. The ability to test a scramjet in the actual environment of hypersonic flight was an important reason the HRE program gained support. The engine's performance would be measured in ground tests, and then measurements would be made in actual flight, from Mach 3 to 8. These data would then be used to validate both the various ground-based test procedures and the projections of scramjet performance.

Using the X-15 also filled a political role. Although scramjet advocates were vocal, there also were a large number of researchers and engineers who were skeptical about the scramjet concept. Many believed that scramjets would never be a viable concept, as they felt the engines' technical problems, such as efficient supersonic combustion, could never be solved. These individuals had less visibility than the scramjet supporters, but had a significant influence nevertheless on attitudes toward any scramjet development efforts.

From these competing demands, opinions, and conflicts, an opinion developed that the only means of overcoming the skeptics would be for the ground-based research program to be tied to development and flight testing of an X-15 scramjet engine. Without such an approach, scramjets would not be considered a reality, no matter how much ground testing was done. Most important of all from a political viewpoint, NASA headquarters would not approve a major scramjet research effort unless the ultimate goal was actual flight tests. This propulsion research would also benefit the X-15 program. By 1964, the aircraft had completed its speed and envelope expansion flights and was beginning to fly a series of scientific and technological experiments. The HRE would provide added justification for continuing the X-15 program.[8]

The troubled history of the HRE illustrates how the complex mix of technology, policy, and happenstance influences aerospace projects. In contrast to the Aerospaceplane, the HRE was a relatively small-scale/short-term effort. It was originally to cost $30 million and take four years. But despite this difference, the HRE had the same basic flaw as the Aerospaceplane—that scramjet technology was still too immature to be workable.

Ideally, a basic research program should have been conducted to fill the technological gaps before any commitment was made to a full-fledged scramjet development program. This had been the recommendation of the 1964 Air Force panel looking at scramjet development. Despite its optimistic tone, the panel had cautioned that any flight-test programs should await establishment of a firm technological basis from ground tests. Instead, the debate between the supporters and critics of scramjets shaped the program. Between the salesmanship of the believers and the doubts of the skeptics, there emerged the political necessity of a flight program.

This debate and the resulting plans for a flight program underline the issue of what drives technological innovation. Is necessity really the mother of invention, or does an invention create its own need? The history of science and technology give examples to support both possibilities, but the underlying trend is often that development is nonlinear. There are many cases where new inventions and scientific concepts were ignored, only to be independently reinvented years or decades later. The often-ignored forces behind such events are social, cultural, political, and national needs and influences.

The X-15's role in the HRE project is one example of this nonlinearity. It was a matter of both happenstance and opportunity. The X-15 was built to investigate the high-speed/high-altitude flight regime. Propulsion research was not considered to have a role in its flight research program. This changed when the second X-15 suffered an engine problem after launch and was forced to make an emergency landing on an uprange lake bed. The aircraft was heavy with fuel, causing one of the tail skids to collapse, and the X-15 to overturn.

Rather than simply repairing the damage, North American Aviation, the airplane's builder, proposed it be rebuilt with a Mach 8 capability. Among the proposed missions for the X-15A-2 were tests of different airbreathing engine concepts. The HRE fitted into this effort. Use of the X-15 also provided a way around the shortcomings of ground facilities for testing scramjet engines. The situation can be likened to the X-1 being used in the late 1940s for supersonic data that existing wind tunnels could not provide.

Initially, the HRE had the support of senior NASA headquarters officials. Hugh L. Dryden, the NASA deputy administrator, had earlier expressed support for research engine activities and had backed the modification of the X-15A-2. Robert Seamans, the NASA associate administrator, also favored the HRE. Approval also addressed a political need. Seamans had been pressured to increase aeronautical funding, and the HRE provided an easy means to this end.

The lack of basic scramjet technology became apparent following the HRE's approval and the selection of the Garrett corporation as the prime contractor for the HRE project. Costs quickly increased, the schedule began to stretch, and the project goals diminished. The technological optimism that marked the HRE project's beginning soon gave way to the reality of tighter budgets amid the social and political turmoil of the late 1960s. The new NASA managers who replaced Dryden and Seamans had little interest in the HRE and were just as quick to cut back the effort when problems appeared. The X-15 program ended, flight tests were dropped, and testing reverted to a limited and trouble-plagued ground-based program before finally being cancelled. Even after a decade of work, the HRE was still years away from being ready for actual flights.[9]

Looking back on the events of the HRE program, a basic question is apparent. Would a generalized research program have been a better approach? Or did the HRE, for all its failures and disappointments, advance scramjet technology more quickly and efficiently than would have a step-by-step research effort? Assessments by the participants differ.

John V. Becker, a senior official at Langley during the HRE period who later wrote a history of the program, offered one perspective. He had initially been positive toward HRE during the project's early years. But he noted that between 1967 and 1970 this opinion changed radically. The Langley researchers' understanding of scramjets had been greatly expanded by their involvement with the HRE. As they learned more about such issues as scramjet engine installations, however, it became increasingly apparent that the pod-shaped HRE, with its zero net thrust and shallow annular flow passages, would provide little useful information for future scramjet designs.

Other viewpoints on the efficiency of step-by-step research vs a focused project like the HRE include those of A. DuPont of Garrett. He designed the HRE and was its first project engineer at Garrett; he believed that the HRE went a long way in proving that scramjets were a reality, even though the engine never flew. H. Lopez, who was Garrett's second HRE project engineer, felt the major value of the HRE was in "putting it all together." This included designing control systems that were compatible with combustor requirements and demonstrating that all of the elements required for a real scramjet could be integrated into a complete system.

E. A. Mackley, the HRE project manager at NASA from 1973 to 1975, argued that a project like the HRE enjoyed a higher level of funding and could operate on faster schedules than general research programs. Thus, he contended, they could provide data that would be either impossible to achieve through general research, or that would take longer and cost more. Mackley gave as an example the ground structural testing done on the HRE; this, he believed, could not have been undertaken as a general research project by the Langley structures groups.

Ferri's comments on the HRE were more wide-ranging. He argued that NASA was inexperienced with scramjets and "did not trust advanced concepts based on the most sophisticated level of technology existing in 1964." Ferri also said that the HRE design was too complicated for the time and money available. The HRE, in his view, was too much like a prototype engine, with all flight subsystems represented. He believed that NASA should have concentrated on a simple aerothermodynamic demonstration using a boilerplate engine structure. A useful flight research program, he thought, could have been accomplished had this approach been taken. He added that this approach could have also been done within the original schedule and cost limits.

Of the HRE ground tests conducted, Ferri felt that the structural testing was the only accomplishment of real merit. Ferri argued that these tests could have been done at any time, however, with any of the proposed engine designs and did not require a flight research program. He considered that the rest of the ground tests were valuable only as examples of what not to do. As for scramjet work at Langley that followed the HRE, he believed that the research was based on the approach he recommended (i.e., advanced concepts based on the most sophisticated level of technology), but that the effort was moving too slowly and cost more than would a more vigorous and better-funded program.[10]

The Aerospaceplane and the HRE offer many lessons to those trying to turn scramjets' potential into operational reality. The first was to not mistake potential for reality. Scramjet backers offered salesmanship that was not supported by a thorough understanding of the physics and technology that were required. Efforts made in this direction during the 1960s did little to resolve this lack of knowledge. Despite the efforts of many researchers, a workable scramjet had yet to be designed by the end of the 1960s. Each of the engine's separate elements had flaws still needing to be corrected.

The rush to undertake a flight research program further complicated the issue. This debate involved the conflict between the optimistic picture painted by the scramjet's supporters, the doubts expressed by the skeptics, and resulting need for a hypersonic flight-test program to demonstrate that a scramjet could work. Shortcomings in the available ground-test facilities was another factor, one that the X-15 flights could address.

There is also the larger issue of what should be the goals of publicly funded research. The NACA had not focused on pure research, but rather on applications. These ranged from wind-tunnel studies of different airfoil shapes, with the data used in designing new aircraft, to wartime efforts to reduce the drag of production aircraft in order to increase their performance. Requesting funding for "pure" research, without a direct, near-term application, posed political difficulties for a government organization. In practical terms, in order to get funding for research on scramjet technology, a flyable engine had to be the end result of the effort. Whatever positive results came from the HRE research, the failure to successfully build a flight engine caused the whole program to be seen as a failure. As a result, scramjet research was set back, and it was impossible to gain political support for many years afterward.

There were many lessons to be learned from these first attempts to build a scramjet. But they were not learned.

AIRFRAME-INTEGRATED SCRAMJET

By the early 1970s, a new scramjet concept began to emerge among researchers at Langley. It was a very different design from those of the proposed HRE scramjets that would simply be bolted onto the X-15's lower fin; researchers realized by the early 1970s that these pod-type engines simply would not work. The new scramjet engine design was called the *airframe-integrated scramjet.* As the name suggests, the new concept was not meant to simply bolted onto the airframe, as separate part, but rather were fully integrated with it. If the scramjet were to make maximum efficient use of airflow and exhaust, the compression process would have to begin at the vehicle's nose and the exhaust expansion continue out to the end of its fuselage.[11]

Unlike the barrel-shaped HRE, an airframe-integrated scramjet engine was rectangular in shape, with an inlet wider than it was high. Several of these scramjet modules were mounted side by side on the underside of the fuselage. Both the inlet shape and the multiple modules were designed to make maximum use of the airflow, which on an aircraft is wider than it is high.

The underside of the vehicle's forward fuselage served as the inlet ramp for the airframe-integrated scramjet. The ramp was divided into several

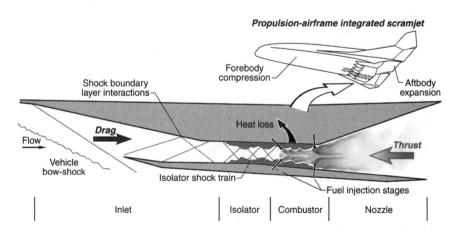

Simplified diagram of an airframe-integrated scramjet engine. Unlike the pod-shaped HRE, the engine and airframe are a single unit. (NASA diagram.)

segments. The nose of the vehicle and each of the segments generated shock waves at shallow oblique angles. Such *forebody compression*, using multiple oblique shock waves, was very effective at slowing and compressing the air. This precompression of the airflow by the forward fuselage also reduced the necessary physical size of the modules by a factor of three at Mach 10. Each scramjet module consisted of the inlet, air duct, fuel injectors, flameholder, and an exit nozzle.[12]

The air then entered the inlet throat and underwent additional compression from interactions between the boundary layers and shock waves. The throat's narrowest point was called the *isolator*. Within this section, a "shock train" of zigzagging shock waves was formed. The airflow had been slowed, compressed, and, as a result, was also at a higher static temperature.

The airflow then entered the *combustor*, and fuel was injected. This could be liquid hydrogen, hydrogen gas, or a hydrocarbon fuel, depending on the specific engine design. But the exposed nozzles or spray bars used in jet engines or ramjets would act as obstructions in the airflow, creating shock waves and internal drag. To prevent this, the scramjet fuel injectors were located in the engine's walls. The position and spacing of these injector nozzles were dependent on the scramjet's speed range, the type of fuel burned, and whether both subsonic and supersonic combustion (dual-mode engine capability) was used. Although the fuel/oxygen mixture was combustible, an external ignition source was still required. Silane (SiH_4), which ignited on contact with oxygen, was used for this purpose. (The combustion of the silane and oxygen produces fine sand.) Once the combustion had stabilized, the silane flow was shut off.

When scramjets were first proposed in the 1950s, many researchers doubted that stable combustion could be maintained in a supersonic airflow. In conventional ramjets, in which combustion occurred at subsonic speeds, the pipes used as flameholders were in the airflow. Just as with the fuel injectors, flameholders in a scramjet could not be used in the supersonic airflow because of their effects on airflow and drag. Instead, a small step or ramp was typically used in scramjet designs as the flameholder. As the boundary layer passed over it, an eddy was formed (much like eddies that form in water flowing around a rock in a stream). This eddy allowed stable combustion to occur. During the process of combustion, a great deal of heat was released. Some of this was absorbed by the engine's structure, and this heat loss had to be minimized because the transfer cooled the exhaust gas. This reduces the amount of expansion as the hot gas entered the exhaust nozzle to generate thrust.

Just as the inlet had to be integrated with the lower forward fuselage to maximize the amount of air supplied to the engine, a similar technique had to be used in the nozzle design to extract the maximum amount of thrust from the expanding exhaust gas. This, along with the rectangular shape of the engine, ruled out a standard conical-shaped nozzle, as used on rockets and conventional ramjets.

Instead, the aft fuselage of an airframe-integrated scramjet had a sloping shape. This formed the top half of a nozzle, which extended out to the tail of the vehicle. The bottom half of the "nozzle" was formed by the ambient air pressure. The shape of the exhaust plume would change with altitude because of the different air pressure. As a result, the optimum expansion would occur. This would not be the case with a conical nozzle because of its fixed shape. In addition to maximizing the efficiency of the exhaust expansion, the half-nozzle reduced the vehicle's weight, size, heat-transfer load, and the engine's external drag. The same principle of an expanding exhaust plume and a half-nozzle is also used in a linear aerospike engine.[13]

The airframe-integrated scramjet engine can be described as "precisely simple." The scramjet module was an empty rectangular box. But behind this apparent simplicity was a daunting engineering task. For an airframe-integrated scramjet to work properly, all the elements—the forebody ramp, the engine, and the afterbody exhaust nozzle—must work as a single whole. A single error will result in an inefficient engine.

NATIONAL HYPERSONIC FLIGHT RESEARCH FACILITY

The development of the airframe-integrated scramjet came at a time of little interest in such advanced concepts. The 1970s saw the end of NASA's Apollo program and a halt in U.S. manned spaceflights for half a decade. The unmanned planetary missions approved in the late 1960s and early 1970s were launched, but proposed advanced follow-on flights failed to gain approval.

Aeronautical research experienced a similar decline. The X-15 program ended in 1968. The lifting-body program was still underway in the early 1970s, with research flights by the HL-10, X-24A, and M2-F3 vehicles, but its end was approaching. The final lifting body was the X-24B. This was actually the X-24A fitted with a modified long-nose delta fuselage. This shape had two applications. It gave a better cross-range capability to a vehicle reentering from orbit and could also be used by a hypersonic cruise vehicle powered by advanced airbreathing engines. Flight tests of the X-24B began in 1973 and ended in 1975, bringing the lifting-body program to a close.[14]

The end of the X-15 research and the winding down of the lifting-body programs left a void in aeronautical research. The development of a new hypersonic vehicle had wide appeal within both the Air Force and NASA. In 1972 the Air Force Flight Dynamics Laboratory (FDL) proposed a delta-wing test vehicle that would fly at speeds between Mach 3 to 5. The following year, the FDL offered a plan for an incremental growth vehicle, so named because it would initially fly at Mach 4.5, but then be upgraded to reach Mach 6, and finally Mach 9. At the same time, Langley Research Center

The X-24B lifting body flight tested a fuselage shape for a possible hypersonic cruise vehicle. This new fuselage was similar to that originally planned for the X-24C vehicle, which was to test airbreathing engines at hypersonic speeds. (NASA photo E75-28524.)

engineers had ideas of their own. Their initial vehicle concept was the Hypersonic Research Facility (HYFAC), which was designed to reach a top speed of Mach 12—twice the X-15's maximum speed. This was followed in 1974 by a proposal for a less exotic vehicle, called the High-Speed Research Aircraft (HSRA), with a top speed of Mach 8.

All of the FDL and NASA proposed concept vehicles had provisions for testing of airbreathing propulsion systems. The proposals differed in their research goals, however. The FDL vehicles focused on designs that would be suitable for military roles such as interception, reconnaissance, or strike. The NASA proposals were for long-range hypersonic cruise vehicles and space launchers. None of the concepts received official support to begin development.

This nearly changed with another FDL proposal, which overlapped the more advanced concepts. At about the time the X-24B made its first flights, the FDL engineers, who had developed the X-24B shape, began studying a hypersonic version called the X-24C. Two different vehicle concepts were proposed—one with cheek inlets for an airbreathing engine and a second powered by an XLR-99 rocket engine. The target speed would be Mach 5. X-24C program costs were estimated to be around $70 million.

The advantage of the X-24C proposal was that it was largely an "off-the-shelf" design in terms of shape, equipment, and technology. This made it a much more practical design than the more complex FDL and NASA proposals.

The X-24C gained the support of Gen. Sam Phillips, the head of the Air Force Systems Command and a former senior official in the Apollo program.

Both the X-15 and lifting-body programs had been run as joint NASA/Air Force efforts, so it made sense to do the same for the emerging X-24C. In December 1975, a month after the final X-24B flight, NASA and the Air Force formed an X-24C Joint Steering Committee. This consisted of the commanders of the Air Force Flight Test Center and the FDL and the directors of the NASA Flight Research Center (now Dryden Flight Research Center) and Langley Research Center.

Over the next several months, the group moved away from the relatively simple X-24C concept, toward the larger, more complex vehicles proposed by Langley and the FDL. The rationale was that a joint NASA/Air Force research facility should be designed to undertake research into a wide range of pacing technology in hypersonic flight and serve as a focus for U.S. research efforts in the field. This, planners envisioned, would combine a wide range of research goals into a single vehicle.

The Air Force wanted to test military-related technology experiments—photography, weapons separation, radome heating, nose-tip erosion, thermal protective systems, and removable fins. Different airbreathing propulsion systems were to be tested, including integrated rocket ramjets, as well as subsonic combustion ramjets. To do this, designers moved away from the X-24C shape, toward a design more akin to those of the Langley concepts. The vehicle would have a modular configuration, with a removable center section of the fuselage, to accommodate the different experiments. With the connection to the original X-24C vehicle now gone, the program received a new name. The traditional X-plane designation was abandoned and replaced with the awkward National Hypersonic Flight Research Facility (NHFRF, but pronounced "nerf").

The proposed NHFRF gained favor within NASA, as it fulfilled a number of research and institutional needs. For the NASA Flight Research Center, the X-24C was a continuation of the previous three decades of research into high-speed flight, revitalized the role of aeronautics within NASA, and provided a major role for the center during the shuttle era. For Langley aeronautical and propulsion engineers, the vehicle was the culmination of all of their efforts in high-speed flight and airbreathing propulsion systems. They also saw it as a means to "cover the whole hypersonic waterfront and do it before we've lost all the hypersonic talent we developed from the X-15 program."

The planned performance of the NHFRF was impressive. After launch from the B-52B mothership, the vehicle could reach a maximum speed of Mach 8 under rocket power. It also was designed to cruise at a speed of Mach 6+ for 40 seconds. This was an extremely demanding requirement. The project engineers envisioned construction of two NHFRF vehicles, to be used in a 200-flight research program beginning in 1983, and spanning a decade. This effort was estimated to cost $200 million.

Despite the support for the NHFRF by both NASA and the Air Force, however, trouble for the project was ahead. Much of NASA's budget was committed to the space shuttle, and both technical problems and high inflation were causing the program's costs to balloon. At the same time, the Air Force was introducing a new generation of fighter aircraft, against a background of funding cutbacks and poor morale. The increasing complexity of the NHFRF had, by early 1977, raised the estimated cost to as much as $500 to $600 million. NASA Headquarters was unwilling to foot the ever-growing bill and in September 1977 cancelled the agency's participation in the project. James J. Kramer, the acting NASA associate administrator for aeronautics and space technology, stated that, "the combination of a tight budget and the inability to identify a pressing near-term need for the flight facility had led to a decision by NASA not to proceed to a flight test vehicle at this time." The Air Force could not take over full funding of the NHFRF and ended its support for the effort.[15]

Although the X-24B was the last rocket-powered research aircraft to fly, it was the failure of the X-24C/NHFRF to receive approval that ended the 30-year era of rocket planes, flying to ever higher speeds and altitudes. The era had begun in 1946 with the glide flights of the X-1, in a blaze of publicity. The era ended with a memo, and its passing went unnoticed. The end of NHFRF dealt a hard blow to morale at the Flight Research Center, and recriminations soon followed. Some blamed overmanagement. Objections were also raised about the 40-second cruise requirement. This added considerable cost and difficulty to development of the NHFRF. Some argued it would have been better to build the original X-24C design rather than a more advanced and complex vehicle designed to be all things to all people.[16]

In retrospect, it seems unlikely that even the original X-24C concept would have been approved. The reasons were not technical, as with the Aerospaceplane. There would certainly have been difficulties and setbacks, especially with the more complex NHFRF concepts, but engineers could have drawn on the technology and experience from the X-15 and lifting-body programs in solving those difficulties. The real problem preventing the project from gaining support was that the time was simply not right for a project like the X-24C/NHFRF. At the time, the research focus at NASA was shifting to such projects as supercritical wing designs, winglets, and digital fly by wire. Although a scramjet-powered vehicle could serve as a second-generation space vehicle, the space shuttle had yet to fly; it was far too early to begin work on a replacement. Finally, the "me-generation" mentality that marked the 1970s was unfavorable to the bold challenges of flying at high speeds and altitudes that had so captivated engineers in the previous three decades.

Among the lessons that can be drawn from the X-24C/NHFRF is that it is not enough for a project to be technically feasible, and that its data would be valuable. As with the NACA's research activities, NASA aeronautical efforts were publicly funded projects. They had to relate to national needs. The supercritical wing designs and winglets both offered major improvements in fuel economy, a major public and commercial issue in the wake of the sharp increase in fuel costs in the early 1970s. Fly-by-wire technology opened new possibilities in aircraft design, in that this removed the need for an aircraft to be inherently stable.

Over the following decades, supercritical wings became standard on business jets, airliners, fighters, and heavy transports. Winglets appeared on sailplanes, light aircraft, business jets, airliners, and heavy transports. Virtually all new military and many airliners built during this period used fly-by-wire control systems. In terms of the impact on aeronautics, the government research funding provided for these areas was justified.

The "need for speed" and ever-higher altitudes, in contrast, which had been driving forces in both civilian and military aircraft design, were no longer critical issues. Supersonic transports were uneconomical to operate because of high fuel prices. Strategic bombers now flew at low level to strike their targets, while the emerging stealth technology was incompatible with supersonic flight. The airliners, fighters, and bombers built in the latter part of the 20th century all flew within the speed and altitude envelopes of aircraft built during the late 1950s and early 1960s.

Beyond these public policy issues, another factor was the lack of focus in the research goals for the X-24C/NHFRF. Trying to accomplish a wide range of goals made the vehicle more complex, and the heritage from the X-24B shape and systems was lost. This resulted in rapid cost increases even before the program was approved. In contrast, with the X-15, the original research goals were limited to high-speed/high-altitude flight. The vehicle had enough "stretch" built into it to later accommodate scientific and engineering experiments.

As a result of the failure of the NHFRF to gain approval, nearly a decade would pass before a major scramjet development effort would again be made. The new effort was to be much more ambitious, but would still suffer from the same old flaws.

NATIONAL AEROSPACE PLANE

The attraction of a single-stage-to-orbit vehicle, powered by scramjet engines, still beckoned, and still had its supporters. Beyond the advantages such a vehicle could provide for space access, the technology could also be used for a high-speed transport, a reconnaissance aircraft, or a strike vehicle. Not surprisingly, given the potential for the latter two roles, it was the U.S. military that first turned its attention back to the possibilities offered by the scramjet.

The aircraft that would become the National Aerospace Plane (NASP) had its roots with the Air Force Aeronautical Systems Division in 1979. The original study on which the NASP was based was of second-generation shuttle vehicles. At the same time, Air Force Systems Command was looking at a concept called the Transatmospheric Vehicle. In early 1982, the two efforts were combined under the Defense Advanced Research Projects Agency (DARPA). This group subsequently oversaw a study called Copper Canyon.

A key event occurred in 1983, when a small aerospace firm specializing in engine cycle studies was undertaking a NASA study of scramjet-powered vehicles. The study's computer analyses indicated that a single-stage-to-orbit vehicle actually could take off from a runway and fly into orbit. The study vehicle's gross takeoff weight was an astonishingly low 50,000 pounds, about that of the X-15A-2, had a payload of about 2500 pounds, and could be ready to fly in 1990. The study vehicle would use a multicycle engine, a low-speed subsonic propulsion system, a midspeed ramjet, and finally a scramjet to reach orbital speeds. The three propulsion systems would have to switch modes during the ascent. This study vehicle became the "initial government baseline design."[17]

By 1986, government approval was given to NASA and the Air Force to begin work on the NASP. Like the Aerospaceplane of more than two decades earlier, this was to be a single-stage-to-orbit vehicle. The NASP program called for using wind tunnels and computational-fluid-dynamics (CFD) analysis to develop technology for a single-stage-to-orbit configuration, an airbreathing propulsion system, hypersonic cruise, and aircraft-like operations.[18]

The only National Aerospace Plane "vehicle" to ever reach the NASA Dryden Flight Research Center. This was a full-scale "footprint" intended to check the ability of the ground crew to move it inside the hangar. (NASA photo EC91-0354-01.)

The NASP research program soon grew into the largest development effort in the history of scramjet propulsion, involving, at its peak, more than 5000 engineers and scientists. In addition to aerospace contractors, a broad-based university program in hypersonic research also received federal support and funding. Through these efforts, an entire new generation of scramjet researchers was trained.

Among the results of the NASP program were design and ground testing of several small and large-scale dual-mode scramjets, at Langley Research Center, which worked both as a conventional subsonic combustion ramjet at lower speeds and as a scramjet at higher speeds. This work led to construction of a large-scale concept demonstration engine (CDE) measuring 10 × 16 × 142 inches. The CDE was tested in Langley's 8-foot High Temperature Tunnel (HTT) at simulated Mach 6.8 flight conditions. The CDE test objectives were to demonstrate the performance and operating limits of a large integrated scramjet as well as to verify flowpath design methods.[19]

Tests were also done on small-scale scramjets at speeds up to Mach 18 and large-scale ramjets at up to Mach 8 speeds. Computational-fluid-dynamics analysis techniques were developed, validated, and used to make predictions and analyze data. During the course of the research, several new hypersonic test facilities and wind tunnels were built in the United States. Existing facilities were also modified to allow testing of large-scale scramjets at speeds of Mach 8. Engineers developed and tested several new instruments that could measure temperatures and pressures in a variety of materials. These instruments included combustor diagnostics and gauges to measure engine thrust above Mach 8. In the area of materials, wing leading-edge composites that could withstand the heating required for flight were developed as part of the NASP program. The new materials included carbon–carbon composites, titanium alloys, metal matrix composites, copper niobium, and beryllium fiber composites.[20]

Yet despite these achievements, the NASP program was flawed in ways similar to those of the earlier Aerospaceplane and HRE programs. The NASP was a fully integrated aircraft research and development program. Its ultimate goal was to build two X-30 research aircraft with the second of these to be capable of flying directly into orbit. A decision was made that building an orbital vehicle, rather than building rocket-boosted subscale test vehicles or conducting ground research into such issues as boundary-layer transition, was the only path to gaining the necessary support for the scramjet and hypersonic research efforts from the Reagan administration, Congress, and public.

The vehicle was described by NASP program management as a "forcing function," which would serve to mature the technology faster than would a pure research program. There were several difficulties with this approach. For it to become a reality, technological breakthroughs were needed in virtually every discipline connected with the NASP. These included "slush" hydrogen, advanced materials, avionics and control systems, and actively cooled structures. The breakthroughs required to build the NASP were also made more difficult by external factors.

Hypersonic expertise at Langley and aerospace contractors had largely been dispersed by the early 1980s. The older engineers and scientists had left the hypersonic field, and new talent was not replacing them. There were also questions in the early 1980s about whether the data from small engine modules, tested for a few seconds in wind tunnels, could be accurately scaled up to a full-scale scramjet, operating for several minutes under real flight conditions in the actual atmosphere. Given doubts that subscale scramjet models would provide accurate data, many believed that the only development of a full-scale NASP would allow scramjet technology to be tested.[21]

Despite the unknowns, many of those working on the NASP truly believed that the project would be easy and could be achieved at a relatively low cost. Advocates of the NASP claimed that new technologies required had been adequately developed to resolve the numerous problems inherent in hypersonic flight and the single-stage-to-orbit mission profile. In retrospect, however, these technologies seemed to have been merely extrapolations of ground-test data.[22]

A prime example of this was the initial government baseline design for the National Aerospace Plane. The claim that the vehicle could reach orbit was based on "highly questionable assumptions, optimistic interpretation of results, and convenient omissions." The initial government baseline design vehicle had no landing gear, no safety equipment, and no margin for an increase in size or weight growth. It even lacked thrusters to stabilize it once in space. The scramjet combustors had to be a specific size. If they were made larger, injector struts would have to be used, creating flowfield problems. If the engine were smaller, it could not fully burn the fuel. The scramjet could not serve as a prototype for any other engine. The vehicle required a takeoff speed of 300 miles per hour. Finally, the wing structure passed through the hydrogen tank subjecting the wing to both extreme heat (from high-speed airflow) and extreme cold (from the hydrogen). None of the other NASP contractors were able to replicate the computer results, which were used as proof that the initial government baseline design was feasible.

This led to a split in program personnel between the entrepreneurs and the engineers. The former saw the potential of an airbreathing single-stage-to-orbit vehicle and worried little about the technical difficulties of actually building it. The latter focused on the technical problems of actually constructing the National Aerospace Plane. The result was that the entrepreneurs accused the engineers of lacking vision, while the engineers said the entrepreneurs were going beyond technical realities. Yet the split was neither black and white, nor did it produce a stalemate. Even engineers who were pessimistic about NASP saw no physical reason why a scramjet-powered vehicle could not reach orbit.

Ultimately, program personnel came to believe that although the baseline single-stage-to-orbit design was unworkable, it still might lead to a workable vehicle. This idea was expressed with the inelegant phrase that "there was a pony in the pile." Others thought that the main contribution the NASP would make was not the scramjet itself, but the development of computational-fluid-dynamics codes that would allow researchers to calculate the aerodynamic, heating, fuel mixing, and combustion effects on a computer. With such a powerful design tool, the shortcomings in the baseline design could be eliminated. Still other researchers saw the NASP's contribution in terms of expanding the technology base; this faction believed that even if NASP never flew, the effort would be worthwhile. This was counter to the NASA imperative to work on applied research, rather than pure research.

These divisions highlighted a basic question: what would NASP actually be. Officially, it was to be a single-stage-to-orbit aircraft. Yet it was often depicted as the "Orient Express"—a hypersonic airliner able to fly across the Pacific Ocean in a few hours, not least of all by President Ronald Reagan himself. Others thought it should be an experimental aircraft with a top speed of about Mach 12. This was well below orbital velocity but still double the speed of the X-15. The level of these doctrinal differences was made clear in a November 1986 Langley memo. It noted that a variety of program goals had been offered for NASP: 1) single-stage-to-orbit, 2) low-cost delivery of payload to low-Earth orbit, 3) long-duration supersonic cruise, and 4) experimental hypersonic research vehicle. Of the four, the Langley memo indicated the third and fourth goals were "considered sufficient" to justify NASP. Regarding the first and second goals, the memo noted "many feel that 1 and 2 are not feasible or even a serious requirement."

The single-stage-to-orbit concept had been the reason the NASP had gained support by both the Reagan administration and Congress. That Langley managers did not judged this to be "a serious requirement" was the result of a "big tent philosophy" that tolerated a significant level of ambiguity about the program's goals in order to keep options open and encourage creativity.[23]

As time passed, the intractable difficulties inherent in the program became increasingly apparent. It was ultimately cancelled in October 1994, after some $2.4 billion had been spent. The end of the NASP program, however, left a legacy of accomplishment as well as disappointment. Despite eight years of work and over two billion dollars, a workable NASP design had not been developed. Yet many unknowns about scramjets and related technologies had been explored, and in some cases solved.

SCRAMJET DEVELOPMENT — LESSONS NOT LEARNED FROM 1958 TO 1994

The first four decades of U.S. scramjet development provide examples of lessons that were not learned, several of them, several times. These included goals not supported by the available technology and "overselling"—mistaking potential for reality—as well as an overall lack of focus about program goals, attempting to be all things to all people, and the influence of change in the larger society. There were also the issues of the difficulties inherent in the public funding of cutting-edge research, with the high degree of uncertainty over success and the ultimate application of the new technology. Finally, there remained a perceived political need to expand a basic research effort to include construction of an aircraft as the ultimate goal.

In retrospect, the flaws in the early and overambitious scramjet development efforts were many and multilayered, and any one would have been enough to cause the effort to end in disappointment. Yet despite all of the setbacks and disappointments that had marred the initial decades of scramjet research, much had been accomplished. It had not been done in an orderly process, but by the mid-1990s there was a body of knowledge sufficient to undertake flight tests of scramjet engine designs.

The question then became what to do next.

NOTES

[1]*The Hypersonic Revolution Case Studies in the History of Hypersonic Technology,* Vol. II, edited by Richard P. Hallion, Air Force History and Museum Program, Bolling AFB, Washington, DC, 1998, pp. VI-ii–VI-iii-a.

[2]Fletcher, Edward A., Robert G. Dorsch, and Melvin Gerstein, "Combustion of Aluminum Borohydride in a Supersonic Wind Tunnel," NACA RM E55D07a, June 20, 1955.

[3]Weber, Robert J., and John S. MacKay, "Analysis of Ramjet Engines Using Supersonic Combustion," NACA TN 4386, Sept. 1958. Weber and McKay referred to this as a "SCRJ" (supersonic combustion ram jet). "Scramjet" quickly emerged as the preferred name for the new engine.

[4]*The Hypersonic Revolution,* Vol. II, pp. vi–xiv, 749–751, 753–756.

[5]The film *2001 A Space Odyssey* is an example of this early 1960s view of the future.

[6]*The Hypersonic Revolution,* Vol. II, pp. vi-iiia, 752, 948–952.

[7]Ibid, pp.774–776, 792, 817, 836, 847, 851.

[8]Ibid, pp. 754–756, 759, 760, 761, 847, 848.

[9]Ibid, pp. 755, 762, 764, 765, 832, 841.

[10]Ibid, pp. 845–851.

[11]Ohio State Univ., "A Conceptual Design of an Unmanned Test Vehicle Using an Airbreathing Propulsion System," NASA-CR-195550, 1994, p. 3.

[12]Mehta, Unmeel B., "Air-Breathing Aerospace Plane Development Essential: Hypersonic Propulsion Flight Tests," NASA TM 108857, Nov. 1994, p. 3.

[13]Henry, John R., and Griffin Y. Anderson, "Design Considerations for the Airframe Integrated Scramjet," NASA TM X-2895, Dec. 1973, p. 4., and George Emanuel, "A First Scramjet Study," NASA Contractor Report NAG 1-886, 1985, pp. 5, 10. Combustion in a

scramjet has been likened to keeping a match lit in a hurricane. This is an incorrect analogy, as a major hurricane's wind speed is about 150 miles per hour, vs the supersonic speed of the scramjet airflow.

[14]Hallion, Richard P., and Michael H. Gorn, *On the Frontier: Experimental Flight at NASA Dryden*, Smithsonian Books, Washington, DC, 2003, pp. 163–167, 419, 420.

[15]Ibid, pp. 169, 170, and *The Hypersonic Revolution,* Vol. II, pp. 930–938.

[16]Hallion, Gorn, *On the Frontier*, p. 170.

[17]*The Hypersonic Revolution Case Studies in the History of Hypersonic Technology*, Vol. III, edited by Larry Schweikart, Air Force History and Museum Program, Bolling AFB, Washington, DC, 1998, pp. 11, 19–23, 153.

[18]Mehta, "Air-Breathing Aerospace Plane Development Essential: Hypersonic Propulsion Flight Tests," p. 6.

[19]Kumar, Ajay J., Philip Drummond, Charles R. McClinton, and James L. Hunt, "Research in Hypersonic Airbreathing Propulsion at the NASA Langley Research Center," ISABE-2001: Invited Lecture 4, p. 2.

[20]*The Hypersonic Revolution,* Vol. III, pp. 324–326.

[21]Ibid, pp. 4, 11, 14, 15, 18, 25, 26.

[22]Iliff, Kenneth W., and Curtis Peebles, *From Runway to Orbit Reflections of a NASA Engineer*, NASA Headquarters, Washington, DC, 2004, pp. 305–310.

[23]*The Hypersonic Revolution,* Vol. III, pp. 8, 24, 29–31, 59, 63.

Chapter 2

PHOENIX FROM THE ASHES

To invent an airplane is nothing. To build one is something. To fly is everything.
Otto Lilienthal, aviation pioneer, 1848–1896

What would eventually become the Hyper-X project had its start within the National Aerospace Plane. This was ironic, as NASP project managers rejected the very idea of a short-term, limited-goal effort built around a sub-scale vehicle. It took a long time for them to finally accept this approach.

Among reasons that the NASP program was focused on development of a full-scale test aircraft was the belief of many researchers and contractors that data from a subscale scramjet could not be scaled up to a full-size engine without introducing errors. Indeed, as time passed, the contractors found that they became less confident that they could predict general performance from specific data points. There were uncertainties in many data points, and those uncertainties changed. For these reasons, all of the contractors believed that only a prototype, near-full-scale vehicle with a maximum speed above Mach 20 would give them real confidence in their performance predictions for a single-stage-to-orbit design.

This view effectively eliminated the possibility of an incremental development approach. Such a graduated approach would have involved ground tests to speeds of Mach 8, then computational-fluid-dynamics analysis at from Mach 8 to Mach 15, and finally subscale flight tests of small vehicles at speeds above Mach 15. These would be made with rocket-boosted vehicles similar in design and shape to the NASP, but much smaller than the actual vehicle.

But an incremental plan was supported by many NASA researchers, who had long believed that a Mach 15 vehicle would be sufficient for providing most of the data necessary to predict the requirements of an orbital NASP. This concept also allowed for a step-by-step approach. The data from the low Mach flights could then be used to refine the design of the orbital NASP. Such an effort also fit the belief of many NASA researchers that expanding the hypersonic technology base was more important than building and flying an actual vehicle.[1]

SMALL-SCALE HYPERSONIC VEHICLES

Despite the rejection of an incremental development approach for the National Aerospace Plane, various subscale proposals were still made over the years. The most ambitious was the hypersonic air-launch option (HALO). This was a Dryden proposal for a piloted vehicle launched from the back of an SR-71. The HALO concept and the flight plan reflected Dryden's experiences with rocket planes since the late 1940s. The influence of Dryden's past was apparent in the HALO's planned mission profile, which was similar to that of the X-15 of the 1960s.

The profile called for the SR-71/HALO to take off from Edwards Air Force Base and fly to the Boise, Idaho, area. The launch would be made at Mach 3 and 70,000 feet. The HALO would be boosted to test speeds—from Mach 8 to Mach 10—by a liquid-hydrogen-fueled RL-10 rocket engine. The nose of the vehicle was detachable, so that the ramp angle of the inlet could be altered according to the tests being made. Different modular scramjet engine designs would be fitted to the HALO's underside. The engines would be tested during a two-minute cruise at test conditions. During this period, the scramjet's response to variations in the angle of attack and sideslip, as well the effects of different yaw, pitch, and roll rates. The test data from each of the scramjet designs could then be compared, to show their individual advantages and shortcomings. Once the speed run was completed, the HALO would pitch up to reduce dynamic pressure and heating on the vehicle. The HALO would glide south across Utah, then make a sweeping turn across California before landing back at Edwards Air Force Base.

The goal was to show that scramjets could operate at varying conditions, could avoid unstarts, and could operate while maneuvering. In addition, the profile would test different injector designs. Data on the physics of hypersonic flight, such as the real gas, catalytic, and boundary-layer effects, would be collected, and the thermal protection system also would be tested. About 50 to 100 flights would be made during the program.

To keep costs down, off-the-shelf equipment such as actuators, landing-gear systems, and the pilot's ejection seat would be used. The RL-10 rocket engine was well proven and very reliable as evidenced from its use in the Centaur upper stage. Costs to build the hypersonic air-launch option were very roughly estimated by Dryden engineers at around $300 million. To refine this further, Ben Rich of Lockheed's Skunk Works was asked by Dryden managers to review the HALO design, assess its feasibility, and provide a cost estimate for the vehicle.

Rich viewed the vehicle as technically feasible, including the Mach 3 separation from the SR-71. Dryden engineers were shocked, however, when he gave a cost estimate of $1 billion to build the HALO. Rich explained that this was because anything worth doing usually cost this much, with most of the money going to satisfying the bureaucracy. National

Aerospace Plane personnel added to the cost problems when they estimated that the scramjet modules would also cost $1 billion. As the modules
were of relatively simple design, with fixed geometry inlets, injectors, and
exhaust nozzles, there were suspicions among Dryden personnel that the
cost estimate was an effort to kill the HALO project, and thus eliminate a
NASP program competitor.

There were also problems within NASA regarding the HALO. Dryden's
proposal had been developed with assistance of engineers at NASA Ames
Research Center. (At that time, Dryden was not an independent center, but
rather a research facility managed by Ames.) An approach was made to
Langley engineers to refine the HALO design. This was as much for political
reasons as for anything related to engineering. The project would never be
approved by NASA Headquarters unless it had Langley's backing, and
Langley managers found much to dislike about the HALO. Their reservations
included launch from an SR-71, the fact that the HALO would be a manned
vehicle, and the proposed aircraft's large size.

In an attempt to win Langley's approval, Ames engineers redesigned the
vehicle to take into account these objections. The SR-71 launch option was
retained, but the vehicle was now smaller, unmanned, and renamed the
HALO II. Their efforts, however, were to no avail. Langley and NASA
Headquarters would not back the project.

At the other end of the scale from the HALO were proposals for small-
scale hypersonic experiments to be launched by the Pegasus booster. These
concepts were explored by Dryden engineers Kenneth W. Iliff and Henry
Arnaiz. The Pegasus booster would be available soon, and it had a substantial
performance capability. A large vehicle with deployable scramjet experiments
could reach speeds between Mach 10 and 15. There was a wide range of proposed vehicles that could be used to test inlet performance, boundary-layer
transitions, shock impingement heating, and advanced thermal protection
systems. They also would provide aerodynamic and aerothermodynamic
data. The resulting flight data could be used to verify that the ground tests and
computational-fluid-dynamics codes were accurate. Between the HALO and
the Pegasus-launched vehicles, the entire hypersonic flight region could be
explored.

None of these ideas was funded, however, for several reasons. Beyond the
doubts about the accuracy of subscale tests, National Aerospace Plane supporters
claimed that the physics of hypersonic flight was completely understood and
such tests were therefore unneeded. Wind-tunnel researchers took exactly the
opposite position, believing that unless subscale flight tests were done at very
precise, defined conditions the resulting data would not be useful.[2]

As the NASP program encountered increasing budget and technical difficulties, program managers came to realize that the requirement to build a
full-scale test aircraft was becoming a detriment. After 1992, NASP program

efforts began to focus on the more immediate goal of keeping some level of hypersonic research underway. The idea of building a full-scale X-30 able to fly into orbit was effectively abandoned. Instead, a number of ideas began to surface that focused on a subscale vehicle for scramjet flight tests.

What ultimately emerged was a shift toward subscale but still large, NASP-like unpiloted vehicles launched by Minuteman ballistic missiles. The engineers envisioned that the vehicle would separate from the missile and flight test a scramjet engine. Even a limited-duration test would represent a major advance, as no scramjet had yet made a free flight. All existing data had been acquired through wind-tunnel testing. This shift in focus brought a sense of optimism. It seemed that the NASP program was finally focused on a near-term effort that Congress would fund.

The initial ballistic missile-launched test program was dubbed HYFLITE (Hypersonic Flight Experiment) and had three elements. HYFLITE I would determine boundary-layer transition. HYFLITE II would incorporate the engine flowpath, in order to determine inlet operations and airflow characteristics, and to show that the scramjet could actually produce thrust. The goal of HYFLITE III was to demonstrate integrated propulsion at high speeds, produce more thrust than drag, and test stability and control of a free-flying vehicle. The three vehicles were to be wedged-shaped, simulating the X-30's forebody. The launch vehicle would be a Minuteman II intercontinental ballistic missile (ICBM).

The HYFLITE program research goals were ambitious. NASP officials estimated that the program would meet 50% of the research objectives for scramjet performance in aerothermal validations; nearly 50% for boundary-layer and computational-fluid-dynamics validation for local flow; 40% of overall engine/airframe integration; about 25% of scramjet operability and performance; and 20% of engine-mode integration.

But although the research goals were substantial, so were the estimated costs. HYFLITE I and II's combined costs were estimated to be as high as $579.8 million. This, however, was dwarfed by the cost estimate for the more complex HYFLITE III, projected to be $1.4 billion for the single mission. Although some within the program argued the cost estimates were exaggerated, it was clear that HYFLITE also faced major technical challenges.

The Minuteman booster normally followed a high, arching ballistic trajectory to its target. But for the HYFLITE programs, the booster would have to pitch over soon after launch in order to reach proper Mach number, dynamic pressure, and flow conditions for the tests. This would require significant booster modifications, which raised a large number of technical issues as well as questions about the amount of data that the flights would produce. With the National Aerospace Plane program in serious trouble, subscale tests had become the only option. HYFLITE I and II phases were approved, whereas work on HYFILTE III was put off.[3]

The HYFLITE effort proved short lived, however. With defense funding continuing to decline with the Cold War's end, Congress directed that the NASP effort be closed out by the end of fiscal year 1994. The legislative conference committee debating the issue noted that although conferees did not feel the United States could afford to develop a hypersonic research aircraft, they did encourage continued hypersonic research. The level of funding provided was below that needed for HYFLITE, however. Additionally, debate continued, focusing on basic research vs demonstration of operational systems.

Ultimately, boundary-layer research efforts were dropped, and a new proposal, the Hypersonic Systems Technology Program (HySTP), which was focused on the basic question of whether a scramjet could really work, emerged. This would be accomplished by launching a 25%-scale scramjet to speeds of Mach 12 to 15 using a Minuteman or Peacekeeper intercontinental ballistic missile. Total cost to the Air Force of HySTP would be $450 million over five years. Additional money would be provided by NASA. The key research goal would be to see whether the scramjet could produce "useful" thrust, defined as thrust from combustion beyond that produced by the mere venting of hydrogen gas through the engine's nozzle. When compared to the National Aerospace Plane goal of building a vehicle able to take off from a runway and enter orbit, it was clear how far U.S. hypersonic ambitions had fallen since the 1980s. Yet not even this modest effort would prove successful. Funding initially designated for the HySTP was transferred to other Defense Department commitments. The program ended in May 1995, joining the now-cancelled NASP.

In retrospect, several lessons can be drawn from the NASP saga over and above those of the problems it had shared with previous efforts like the Aerospaceplane. The focus of the NASP on the "be-all and end-all" goal of a single-stage-to-orbit demonstration proved to be a trap. This goal grew out of the belief by some individuals within the Air Force, the aerospace industry, and government that development of this type of vehicle could be accomplished with relative ease and at low cost. There was also the belief that this approach would "force" development of hypersonic technology faster than would a general research program. Finally, this approach was seen as the only way to get needed technical data and to politically "sell" the program.

The actual result was later likened to the Wright brothers deciding they would build an SR-71 as their first airplane. A huge number of technological breakthroughs were required in order to go from the Wright Flyer to the Blackbird. Had the NASP program adopted an incremental approach from the start, the program could have had a nonorbital vehicle flying in very short order and at relatively low cost. These flights could have demonstrated progress, necessary from the political point of view, and would have provided both flight data and a cross check on the computational-fluid-dynamics and wind-tunnel tests.

Similarly, such an approach could also have allowed planners to forego the potential of a single-stage-to-orbit vehicle for the more attainable profile of a scramjet-powered first stage and an expendable rocket second stage. This evolutionary approach would still have been technologically demanding, but far less grandiose than the notion of flying directly into orbit.

By the time NASP managers realized an incremental effort was required, the program was nearing its end. Worse yet, even an incremental approach still involved the need for a large vehicle, which required a large booster. The potential economy of a small-scale effort was effectively lost. More than four decades had passed since the scramjet had emerged as a potential propulsion system. Yet despite all of the research and development efforts undertaken during that time, a scramjet still had not been proven viable. A very different approach would be required before successful scramjet test flights would actually be achieved.[4]

GOLDIN'S RULES

Daniel S. Goldin has been the longest-serving NASA administrator to date and the most controversial individual to hold the position. This was caused in large part by the "faster, better, cheaper" approach to space missions that became his signature. By the early 1990s unmanned space probes, touted as low cost and more scientifically productive, were caught in a cost spiral.

When a planetary mission received approval, project scientists would inevitably add every instrument possible to the mission. Just as inevitably, this increased the probe's mass, which then meant a larger booster would be required, which in turn increased costs. Because the probes were one of a kind, the risk of failure meant potential loss of a huge investment of time and money. As a result, more system redundancies, as a hedge against disaster, were added, which further increased costs. In an effort to reduce risks to the mission, only established technologies were to be used. Finally, the entire process took years to complete, increasing costs still further.

A prime example of this spiral was the Cassini mission to Saturn, launched in October of 1997. Total mission cost was $3.3 billion. The probe took eight years to design and build and weighed 12,346 pounds fully fueled. This required a Titan IVB/Centaur booster as the launch vehicle. But even powered by the largest expendable U.S. booster, this massive probe could not fly directly to Saturn. Instead, it needed a gravity assist derived through two flybys of Venus, a flyby of Earth, and another of Jupiter to gain sufficient velocity to reach Saturn, resulting in a flight time of nearly seven years. Only in July of 2004, after a decade and half of work and a cost greater than construction of a space shuttle, could the Cassini mission begin its studies of Saturn.

Goldin's approach, whatever the shortcomings later ascribed to it, had its roots in practicality. He argued that this approach to planetary exploration was self-defeating, as fewer and fewer probes would be built, each costing more and more, until the cost was too high to be politically feasible. The faster, better, cheaper approach Goldin developed included a tight schedule and cost limits, keeping the probes' weight to that which could be carried by a Delta II booster, reducing the number of project staff, using advanced technologies, and accepting a greater degree of risk than was traditional with satellites and planetary probes.

The results of Goldin's efforts were mixed. On the positive side, for a cost equal to that of the single Cassini mission, a total of 16 space probes and satellites were launched by 2000 under the faster, better, cheaper approach. These included five Mars missions, one moon mission, three space telescopes, two asteroid/comet rendezvous missions, four Earth satellites, and an ion-propulsion test mission. This series of achievements represented a rebirth of the U.S. planetary research program after almost two decades of near inactivity. The risk inherent in the concept was also apparent, however. Of the 16 missions, six failed for various reasons, translating into a relatively meager success rate of 63%.[5]

Although the faster, better, cheaper concept has come to be associated more with space probes than with aeronautical research, Goldin saw it as an approach that would also be useful in untangling the U.S. scramjet effort in the wake of the National Aerospace Plane's cancellation. Goldin was briefed on the hypersonic air-launch option and Pegasus-launched vehicles at Dryden on September 3, 1992. Iliff began what was planned as a half-hour presentation. He recalled later that he had barely gotten to his second chart before Goldin began challenging what he was saying. For the next hour and a half, Goldin questioned Iliff about single-stage reusable vehicles, rockets vs airbreathers, and what Iliff thought were the good ideas and what were the bad ideas. Finally, with lunch time approaching, Iliff asked if he could be permitted to finish his hypersonic briefing.

Iliff thought his briefing was well received. He also commented later that Goldin clearly did not like the NASP concept and was looking for an "off ramp." The HALO proposal looked like the best available option. Goldin made this clear in an off-the-cuff comment to a reporter with the local *Antelope Valley Press,* when he indicated that he favored an alternative to the NASP, and suggested the possibility of using the HALO concept. The NASP personnel's morale already had been adversely affected by the retreat from the single-stage-to-orbit approach and ongoing budget cuts. "The vultures are circling," a NASP briefing paper noted. Goldin's comments did nothing to improve their outlook. Although the NASP was often thought of as a NASA project, the bulk of the funding and management was provided by the Air Force. Congress had previously prohibited the Department of Defense from spending more that twice the amount NASA did on the program. Now, with Goldin's comments implying NASA funding was about to end, NASP's future was now bleak.[6]

Two views of the first X-43A. The shape was derived from the DF-9 Mach 10 concept vehicle, producing one of the sleekest research aircraft ever built. (NASA photo EC99-45265-11 and -18.)

With the end of NASP and the Hypersonic Systems Technology Program, the Air Force and NASA took divergent paths in hypersonic research. The Air Force planned to spend $20 million annually between fiscal years 1995 and 2000 for "generic" hypersonic research. The focus was to be on hydrocarbon-fueled scramjet testing at speeds of from Mach 4 to 8 in support of missile-related work. This effort was to be called HyTech (hypersonic technology) and involved the Aerojet Corporation and United Technologies.[7]

Having previously studied flight vehicles for hypersonic research, NASA opted for a small rocket-boosted research vehicle concept that it could pursue on its own. Unlike the HYFLITE and HySTP, however, this effort would be

Two additional views of the first X-43A. (NASA photo EC99-22 and 23.)

structured to meet cost constraints while fulfilling data requirements. Costs were to be limited by making use of technology, hardware, vehicle concepts, databases, design tools, and other research data from the NASP program.

NASA's new effort was called the X-43A Hyper-X project. It was not a huge, long-term, multibillion-dollar effort like that of the NASP, but a small, short-schedule, low-cost/high-risk project modeled on Goldin's faster, better, cheaper approach. To limit risk, preflight analysis and experimental verification would be done in ground tests. These would be followed by flight tests of a sub-scale vehicle to test scramjet engine performance in flight. The Hyper-X goals were flight validation of design predictions, development of the advanced tools needed to further refine scramjet engines and hypersonic vehicles, and risk reduction through preflight analysis and verification of predicted aerodynamic, propulsion system, structural, and integrated scramjet/airframe performance. The ultimate purpose was to advance hypersonic development from laboratory to flight-test level. This was necessary before NASA, the Defense Department, or private industry could pursue development of a larger, piloted hypersonic vehicle.[8]

The faster, better, cheaper approach became known for both remarkable achievements and heart-breaking failures. The Hyper-X would follow the same path.

ORIGINS AND DECISIONS

Several roads lead to the start of the Hyper-X project. One began with a group of people at Langley led by Lana Couch, an engineer who had worked on the National Aerospace Plane, and included John Hicks, Charles R. "Chuck" McClinton, and Vincent L. Rausch (who had worked on the NASP while in the Air Force, before taking a position at Langley Research Center). They knew how much data the NASP program had produced, despite the unsuccessful attempt to build a research aircraft. The group came together and lamented that it was too bad that they could not take this huge database and apply it to a vehicle that could be flown in the near term.[9]

The first stack on its trailer. From front to back, the X-43A, the adaptor, and the HXLV. (NASA photo EC01-0164-02.)

At this same time, Langley's James L. Hunt and Edward A. Eiswirth of McDonnell Douglas Aerospace were making a study of a family of hypersonic vehicles. Titled "NASA's Dual-Fuel Airbreathing Hypersonic Vehicle Study," the study's first phase called for developing a conceptual design for a scramjet-powered reconnaissance/strike aircraft. The vehicle would be based in the United States and have a range of 10,000 nautical miles. It would use hydrogen fuel, hydrocarbon fuel, or a combination of the two for different mission phases (thus the term "dual fuel" of the study's title). Phase II was built around a two-stage-to-orbit booster design concept, whereas Phase III called for an X-plane concept through which flight data could be acquired.[10]

Over the previous four decades, many similar proposals had been made. These went back to advanced X-15 concepts, the X-24C/NHFRF, hypersonic air-launch option, the Pegasus-launched vehicles, and the Hypersonic Flight Experiment and Hypersonic Systems Technology Program proposals. What was different in the wake of the National Aerospace Plane's end was that events and circumstances had now aligned to make a hypersonic flight research program possible. The repeated failures of the overambitious plans finally resulted in a change in mindset. Researchers were now willing to accept the utility of a simple research project that had a real chance of getting funded, instead of an all-or-nothing gamble. NASA Administrator Goldin had initiated a series of X-plane competitions. Management officials in Langley's Hypersonic Vehicle Office learned during phase I work that support was building at NASA Headquarters for a hypersonic flight demonstration program.

Hicks, McClinton, Rausch, and team leader Couch put together a NASA proposal for test of a small-scale airframe integrated scramjet, using the phase I design concept and the National Aerospace Plane database. The team also did a large amount of wind-tunnel testing and computational-fluid-dynamics analysis in support of the proposal. The X-plane programs, like the faster, better, cheaper space missions, were to be small scale/high risk, with small budgets and short schedules; the basic parameters were about $200 million and four years. The team's proposal was selected by NASA Headquarters in July 1996, and then they faced the question, "Oh gee, now what do we do?"[11]

Studies were also made to determine minimum research-vehicle size. This was a major issue, as the larger the vehicle, the higher the cost. The studies found that optimal size would be from 10 to 12 feet long, with either size being compatible for the rocket booster that would be used. The larger size was selected, as it promised small performance gains over the smaller model. The increased size also meant additional volume for internal systems, without adding significantly to total costs.

The team also had contracted with McDonnell Douglas for conceptual design studies, which were done between February and May of 1995. This was followed by development of a preliminary design for the "government candidate design" vehicle, completed at McDonnell Douglas between March and October of 1996. The design was based on the phase III concept of the dual-fuel airbreathing hypersonic vehicle study. The Hyper-X research vehicle was scaled down in size from the previous phase I study concept, which was referred to as the DF-9. This allowed the existing database of National Aerospace Plane information to be used and for the design to rapidly converge into that of a controllable small-scale test vehicle.[12]

The degree of reduction was significant. The McDonnell Douglas DF-9 vehicle was envisioned as being 202 feet long, with a fueled takeoff weight of about 532,000 pounds. A 747 airliner, in contrast, is 225 feet long and has a takeoff weight of 800,000 pounds.[13] For the research vehicle to be capable of demonstrating a scramjet engine in flight, the DF-9 design concept had to be scaled down from 202 to 12 feet in length.

Although the DF-9 shape could be reduced in size with relative ease, the same was not true of the scramjet engine flowpath. The engine's inlet contraction, fuel-injector details, and combustor length had to be revised to account for scale, wall temperature, and other effects. The scramjet engine flown on the subscale research vehicle would be made of copper-alloy materials like those of wind-tunnel scramjet models. Because the scramjet engine would only operate in flight for about 10 seconds, a simple cooling system using a water-glycol mix would be sufficient. This resulted in a far simpler design than that of a flight-weight, actively cooled engine.

If the Hyper-X scramjet engine performed in flight as predicted in the ground tests and theoretical analysis, design methods would be validated. This, in turn, would indicate that those methods could be used to design and build more advanced operational systems.[14]

Beyond the preliminary designs of both the research vehicle and scramjet, there was the issue of selecting the booster rocket. As in the Minuteman-boosted HYFLITE/HySTP programs, the booster would be required to propel the research vehicle to the proper altitude, speed, dynamic pressure, and other flight conditions. The vehicle would then separate from the booster, stabilize, and begin the engine test. There would be four flights, with very different mission profiles.

The first Hyper-X flight would reach a speed of Mach 7, demonstrate the scramjet's ability to produce more thrust than drag, and show positive acceleration. The flight data would validate the scramjet design tools. Leading up to the actual flight, the entire scramjet engine would undergo a full-duration simulated Mach 7 burn in Langley Research Center's High Temperature Tunnel. These ground data would then be compared with those from the flight. As a result, the Mach 7 flight was considered the "easiest" mission.

The second flight, with a top speed of Mach 5, would test a dual-mode scramjet. This involved changes in the injection of the gaseous hydrogen fuel into the combustor. The scramjet would have to operate initially as a ramjet, with subsonic combustion. It would then have to transition to supersonic combustion, without any instability.

The final two flights were to be at Mach 10. These flights were considered the big unknowns. Ground testing in wind tunnels could not simulate continuous Mach 10 engine operations. Only blowdown tests, lasting for a millisecond, could be made. To create a performance curve required many, many tests because each test provided only a single data point. Engineers viewed the Mach 10 flight as the riskiest element of the project, for they had little ground data, and, as a result, two flights were planned to allow for a possible failure on the first flight.[15]

For the booster rockets, several candidates were available. In addition, the possibility of either a ground launch or an air launch from the NASA B-52B also was considered. Studies were made by both government and contractor teams of the different booster candidates. Although the target Mach numbers differed for the flights, the separation conditions were the same—a dynamic pressure of about 1000 pounds per square foot and a flight angle path of about +2 degrees.

Three different ground-launched solid rocket boosters were examined. Unlike liquid-fueled rockets, which could be throttled and then shutdown when the correct speed was reached, solid rockets continued to burn until all of the propellant was consumed. To adjust the burnout speed at which this occurred, ballast would have to be carried. The first candidate rocket was an Orion 50S GL. It was a Pegasus first stage that had been modified to serve as the second stage of the Taurus launch vehicle. The Orion 50S GL was capable of reaching all three separation speeds. For the Mach 5 flight, this required 11,000 pounds of ballast. The Mach 7 launch would require 5350 pounds and the Mach 10 flight only 500 pounds of ballast.

The difficulty with the Orion 50 S GL was in aerodynamic control during ascent and separation. It lacked the fins used for aerodynamic control on the standard Pegasus. A thrust-vectoring system with fins and ailerons would have to be added to the rocket. This would be a new development, with companion increases in both cost and risk.

The other two ground-launched boosters, the ATK Castor IVB and the ATK GEN-VN, had even greater shortcomings. The Castor IVB, used on the Maxus sounding rocket, had a maximum speed of Mach 8, well short of the required Mach 10 test conditions. Its use also would require addition of a thrust-vectoring system with four fins and ailerons, which could be provided by upgrading the existing control system. The GEN-VN was only slightly better. Its maximum velocity was Mach 9.8, just below the planned test speed. However, like the Orion 50S GL, the GEN-VN would also require a completely new thrust-vectoring system with fins and ailerons. Additionally, the GEN-VN had been used only as a strap-on booster for the Delta II rocket. These were ignited at liftoff and then separated after burnout from the Delta II's first stage. The GEN-VN had never flown as an independent rocket, and NASA considered its use for Hyper-X applications as too risky.

Because of the performance shortcomings of two candidate boosters, the risk of using the GEN-VN rocket in an entirely unproven role, and the need to add aerodynamic controls to all three boosters, the ground-launch option was eliminated for the Hyper-X.

The obvious option, engineers saw, was air launch of the X-43A from the NASA B-52B, using a modified Orion 50S first stage of Orbital Sciences Corporation's Pegasus launch vehicle as the Hyper-X launch vehicle (HXLV). Among the advantages were that the initial study indicated a single booster configuration would be developed to fly all three profiles. The only difference was the amount of ballast carried by the HXLV to adjust burnout speed. This translated to a perceived low risk of booster failure. Furthermore, the Pegasus already had made a number of successful satellite launches, so that the rocket was a judged to be a reliable system.

The three triangular fins on the Pegasus first stage would provide aerodynamic control during the flight. With the Hyper-X, the fins would be used to keep the booster stable during ascent, solid-fuel rocket burnout, and separation from the research vehicle. An air launch from beneath the wing of the NASA B-52B, which a modified Pegasus would facilitate, also meant flexibility in launch location. The B-52B had been used for the first six Pegasus satellite launches; the air-launch procedure also had a successful record. An additional advantage of using the air-launched Pegasus was a lower heating load during ascent, as compared with that of the three ground-launched boosters.

Although the Pegasus first stage offered the advantage of being an "off-the-shelf" booster, it would have to be modified for the Hyper-X mission profile. The extent of the modification that would be required, however, was not immediately apparent. For its role as the HXLV, the Pegasus first stage would be used, and the second and third stages, used for satellite launches, were removed.

Attached to the front of the HXLV booster was a two-part adapter. The first part was a cylinder that held most of the flight avionics. These included the inertial navigation system and other flight controls, the flight termination system, ordnance initiation, and electrical power subsystems. The cylindrical section of the adapter carried ballast plates, which weighed as much as 5000 pounds and adjusted the final vehicle mass, center of gravity, and pitch moment of inertia. Finally, the cylinder was fitted with thermal, stress, and acceleration transducers, which were monitored by the flight encoder.

At the front of the cylinder was a second element that served as the attachment point for the X-43A Hyper-X research vehicle (HXRV). A cone-shape section blended into a flat wedge that matched the differing shapes of the rear engine section, the half-nozzle, and the aft end of the X-43A's fuselage. This flat wedge contained the separation mechanism and connections to the X-43A's onboard systems. The complete adapter also served as the interface with the HXLV, allowing electrical and fluid connections between the two. The complete HXLV, adapter, and X-43A were called the "stack." The X-43A and adapter were referred to as the "short stack."[16]

Although the Pegasus had a solid reliability record, it did have limitations. The vehicle used "single-string" systems—no backup system that could be activated in the event of a failure. As a result, a single problem could cause the flight to be lost. (The only exception was the booster's flight termination system, which could be activated to destroy it in the event of a failure.) Adding redundant systems to the HXLV was not an option; software complexity issues would have made them very costly and time consuming to develop, and time and money were in short supply.

Once the X-43A's preliminary design was complete, NASA sought contractors to build it. Officials were determined that the procurement process for the project would be rapid. A request for proposal (RFP) based on McDonnell Douglas's preliminary design study for the vehicle was issued for construction. Terms of the RFP stipulated that if a contractor accepted the design study, submission of a detailed technical justification would not be required. Contractors who did not accept the existing design study, however, would be required to explain their objections and offer alternatives.

Two teams competed to build the fastest airplane in the world. The first was McDonnell Douglas and Pratt and Whitney. The second was led by MicroCraft, Inc., of Tullahoma, Tennessee, which would build the airframe, and included Rockwell International's Seal Beach division (systems), and General Applied Sciences Laboratory (scramjet engine).[17]

McDonnell Douglas had worked on the National Aerospace Plane, the DF-9, and the initial Hyper-X design studies, and had a long history of creating successful aircraft designs. Pratt and Whitney was a major U.S. engine manufacturer. As for the other team, Rockwell International had a distinguished history, and General Applied Sciences Laboratory had been involved in scramjet research since its very first stages in the 1950s. In contrast, MicroCraft had never built an actual airplane. Its specialty was construction of wind-tunnel models. McDonnell Douglas seemed a sure bet to win the Hyper-X contract, yet both teams had accepted the design study, so that there were no significant technical issues that would make one team preferable over the other. The contract was therefore awarded based on cost.

MicroCraft's rates were lower than those of the much larger McDonnell Douglas. As a result, NASA selection officials awarded the contract to MicroCraft. Thus, a small, woman-owned business in a little town in Tennessee that had never built an airplane would build the fastest airplane ever to fly. A formal contract was issued to the MicroCraft team in March 1997 for fabrication of the X-43As. Orbital Sciences had already received a separate contract, in February 1997, to fabricate the modified first stage Pegasus/HXLV boosters.

FROM PAPER PLANS TO A PRELIMINARY DESIGN

The initial Hyper-X design concepts and mission planning now had to be transformed into a preliminary design of a flyable airplane. The design and manufacturing phase was initiated in March of 1997, with the awarding of the contract to MicroCraft. Within NASA, there was a division of authority for the Hyper-X project. Langley was assigned overall program management responsibility and would oversee engineering for the project. Testing of the X-43A's scramjet would be done in the Langley wind tunnels, work that included engine flowpath development tests and integrated engine flowpath and control system tests. Much of this was done in Langley's 8-foot High Temperature Tunnel (HTT). The 12-foot length of the X-43A allowed full-scale testing of the scramjet engine in the HTT, eliminating the potential for problems of scale.[18]

Dryden had responsibility for integration and checkout of the X-43A vehicles, the booster, and the adapter once they were delivered. Dryden also had overall responsibility for the flight program, operating the B-52B launch aircraft, the chase planes, and the control rooms. Dryden was also to coordinate with the U.S. Navy-operated test range that would receive data from the X-43A in flight, which was then relayed to Dryden itself.[19]

The working relationship between Langley, Dryden, and the different contractors proved highly successful. Hyper-X project personnel came to view the result as a very highly integrated team. Langley, Dryden, Rockwell International (which soon merged with Boeing), MicroCraft, and General Applied Sciences Laboratory each did what they were best suited to do. (MicroCraft and GASL both became part of ATK Aerospace Company near the end of the Hyper-X project. ATK was the contractor for the HXLV rocket.) If NASA or one of the contractors had a question, all would meet and decide who could solve the problem most effectively. In some cases NASA possessed the necessary facilities or expertise, while in other cases it was the contractors who either had the expertise or could do the job more cheaply than the government.

An adapter in a Dryden hangar. This structure contained the separation system, any ballast required for a flight, the tanks for the high-pressure nitrogen gas and water-glycol coolant, and the electrical and fluid connections with the X-43A. (NASA photo EC99-44947-03.)

Paul Reukauf, Hyper-X deputy project manager at Dryden, noted that NASA, for example, had established certain procedures for using fasteners and safety wires and for running wires inside a vehicle. These procedures were based on decades of experience in building research vehicles. He later recalled that when NASA disagreed with how a contractor was doing something, a meeting would be held. The NASA representative would give their reasons for why they wanted the procedure done a specific way, go into the history of why NASA did it this way, and give examples of how NASA had learned these lessons in the past. Reukauf said that he could not recall a case in which the contractor did not acknowledge that NASA had more experience in the area of the issue being debated and that they would make the change. The flip side of this was that NASA personnel realized that every time the government asked for a change, the government also had to pay for the change. "So," Reukauf added, "bringing everybody with expertise to the table really made sense."[20]

During National Aerospace Plane, much effort was expended at building a national team made up of the different airframe and engine contractors. In reality, this was based on the late-1980s fad for what was called Japanese-style management, which was itself based on group consensus. The NASP program, along with its many and diverse goals, was to serve as a test of such management techniques. The test, like much else with the effort, proved unsuccessful, as employing the Japanese management style put NASP behind schedule by as much as a year.[21]

The management of the Hyper-X project, in contrast, was grounded in the different capabilities of the partners and a basic sense of fair play. Each team member did what they were best at, or could do just as well but at a lower cost than other members. In disagreements between NASA managers and contractors, rather than the government simply giving orders, the reasons and historical background were provided. The contractors saw why the changes were being requested. In the same way, the government was obligated to pay for the work it wanted done. Another advantage was that this management approach has as its central goal the construction of the Hyper-X, rather than trying to prove a doctrinal point in abstract management theory.

PROPELLANT OFF-LOADING

As the Hyper-X team set to work in March 1997, it faced the task of transforming paper concepts and design assumptions into real hardware. These included the actual weights associated with such features as hinges, fairings, joints, avionics, and other systems, and changes in design and thrust, drag, and total weight of the vehicle that would occur as the design was further refined. This entailed a great many tasks, but four issues stood out in the early days of the project: propellant offloading, vehicle recovery, stack stiffness, and separation.[22]

The booster selection analysis had assumed that adding ballast to the Pegasus first stage would be enough to reduce the burnout speed for the Mach 7 and 5 flights and to allow a nominal 40,000-foot launch altitude from the B-52B. The ballast needed for the Mach 7 flight was 10,600 pounds, whereas the Mach 5 flight required a total of 20,000 pounds of added weight. The two Mach 10 flights each would require just 2000 pounds of ballast.

The burnout speed of the modified Pegasus first stage was ideal for the pair of Mach 10 flights, but less so for the two other, slower tests. The proposed ballast loads for the Mach 7 and 5 missions increased the stack weight to the point that it would exceed the B-52B's maximum 41,400-pound limit on the X-15 pylon with the Pegasus adapter. In addition, the Hyper-X launch vehicle was required to coast after burnout. Air drag would slow the stack to the planned separation speed. The resulting aerodynamic heating during the coast period would have put too great a thermal load on the stack for its structure to withstand.

The stack weight and center of gravity would have to be kept within the B-52B's pylon limit, meet the limitations of the HXLV systems and/or structures, and result in the Mach 7 and 5 burnout speeds. Although the B-52B pylon weight limit was later raised, adding ballast was not the solution engineers initially thought it would be. Instead, another, more complicated approach was required to achieve the planned separation speed. So the Hyper-X design team made a number of studies to meet the requirements. Three potential approaches emerged: 1) offload propellant from the Orion 50S rocket motor to reduce the total impulse and thus the amount of ballast required; 2) perform energy-management maneuvers during ascent in order to reduce its velocity at burnout; and 3) reduce the launch altitude and Mach number in order to increase the amount of impulse needed to reach the planned separation speed.

The team's analysts showed that different approaches would have to be taken for the Mach 7 and 5 flights. Option 2 was eliminated for both launches. Unless major modifications were made, the energy-management maneuvers would exceed the structure and control-system limitations of the baseline Hyper-X launch vehicle. This was viewed as undesirable, as project engineers wanted to minimize any changes made to the booster.

For the Mach 5 flight, the third option of reducing the launch altitude and speed was also eliminated. The drop would have to be made at an altitude of less than 10,000 feet to result in a Mach 5 burnout speed. This left only the first option, the off-loading of propellant. This option set in motion a second round of design activity. One advantage engineers had in developing possible solutions was that the Hyper-X launch-vehicle boosters had yet to be built. Thus, engineers could start from scratch in developing a procedure.

ATK Thiokol, the contractor for the Orion 50S motor, developed a simple approach to reducing the propellant load for the Mach 5 launch. Inside the motor casing was a layer of insulation that separated the casing from the propellant. By increasing the thickness of this insulation, some 7000 pounds of solid propellant would be displaced. This reduced the total impulse, allowed standard casting tooling for the Orion 50S to be used, and eliminated the need to machine the propellant out of the casing. Additionally, the Hyper-X launch-vehicle ballistics at ignition and during most of the burn would follow the baseline profile. ATK Thiokol successfully demonstrated the fabrication technique necessary for the thicker insulation layer in the latter part of 1997. It was considered a feasible and moderate-risk procedure for building an off-loaded booster.

In contrast to the Mach 5 flight, both the propellant off-load and new launch profile options were available for the Mach 7 flight, but the preferable choice was not clear. Regarding off-loading, the same basic procedure of increasing the insulation thickness could be used as on the Mach 5 flight. Although the amount of off-loading required for the Mach 7 flight was not as great as that with the Mach 5 flight, a substantial amount of propellant would still have to be eliminated. This procedure would, however, allow the launch to be made at the baseline conditions of 40,000 feet and at a speed of Mach 0.8.

The other possibility was to use a standard Orion 50S motor, but launch using the lower-and-slower profile. Taking this approach dictated that the launch would be made at about 20,000 feet, and at a speed of Mach 0.5, reducing the burnout velocity to the planned Mach 7. This also would mean a standard Orion 50S motor could be used, but the launch itself would be made under conditions significantly different from those used with earlier Pegasus boosters. Higher air density at the lower altitude would increase dynamic pressure on the vehicle during the first part of the ascent. Additionally, the slower launch speed meant the stack would fly at transonic speeds for a longer period.[23]

The question of whether to off-load propellant from the Orion 50S booster and launch under standard conditions, or use the standard rocket with a new launch profile, underlined the issue of risk assessment. Although the Pegasus had started out as an off-the-shelf component for the Hyper-X launch-vehicle role, it had now become a very different booster. Whichever option was selected for the Mach 7 flight, the Hyper-X launch vehicle no longer had the heritage of the off-the-shelf Pegasus. The question became which of the new conditions were seen as the most likely to end in failure.

Reukauf recalled later, "We all said, no, no, no. We don't want to off-load a booster. That would be like having two simultaneous research experiments. We would have a Hyper-X and we would also have an off-loaded Pegasus booster, which had never been flown that way before."[24] As a result, the lower/slower launch profile was selected.

VEHICLE RECOVERY

While the debate over launch options for the Mach 7 flight was underway, another issue arose. The request for proposal stated that the X-43A vehicles were to be expendable. Once the scramjet test was over, each vehicle would perform maneuvers to acquire aerodynamic data and then splash into the Pacific Ocean and sink. NASA did not consider it necessary to recover the X-43A intact after the flight. The request for proposal went on to say, however, that if a contractor did come up with a way to recover the vehicle, NASA would consider adopting the suggestion. (The term "land" was not specifically used.) Recovering the vehicle did seem to have advantages; the telemetry system would provide data on how the vehicle withstood the flight and register any anomalous events. Even so, a physical examination of a vehicle's postflight condition could be of potential value.

Both McDonnell Douglas and MicroCraft suggested recovery methods, with the focus on retrieving the Mach 5 vehicle. Because of the X-43A's small size, neither contractor proposed using recovery parachutes. There simply was not enough room inside the vehicle for the parachutes to fit. Instead, Reukauf later recalled, McDonnell Douglas suggested flying the X-43A to a water landing in an area that was relatively shallow. The vehicle would splash down and sink to the bottom. The U.S. Navy would then send trained seals for the recovery. The marine mammals would swim down, find the vehicle on the sea floor, and attach a line to it. The X-43A could then be brought to the surface. The Navy had considerable experience and success using seals for such recovery work. As the McDonnell Douglas team was not selected for the contract, their approach was never examined in any detail.

MicroCraft also proposed a recovery scheme, but instead of a splashdown, skids would be fitted to the X-43A for a runway landing. MicroCraft engineers wanted to protect the scramjet engine from damage on touchdown, and so an unusual design was offered. Rather than long skids that extended from the bottom of the X-43A, engineers proposed very short skids mounted on top of the vehicle. The X-43A would roll inverted, the skids would extend, and the vehicle would make a touchdown.

A limited amount of work was done on refining details of a Mach 5 vehicle recovery for about six months. Engineers were faced with a number of higher-priority issues, and, as Reukauf recalled, "nobody really wanted to mess with the landing concept very much." However, Boeing (which had merged with North American by this time) had a considerable desire to land one of the X-43As and pressed hard to keep the recovery option alive.

NASA engineers did talk with the U.S. Navy about possible recovery efforts. By this time the Navy test range off the California coast had been selected for the Hyper-X launches, and San Nicolas Island was a suitable candidate for the recovery site. Hyper-X project engineers asked Navy officials if, after getting the Mach 5 vehicle to San Nicolas Island, they could then land it on the base runway. Navy officials granted permission for NASA to use the runway, but specified several major limitations. First, the Navy insisted that NASA guarantee the X-43A would land on San Nicolas Island, making it clear that the X-43A could not splash down in the ocean surrounding the island because the area contained a marine mammal sanctuary. (This stipulation would have eliminated the McDonnell Douglas recovery proposal.)

The Navy no longer used the waters around San Nicolas Island for operations, as anything splashing into the ocean created enough noise to disturb the whales, sea lions, and elephant seals that inhabited the area. If a marine mammal were to be hit by the X-43A, Reukauf recalled "that would be a major problem." He added, "I came away from that meeting feeling like they [the Navy] didn't care if we wiped out their cafeteria which was just off the end of the runway, but that we better not get in the water."

Despite this, the possibility of recovering an X-43A continued to be discussed as late as the spring of 1999. Instead of San Nicholas Island, the sounding rocket launch site at Poker Flats Research Range in Alaska was proposed as an alternative recovery site. Despite continued interest, however, the effort could not be justified. Reukauf noted later, "We didn't have a very good low-speed database. We didn't have a subsonic database for this vehicle upside down, and it wasn't even clear that we could control the vehicle well enough. ... [W]e said, 'we're creating another research experiment trying to land.' We finally said no. Landing is going to cost us way too much money and it's going to detract from the primary experiment. Just make sure we get the data and we will not land the vehicle. We essentially had to say landing is off the table; we're not going to land."[25]

By this point, not only recovering the X-43A was off the table, but the Mach 5 flight itself was as well. The transition from subsonic to supersonic combustion was important for development of a scramjet that could operate across a range of speeds. This capability was the goal of the X-43A's Mach 5 flight. But an operational scramjet was still a long way off. The operability of a scramjet had yet to be proven with the Hyper-X. To do this, it would be flown at specific speeds, to benchmark the design tools and techniques. The dual-mode data, again, were nice to have, but the Hyper-X team realized that to meet the project goals they would need to gather as much flight time at Mach 7 as possible.

The revised plan, which was approved by NASA in December of 1997, called for only three flights. The first two would be made at Mach 7 and were to demonstrate that the scramjet engine could produce enough thrust to overcome the vehicle's drag, producing positive acceleration. By launching the pair of Mach 7 flights at lower altitude and speed, the unknowns of the off-loaded booster would be eliminated. The third flight was to be the Mach 10 maximum-speed flight. The DF-9 vehicle was designed to cruise at Mach 10, and the X-43A flight would demonstrate whether the engine's thrust would match the amount of drag, allowing the vehicle to maintain its speed. Under the revised schedule, the Mach 10 flight was not viewed as being as critical as originally thought; the Mach 7 flights were to be the main focus, and the dual-mode Mach 5 research flight would have to wait for another program.[26]

STACK FREQUENCY

The issues of the propellant off-loading and the Mach 5 flight were not the only ones that had to be addressed early in the design effort. Before Orbital Sciences received the contract for the Hyper-X launch vehicle, their structural modeling of the initial design indicated that the first longitudinal bending mode of the stack was well below the design requirements of its control system. This was called the "stack frequency." The stack had the heavy

X-43A on its nose, and the assembled vehicle would be exposed to significant forces during the 90-second powered flight. As a result, the structure would flex. The Pegasus guidance system was designed to ignore vibrations with frequencies above 7.5 Hz, as these would result from the vehicle bending rather than from course changes. Because the HXLV guidance system had this same constraint, the original HXLV specifications required bending modes above 10 Hz.

Not meeting this requirement could be disastrous. Among other things, the guidance system would "see" the low-frequency vibrations as a change in the vehicle's angle of attack. It would then try to make corrections and possibly end up "chasing" the vibration resulting in computer-induced oscillation. (These are similar to pilot-induced oscillations in manned aircraft.)

The X-43A's large mass, and its location at the front of the stack, meant that the structure had to be as stiff as possible. The major compliance issue was with the forward end of the adapter, where it connected to the X-43A vehicle. The X-43A and adapter designs had to be reevaluated, with major consequences to the project. The primary keel structure of the X-43A and the entire booster adapter were to be made of steel, rather than the lighter-weight materials originally chosen. As would be expected, the change resulted in a dramatic increase in weight. (This is the traditional bane of aerospace projects, dating back to the work of the Wright brothers.)

The pre-contract-award mass properties for the X-43A and the adapter were about 3300 pounds. With the change in component materials, the weight of the final version of the Mach 7 X-43A and adapter had increased to 5130 pounds. The Hyper-X launch vehicle had enough mass margin to absorb this increase, and so a top speed of Mach 7 was still possible. For the Mach 10 flight, however, the weight increase had eliminated any design margin. To retain the capability for a Mach 10 separation speed, the cylindrical section of the adapter for this flight was made of aluminum, while unneeded subsystems were removed from the forward section to which the X-43A would be attached and other components also were constructed from aluminum instead of steel.

The unexpected weight increase caused by the stack-frequency issue revealed an advantage in selection of a Pegasus first stage to power the Hyper-X launch vehicle. The ground-launched Castor IVB also had the 7.5-Hz limitation, so that the same modifications would have to have been made to the adapter and X-43A. That ground-launched booster, however, lacked the sizable performance margin of the Pegasus. The weight increase resulting from the beefed-up adaptor and research vehicle would have prevented the Castor IVB from reaching the Mach 7 separation speed.[27]

In mid-December 1997, it appeared that stack stiffness exceeded the requirement. By October of 1998, new predictions indicated that the first flexing frequency of both the pitch and yaw axis were lower than expected, at 7.75 and 9.6 Hz, respectively. This, in turn, would require modification of the Hyper-X launch vehicle flight control system.[28]

Discussions among Orbital Sciences, Langley Research Center, Dryden Research Center, and MicroCraft engineers indicated the best solution was a software modification. However, the stiffness and modal data would not be available until March 1999. To prevent delays, Orbital Sciences began work on an alternative hardware fix that involved moving the existing control system feedback sensors aft. By mid-November, Orbital had agreed that a software solution, specifically a notch filter change, was the preferred option. As a backup, Orbital continued design work for moving the feedback sensors.[29]

In March of 1999, structural tests of the adaptor and complete stack were conducted in the Dryden loads lab. These included structural flutter, mode, bending, and interaction testing. These tests revealed that their stiffness was actually higher than predicted, and the stack stiffness/first bending frequency issue was resolved.[30]

SEPARATING IS HARD TO DO

The most pressing issue in the early stages of the design effort was the separation of the X-43A from the adapter following the Hyper-X launch vehicle burnout. The first difficulty to be addressed was that the separation would take place at a very high speed of Mach 7 or 10, with a dynamic pressure on the vehicle of around 1000 pounds per square foot. When the X-43A separated, a mass of about 3000 pounds mounted well forward of the Pegasus booster's center of gravity would suddenly be gone. This could potentially cause the empty booster to pitch up and strike the X-43A. Another factor was that the two vehicles were asymmetric. Because the aft end of the X-43A served as the exhaust nozzle, its surface was sloped, whereas the rear of the scramjet formed a vertical box. The aft end of the vehicle was attached to the adapter by a wedge-shaped ramp. The result was that during separation the expanding gap between the X-43A and the adapter would create a rapidly changing flowfield that was potentially nonlinear and highly dynamic. No one really knew what would happen as a result because separation of two such asymmetric shapes at these high speeds and dynamic pressures had never been attempted.

The question that emerged centered on the mechanics of the separation. Project personnel realized that the separation issue was the "long pole" of the Hyper-X "tent." There was no lack of either solid proposals or less-than-helpful "bright ideas" proposed to address the problem.

The original separation concept was based on that in phase 3 of the dual-fuel study. The X-43A was attached to the adapter by two explosive bolts in the base of the vehicle. The X-43A also rode on three ejection rails, one at the center of the aft bulkhead and two others at the front end of the adapter.

The rails held the X-43A in place during the powered phase and then guided it during the ejection sequence. This was accomplished by two pistons pushing on the base of the X-43A, with the force directed through the vehicle's center of gravity. Pyrotechnic cartridges that generated high-pressure gas drove the pistons. While the pistons used most of the gas, part of it was diverted through a tube that expelled the gas out the top of the adapter. This counteracted the nose-up moment on the booster caused by the shift in its center of gravity.

Among the other ideas offered up to counteract the potential nose-up moment was putting a flap on the top of the adapter or attaching a small rocket to the aft end of the Pegasus. The separation sequence would require about 0.6 seconds before the aft end of the X-43A no longer overlapped the forward end of the adapter. At this point, any chance the X-43A and the Hyper-X launch vehicle would strike one another was eliminated.[31]

To address the separation issue, a joint NASA/contractor integrated product team (IPT) was established. Mary K. Lockwood of Langley Research Center was the lead for the separation IPT. She and the rest of the team, a group of discipline-specific engineers, began working to understand the dynamics of the separation event. Griff Corpening, Dryden chief engineer for the two Mach 7 flights and a member of the separation ITP, recalled the experience as frustrating. He said that at every meeting in which the issue was briefed a number of people in the audience would offer other ideas about what to do. The IPT members then were required to discuss those ideas. The IPT seemed unable, as a result, to keep the process moving forward toward developing a practical separation design.

Among proposed separation concepts was modification of the ramp-shaped forward end of the adapter. It was to be split down the middle and each side would pivot on piano hinges. At separation, the two sides would swing 180 degrees to clear the X-43A. Another concept called for combining the pistons and guide rails. Two large rods would be attached to the X-43A's aft end. The rods would extend until the vehicle was clear of the end of the adapter, and then explosive bolts would fire to release it.

Two other ideas were intended to make the vehicle separation more symmetrical. Rather than constructing the adapter as a single piece, the unit's wedge-shaped forward end would be attached to the X-43A, and the pair would separate from the cone-shaped aft section of the adapter as a single unit. A thruster would fire to push the Pegasus away from the X-43A forward adapter. Once clear, the forward section of the adapter would then separate from the X-43A. One proposal suggested use of an airbag to push the wedge section of the adapter away. Another was to put drag brakes on either side of the forward adapter, to slow it after its release from the X-43A.

A final idea was much simpler, but odd looking. The X-43A would be mounted on the one-piece adapter, but upside down. The idea was that when the Pegasus pitched up from the inverted X-43A, the movement would be away from the research vehicle. Despite the ingenuity, all of these ideas proved unworkable.

The IPT members also solicited input from both the U.S. Army's Redstone Arsenal and Sandia National Laboratory, asking for insights they might be able to offer. The IPT quickly learned that no organization they could find had any experience with this type of high-speed/high-dynamic pressure/ asymmetrical separation. Their general consensus, however, was that the 0.6-second separation time was too long.

The Sandia engineers did have experience with high-speed missile reentry vehicles. Some of these designs had the ability to maneuver at very high speeds. The tests of these reentry vehicles were done using sounding rockets, which would loft the simulated warhead in a high, arching trajectory. When the payload separated, it did so in space, so that the dynamic pressure was effectively zero. Based on this experience, the Sandia engineers recommended having the X-43A reenter, in order to avoid the separation at high dynamic pressures. Although attractive in principle, later analysis by Hyper-X engineers indicated the Mach 10 flight would require a substantial amount of thermal protection material to cope with reentry heating. Because of the vehicle's 12-foot size, the added thermal protection would have had to be added to its interior, and of course there was no internal volume to spare.

With a reentry profile ruled out, Sandia then suggested adding a long fairing to the Hyper-X launch vehicle that was similar in size and shape to the standard Pegasus booster's second and third stages. The X-43A would then be mounted on the bottom of the fairing. Its top surface would be integrated into the fairing, with only the wings and scramjet protruding. Once at separation conditions, the vehicle would be ejected downward, like a bomb being dropped from an aircraft. The problem with this concept was that the X-43A would have to pass through the fairing's bow shock. The separation IPT members were concerned that the X-43A's guidance system would be unable to cope with the upset this would create.

Sandia engineers also strongly recommended that whatever separation system was eventually picked, the rails not be used in its design. They said that the laboratory's experience was that, no matter how well they worked in ground tests, rails could always be counted on to bind up in actual flight. They proposed that the forward adapter be split down the center with pyrotechnic charges then pushed laterally away from the Pegasus as quickly as possible. Small thrusters also would fire to provide the velocity needed to separate the X-43A cleanly from the Pegasus.

The separation IPT concluded that, of the various concepts, the Sandia split-adapter proposal appeared to be the best and was accepted as a basis upon which the separation sequence could be built.

A manufacturing readiness review (MRR) was held in June 1997 at Dryden Research Center. By this time, the separation team had further developed the original Sandia concept. The sequence would begin with the firing of the two pistons. When the X-43A had moved 2 inches, the two clamshell halves of the forward adapter would be split apart by pyrotechnic pistons or springs. The halves were hinged at the rear edges and would swing back against the sides of the adapter. The halves were made of thin aluminum to maintain the necessary stiffness (caused by stack stiffness requirements), and four explosive bolts rather than the original two were used to secure the X-43A. The hinges eliminated the risk in the original Sandia concept that the two large halves of the forward adapter might strike the X-43A as they separated. Keeping the two halves attached to the Pegasus also allowed them to serve as speed brakes, to decelerate the booster, and to increase the distance between it and the X-43A more quickly.

During the manufacturing readiness review, various participants expressed concern that, even with the clamshell design, there was still a significant period of time in which the X-43A's wings could strike one of the halves. During the discussions, a suggestion was made to change the two-part arrangement to allow the forward adapter to swing down as a single piece. This was the design that was ultimately adopted and became known as the "drop jaw."

Given the long debate about the separation, it was inevitable that the drop jaw would also be questioned. With the jaw hanging down at a 90-degree angle, some engineers expressed concerns that shocks waves from the drop jaw would strike the X-43A's nozzle area, causing the vehicle to pitch downward. The vehicle's control system might not then be able to counteract the motion. Determining whether this was a real risk would require extensive wind-tunnel tests, Monte Carlo analysis, and computational-fluid-dynamics simulations.[32]

INITIAL EFFORTS—A SUMMING UP

The Hyper-X had now been transformed from paper plans to a workable design concept, and the four issues that had emerged during this design effort had been successfully dealt with.

The Mach 7 flights represented a question of risk assessment. Either propellant off-load or lower/slower launch was technically feasible. The judgment of all concerned was that a propellant off-load was too risky on a first flight. Wind-tunnel data with the modified model indicated that the Hyper-X launch vehicle could successfully fly the new profile.

The issue of attempting to recover the vehicle was a much simpler decision. The cost and difficulty were too great, and the value was too low. The matter was dropped.

The stack stiffness issue was much more complicated. A great deal of work had been required to ensure that the stack would have the required stiffness and to develop the means to predict vibration frequency. This issue, like the other two, was now closed.

Separation remained as an open issue, however, but the system design had finally been hammered out. There was to be further analysis of the separation sequence, specifically to determine whether the drop jaw should be used or the forward adaptor should remain fixed. In the end, separation would remain an issue in the minds of the engineers until the actual flight was made.

The Hyper-X project now became a march toward the first flight. There were no "showstoppers" along the way. It was now a matter of conducting the wind-tunnel testing, Monte Carlo analyses, and computational-fluid-dynamics simulations to refine the basic design concept, launch profile, separation, and free flight of the X-43A. The funding profile had been changed to meet the project's demands. The booster, adapter, and X-43A had to be built, their systems checked out, and personnel trained in their operation.[33]

On the negative side, the process of refining the design had resulted in unexpected costs. More work and analysis had been required than was originally believed necessary. This, in turn, forced a restructuring of the project. The Mach 5 flight was dropped; two Mach 7 flights and a single Mach 10 flight would be made.

The long march that the engineers now began would prove to be a difficult journey. As is so often the case in flight research, its outcome would test the team in ways they could never have predicted.

NOTES

[1] *The Hypersonic Revolution Case Studies in the History of Hypersonic Technology,* Vol. III, edited by Larry Schweikart, Air Force History and Museum Program, Bolling AFB, Washington, DC, 1998, pp. 189–191.

[2] Iliff, Kenneth W., and Curtis Peebles, *From Runway to Orbit: Reflections of a NASA Engineer,* NASA Headquarters, Washington, DC, 2004, pp. 310–336.

[3] *The Hypersonic Revolution Case Studies in the History of Hypersonic Technology,* Vol. III, pp. 279, 280, 283, 298, 299, 308, 309, and Dave Lux history interview, March 8, 2005, NASA Dryden Flight Research Center History Office, pp. 15, 16.

[4] Iliff and Peebles, *From Runway to Orbit,* pp. 307, 308, and *The Hypersonic Revolution Case Studies in the History of Hypersonic Technology,* Vol. III, pp. 267, 268, 310–316.

Ironically, the replacement for the NASP was the X-33, which was also a single-stage-to-orbit vehicle. Although the X-33 was rocket powered, it still required a very lightweight structure. Problems with the composite material used to build the X-33's fuel tank led to its cancellation in 2001.

[5] McCurdy, Howard E., *Faster Better Cheaper: Low-Cost Innovation in the U.S. Space Program,* Johns Hopkins Univ. Press, Baltimore, 2001, pp. 49, 50, 53, 106, 107.

[6] Iliff and Peebles, *From Runway to Orbit,* p. 325, and *The Hypersonic Revolution Case Studies in the History of Hypersonic Technology,* Vol. III, pp. 284, 285, 296.

[7] *The Hypersonic Revolution Case Studies in the History of Hypersonic Technology,* Vol. III, p. 316, and *The Hypersonic Revolution Case Studies in the History of Hypersonic Technology,*

Vol. II, edited by Richard P. Hallion, Air Force History and Museum Program, Bolling AFB, Washington, DC, 1998, p. vi-xxvii.

[8] Voland R. T., K. E. Rock, L. D. Huebner, D. W. Witte, K. E. Fisher, and C. R. McClinton, "Hyper-X Engine Design and Ground Test Program," AIAA Paper 98–1532, pp. 2–4.

[9] Reukauf, Paul, history interview, Feb. 17, 2005, NASA Dryden Flight Research Center History Office, p. 10.

[10] Hunt, James L., and Edward A. Eiswirth, "NASA's Dual-Fuel Airbreathing Hypersonic Vehicle Study," AIAA paper 96-4591, Nov. 1996, pp. 1–4, and David E. Reubush, "Hyper-X Stage Separation – Background and Status," AIAA Paper 99–4818, Nov. 1999, pp. 2, 3.

[11] Reukauf history interview, pp. 10, 11, and Voland et al., "Hyper-X Engine Design and Ground Test Program," p. 2.

[12] Rausch, Vincent L., Charles R. McClinton, and J. Larry Crawford, "Hyper-X: Flight Validation of Hypersonic Airbreathing Technology," p. 2.

[13] "Air Force Rocket Laboratory X-43A Data Briefing," Dec. 9, 2005, Unclassified draft version, p. 2.

[14] Rausch et al., "Hyper-X: Flight Validation of Hypersonic Airbreathing Technology," p. 2.

[15] Reukauf history interview, pp. 26–29, Delma C. Freeman, Jr., David E. Reubush, Charles R. McClinton, Vincent L. Rausch, and J. Larry Crawford, "The NASA Hyper-X Program," pp. 4, 5.

[16] Joyce, Phillip J., John B. Pomroy, and Laurie Grindle, "The Hyper-X Launch Vehicle: Challenges and Design Considerations for Hypersonic Flight Testing," AIAA Paper 2005-3333, pp. 3–6. The Adapter's cylindrical section was also referred to as the Ballast/Avionics Module (B/AM).

[17] Harsha, Phillip T., Lowell C. Keel, Anthony Castrogiovanni, and Robert T. Sherrill, "X-43A Vehicle Design and Manufacture," AIAA Paper 2005–3334, pp. 1, 2.

[18] Voland et al., "Hyper-X Engine Design and Ground Test Program," pp. 3–12.

[19] Lux, Dave, private communication, Jan. 12, 2006, NASA Dryden Flight Research Center.

[20] Reukauf history interview, pp. 11–15, 35–37.

[21] *The Hypersonic Revolution Case Studies in the History of Hypersonic Technology,* Vol. III, pp. 159, 163, 167, 197, 198. The basic flaw in NASP was not in the management system, but the gap between the available physics and the goals of the program.

[22] *Aerospace Projects Highlights*, May 20, 1997, NASA Dryden Flight Research Center History Office, p. 3.

[23] Joyce et al., "The Hyper-X Launch Vehicle: Challenges and Design Considerations for Hypersonic Flight Testing," pp. 5, 6.

[24] Reukauf history interview, p. 28.

[25] Ibid, pp. 29–32, and *Aerospace Weekly Report*, April 23, 1999, NASA Dryden Flight Research Center History Office, p. 2.

[26] Reukauf history interview, pp. 28–33.

[27] Corpening, Griff, history interview, Dec. 20, 2004 Dryden History Office, pp. 9, 10, 33, 34, 45, and Joyce et al., "The Hyper-X Launch Vehicle: Challenges and Design Considerations for Hypersonic Flight Testing," pp. 5, 6.

[28] *Aerospace Projects Highlights*, Dec. 19, 1997, and Oct. 16, 1998, p. 4.

[29] *Aerospace Projects Highlights*, Nov. 6, 1998, p. 4, Nov. 13, 1998, p. 3, and Nov. 20, 1998, p. 4.

[30] Ibid, March 19, 1999, p. 3, and March 26, 1999, p. 3.

[31] Reubush, David E., "Hyper-X Stage Separation – Background and Status," AIAA Paper 99-4818, Nov. 1999, p. 2.

[32] Ibid, pp. 2, 7, and Corpening interview, p. 13.

[33] Reukauf history interview, p. 29.

Chapter 3

MARCH TO THE FIRST FLIGHT

It all looked so easy when you did it on paper—where valves never froze, gyros never drifted, and rocket motors did not blow up in your face.

Milton W. Rosen, rocket scientist, 1956

With design of the various elements of the stack completed, work could begin on the numerous simulations, tests, ground checkouts, and other activities that had to be undertaken before the first flight could be made. This was a long and complicated process, one that would prove longer and more complicated than had been expected.

With the Hyper-X launch vehicle, changes to the vehicle shape, the addition of the X-43A, the new flight path, and lower drop altitude chosen for the Mach 7 flights all required extensive analysis and testing. The emphasis was on use of existing technology. Griff Corpening, project chief engineer for the two Mach 7 flights, noted: "what we wanted to do was focus on those changes in the launch vehicle, not on the things that were similar between us and Pegasus."[1]

HYPER-X LAUNCH-VEHICLE MODIFICATIONS AND WIND-TUNNEL TESTING

While the Hyper-X launch vehicle was a modified version of the Orion 50S Pegasus first stage, meeting the demands of the new flight profile and environment required several modifications. These included changes to the booster's materials and structures as well as to the mission profile. The three fins on the Pegasus were constructed from a one-piece foam core with wet-laid graphite-composite construction. A central tapered polygon titanium shaft attached the fin to the actuator assembly, which moved the fin in flight. All three fins were identical in shape, design, and construction.

The Mach 7 and 10 flight profiles required modifications to the fins because of the increased heating they would experience during ascent. The most serious issue was the gap heating between the fin root and the fuselage of the aft skirt. The small amount of space available between the fin and fuselage limited the thickness of thermal protection material that could be added. The fins also received additional thermal protection; silica phenolic tiles were bonded to their leading edges to protect the fins against aerodynamic heating. Addition of the tiles altered the shape of the fins from their standard configuration, and the extra thermal protection increased their leading-edge radius.

The Hyper-X launch-vehicle flight path was very different from the steep climb toward orbit made during a conventional Pegasus satellite launch. Five seconds after the HXLH was dropped from the B-52B, the motor ignited, and the stack flew horizontally for several seconds. Between 8 and 13 seconds after launch, the HXLV made a maximum pull up into a steep climb. But rather than continuing in this trajectory, it then made a push-down into a negative angle of attack. In the process, the stack's velocity increased rapidly. By the time burnout occurred, the stack was flying nearly horizontally. There was a coast period of several seconds before the X-43A separation occurred.

These changes to the flight path resulted in both new heat protection requirements and different loading on the wing assembly and the fillet that were attached to the rocket motor. The standard Pegasus wing had flexible silicone-based room-temperature vulcanizing (RTV) sheets bonded to its leading edges, while the wing's surface (called the "acreage") was covered with cork. These materials were inadequate for the conditions of the HXLV ascent profile.

The wing's leading edges had upgraded thermal protection compared to that of the standard Pegasus. This consisted of molded leading-edge tiles of either silica phenolic, for the Mach 7 flights, or carbon phenolic for the Mach 10 launch. These modifications were required because of both the severe stagnation-point heating on the leading edges and the shock-on-shock heating caused by the vehicle bow shock and the X-43A's control surface shocks. The thermal protection on the wing acreage also had to be changed as a result of these more severe heating conditions. Depending on the area and its heating conditions, cork, RTV, or cork/RTV hybrid sheets were bonded to the composite surface.

The wing was attached to the Orion 50S motor with a fillet structure made of low-stress Nomex foam with graphite-facing sandwich construction. The loading on the fillet was solely caused by aerodynamics. Because of the unconventional flight conditions the Hyper-X launch vehicle would face, the loading on the fillet was extensively analyzed. The higher sideslip loads required an increased ply lay-up in the fillet's forward nose and midsection, which provided localized reinforcement. The change in loading required companion changes to the way the fillet's nose was attached to the rocket motor casing. The Pegasus fillet used an inverted composite T-bracket that was bonded to both the fillet's nose and the rocket casing. For the HXLV, this T-bracket was replaced by a G-10 shoe, which was bolted through both the fillet and the casing.

Allowances also had to be made for deformation of the HXLV in flight that did not occur during a standard Pegasus launch. A sliding joint was added between the wing and the fillet to accommodate changes in the wing shape under maximum aerodynamic loading. The fillet also was modified to accommodate expansion of the motor case during the rocket burn. A 4-inch silicone joint was bonded to both the fillet and motor case. This provided a flexible aerodynamic seal around the perimeter of the fillet.[2]

The stack's transonic aerodynamics posed a major challenge. In the seconds immediately following engine ignition, the stack was flying at a fairly high angle of attack of about 10 degrees. The odd shape of the X-43A on the nose of the abbreviated Pegasus stage also created significant aerodynamic effects at transonic speeds. The wings, fins, and other sharp edges on the X-43A vehicle generated vortices, which interacted with the control fins of the HXLV in unpredictable ways. All of this was analyzed to avoid stability problems.

Wind-tunnel tests were done to determine the aerodynamic forces and moments the vehicle would experience. The way these tests were conducted was a reflection of the project decision to consider the HXLV an off-the-shelf item. The Pegasus wind-tunnel model was modified with the addition of the X-43A vehicle. To project personnel, there seemed to be no reason to build a completely new model, when the existing one would serve just as well with minor modifications. On the Pegasus, the vertical rudder provided yaw control. The two dihedral fins were the control surfaces that provided both roll and pitch control for the vehicle. These fins are turned in opposite directions to roll the vehicle left or right. For pitch control, they would move together up and down. On the wind-tunnel model, these fins were designed to move in five-degree increments.

To determine the aerodynamic effects of the X-43A, a test would be done at a specific angle of attack with the fins neutral, then with the fins at plus or minus 5 degrees, and yet again with the fins at plus or minus 10 degrees. This would then be performed at various angles of attack and sideslip. To complete the aerodynamic database for the complete range of fin settings, the data from the 5-degree deflection intervals would be connected in a linear fashion. As a result, to find the roll authority with the fins at 2.5 degrees, engineers would simply add the forces measured at zero degrees and at 5 degrees, and divide by two for a linear average.[3]

Such linear interpolate between two such wind-tunnel test conditions is standard practice. The data indicated that the lower and slower launch conditions of the two Mach 7 flights, and the resulting higher dynamic pressures and the longer period of time the stack would be flying at subsonic speeds, would not pose a risk of failure. The existing Pegasus fin actuation system (FAS) design would be able to accommodate the conditions with a comfortable amount of torque margin.

In modifying the Pegasus for use as the Hyper-X launch vehicle, engineers were influenced both by technical issues and project management policy. The new ascent trajectory required additional heat protection and structural changes. Decisions such as these were made based on engineering requirements. Other decisions were based on policy about how the project was to be run. Among these policy decisions was to use the existing Pegasus database and wind-tunnel model to confirm that the new HXLV launch profile could be accomplished successfully. The other possibility was to undertake a complete design review. This would evaluate the HXLV as if it were a new vehicle being built from scratch. Managers and engineers chose to focus on Hyper-X-specific issues and based as much of the effort as possible on existing data. This kept the project focused on the research goals. There was nothing to indicate these policies were in error.

HYPER-X SEPARATION ANXIETY

Overshadowing the issue of launch, in the minds of Hyper-X engineers, was that of the X-43A separation during the complicated flow conditions at a dynamic pressure of 1000 pounds per square foot while flying at speeds of Mach 7 or 10. This was seen as the "long pole" of the program. Unless this issue was resolved, and senior NASA management convinced that separation could be accomplished with an acceptable degree of risk, the X-43A might never fly.

Preliminary wind-tunnel testing of the separation conditions was done before the development contract was awarded, of course. These tests were conducted with an early X-43A/adapter configuration in the 20-inch Mach 6 and 31-inch Mach 10 wind tunnels at Langley Research Center. The X-43A model was mounted on a "sting" (a metal rod) that passed through the adapter model. The position of the adapter model could be varied for each run to simulate the movement of the X-43A away from the adapter.

Although the tests provided data as a function of the X-43A's axial position relative to the adapter, they bore several limitations. First, the model adapter and X-43A were held in a fixed position relative to one another. As a result, the tests were steady-state approximations of a very dynamic event. The large sting was also thought to have compromised the data. Additionally, the drop-jaw adapter had been selected following the initial review process, so that concept too needed testing. There also were concerns that the drop jaw could create a large normal force on the aft end of the X-43A, causing the research vehicle to pitch down. The onboard guidance system would not be able to correct for this, and the mission would be lost. As a result, computational-fluid-dynamics studies, as well as additional wind-tunnel testing, were scheduled.[4]

In preparation for the wind-tunnel tests, CFD calculations were made to investigate the drop-jaw configuration. The goal was to model the aerodynamic effects as the jaw rotated to different angles during separation. SAMcfd software was used to generate both two-dimensional analysis of the initial gap flow between the X-43A and the adapter as they begin to separate, as well as three-dimensional stage-separation simulations. The SAMcfd program's grid-generation capability was used for inviscid flow cases. The program created a set of grids simulating the complex shapes of the X-43A and the adapter. Grids with four to five million cells were generated for the stage-separation simulation, and 5000 iterations were made on a Cray C-90 supercomputer until a steady state was reached.

For viscous simulations of steady flow about separate surfaces, the OVERFLOW program was used. Employing an overset grid system, surface patches covering the surface of the vehicle and adapter were generated, as were body-filling volume grids. These were sized to include the X-43A and adapter in their specific positions relative to one another.

The overset grid system was seen as an advantage in generating the different separation configurations. The body-filled grids were simply translated and rotated to move components into new positions. The OVERFLOW program's grid-joining process then reconnected the body-filled and background grids to complete the test. The computer simulations of the X-43A and adapter also were covered with overlapping surface grids representing geometric features. The fin leading and trailing edges, as well as the vehicle and scramjet inlet leading edges, were covered with wraparound strips. The body-filling volume grids were then "grown" 8 inches from the surface. The total grid size was 2.8 million points in 52 component grids, 1.4 million points for the X-43A and blade support hardware, 600,000 points for the adapter, and 800,000 points for the background grid.

The simulation was initially used to establish the low base-pressure flowfields for the X-43A and adapter. A sequence of runs was made for each case, beginning with high smoothing levels and short time steps. To speed the steady-state convergence, grid sequencing and multigrid were used. Between 2000 and 4000 steps were required before the convergence forces and moments were obtained on the fine grid level.

The next steps were to validate the OVERCAST program at high Mach numbers and to gain confidence in the grid system developed for the stage-separation configuration. This was accomplished by making a series of simulations for the X-43A alone, which were then compared with the data from a sting-mounted 1/8th-scale model tested in Langley's 20-inch Mach 6 wind tunnel. The OVERFLOW simulations assumed laminar flow, and data reflecting the effects of the sting were not included in the computations. Measurements were taken for normal force, axial force, and the pitching-moment coefficients (C_N, C_A, and C_M).

When the OVERFLOW simulations were compared with Mach 6 wind-tunnel data, the agreement for the normal force and pitching moment were judged as quite good. The axial-force agreement was fair over a wide range of angles of attack. The stage separation was to take place at a zero-degree angle of attack, while the scramjet test condition was to be at 2 degrees. The level of agreement was deemed adequate for the separation simulations.

In addition to these computations, comparisons were made with wind-tunnel runs with turbulent boundary layers and with flight-range Reynolds numbers. The normal force and pitching moment agreed closely, while the axial force changed as expected. Inviscid flow simulations using the SAMcfd program also were made at angles of attack of zero and two degrees. The computational-fluid-dynamics produced similar levels of agreement in normal forces and pitching moments.

While the initial SAMcfd and OVERFLOW simulations were being made, additional wind-tunnel testing was done in the U.S. Air Force's Arnold Engineering Development Center in Tullahoma, Tennessee. The center's Von Kármán Facility wind tunnel B was used in the tests. Tunnel B was equipped with the captive trajectory system (CTS) rig, which allowed independent movement of both the X-43A and Pegasus models. From this, the aerodynamic loads on both vehicles could be determined. The Arnold tests were made at a speed of Mach 6, rather than at the actual separation speed of Mach 7.1.

As with earlier wind-tunnel data, allowances had to be made for aerodynamic effects caused by the CTS rig. The X-43A was mounted on a blade, which created interference effects in the data. There also was a need to understand the sting mounting effects of the earlier tests in the 20-inch Mach 6 tunnel at Langley Research Center. To this end, a series of tests were done in the 20-inch tunnel using a model that could be held with either a sting or a blade, or with a dummy blade or sting also attached. This allowed the interference effects to be measured, and the data produced were used to correct the earlier tests.[5]

By mid-August of 1997, an initial plan involving approximately 27,000 test points had been put together by Boeing and NASA representatives. At this time, the drop jaw configuration had yet to emerge. Thus, the tests were made with the breakaway adapter and the government baseline design. The test program also was considerably smaller than the original effort, which involved a 46,000-point matrix for the government baseline. The plan called for an October 1997 start to the tests, pending modifications to the wind tunnel.[6]

But the schedule soon changed, and by late October the start had been pushed back to the first week in November. This continued to slip, and the "first wind-on run" was actually on November 17, 1997. The test proceeded slowly after multiple problems were experienced with tunnel B. These problems continued into late November, when the lateral drive motor for the CTS rig burned out. Arnold Engineering Development Center personnel found a replacement motor and installed it. The initial plan was to resume testing during the evening of November 24 and continue into November 26 before breaking for the Thanksgiving holiday. But the plan broke down Tuesday night when the replacement motor suffered a failure similar to that of the captive-trajectory-system rig.[7]

Not until the latter part of January 1998 were the wind-tunnel tests at the Arnold center finally completed. Given the problems, it was ironic that the tests had produced more test points than planned, using the various drop-jaw options.[8]

The Arnold Center tests had validated the steady-state wind-tunnel data on the separation maneuver. As a result, the focus of the computational-fluid-dynamics analysis was shifted to the unsteady aspects of the separation. The first issue examined was the transient at initial separation. Engineers thought that as separation began, the initial airflow within the gap between the adapter and the X-43A might generate pressures greater than the steady-state airflow. As the two vehicles moved apart, the pressure difference would equalize, but there might be an initial "kick" to the X-43A. How significant this kick might be, and its effect on the X-43A trajectory, was dependent on the speed at which the pressures equalized.

To determine the possible effects of the kick, two-dimensional, time-accurate simulations of the flow between the adapter lip and the X-43A's base were done. The width of the gap in the simulations was set at 0.5 and 2 inches, which would occur at 0.044 and 0.060 seconds (44 and 60 milliseconds). In these two-dimensional cases the gap flow was much more restricted than with a three-dimensional geometry. This was because the flow began at the adapter lip, then passed between the adapter ramp, and finally exited at the flat aft end of the X-43A.

The SAMcfd program was used for the 0.5-inch gap simulation, whereas the 2-inch gap case required a viscous flow simulation done with the CFL3D grid flow solver. The two simulations found that the forces within the gap would stabilize in less than 0.01 seconds (10 milliseconds). This time period was short, compared with the overall separation event. The X-43A still would be pushed by the pistons at this point during separation, limiting any pitch or sideslip. The two-dimensional simulation did not take into account the gaps at the sides, which would vent airflow and provide pressure relief. This would produce a steady-state pressure close to the freestream airflow. The conclusion drawn from the simulations was that the time frame in which any kick was produced would be too short to have any effect on the X-43A's stability.

The second unsteady separation issue lay in the dynamics of the stack as the sequence occurred. The Hyper-X launch vehicle and the X-43A would be moving relative to one another during the event, which could potentially affect their aerodynamics. The original intention was to run time-accurate computational-fluid-dynamics simulations of the dynamic separation. An analysis of the actual dynamics indicated such an extensive simulation was not needed. At separation, the stack would be moving at a speed of about 7000 feet per second. The relative speed between the X-43A and the booster at 4 inches of separation would be about 14 feet per second. This difference was only 0.2% of the freestream airspeed. The vast difference in velocities made any unsteady effects immeasurably small compared to the steady-state aerodynamics. At 44 inches of separation, the relative speed had increased to 20 feet per second, but this was still low enough to establish quasi-steady-state flow conditions.

One simulation was done using the OVERFLOW program, with the separation distance set at 4 inches, and the X-43A moving away from the adapter at a forward velocity of 6 feet per second. The simulation indicated that the differences in the normal-force, axial-force, and pitching-moment coefficients were on the order of 0.4 percent. Changes of this size could be expected solely as a result of normal variations in the X-43A's velocity and the resulting dynamic pressure. The assumption of quasi-steady-state flow at separation was considered justified.[9]

The next step in the test process was a series of computer simulations, using a program called SimSoft. The program was developed for Langley by Analytical Mechanics Associates and modeled the highly nonlinear and dynamic events of the separation. The complexity of analyzing the separation maneuver was daunting. A standard computer simulation of an aircraft in flight has what is called "6 degrees of freedom." This means that simulated aircraft can move up or down, left or right, and around the yaw, pitch, and roll axes, as well as increase or decrease speed.

For the X-43A/Hyper-X launch-vehicle separation, the simulation had to provide 6 degrees of freedom for the X-43A, another 6 for the HXLV, and 3 more for the two pistons and the drop jaw, for a total of 15 degrees of freedom. The simulation would involve two independently moving vehicles in very close proximity that would interact with each other in unknown ways.[10]

The Monte Carlo analysis of the separation maneuver used the database of nominal forces and moments determined from wind-tunnel and computational-fluid-dynamics results, as well as the uncertainties and three-sigma variations in each measurement, and covered 97% of all possible variations in all of the measurements. As part of this, what were called "stress cases" or "stack-ups" also were made, which meant that the maximum value of each of the variables was used, and they were all added up in the "wrong" direction.[11]

Assembling the database for the Monte Carlo analysis was a daunting task. The wind-tunnel tests were used to develop models of the vehicles' mass properties, separation mechanics, and aerodynamic forces. The computational-fluid-dynamics data were used to quantify the ground-to-flight scaling and unsteady-flow phenomena during the dynamic separation. Additionally, the computational-fluid-dynamics data was used to expand the wind-tunnel database to include vehicle orientations that could not be tested in the wind tunnel. The uncertainties in the aerodynamic data were developed by Rodney Bowersox of the University of Alabama.

The mass properties of the Pegasus booster were obtained from the Orbital Sciences Corporation database, with the modifications required for the X-43A. The adapter mass properties were from MicroCraft. The X-43A mass properties were determined from weight and inertial tests conducted at Dryden Flight Research Center. The varying initial-separation conditions, such as Mach number, altitude, dynamic pressure, and body angles of the stack were fed into the SepSim program. Called the "stack states," these were produced by a separate Monte Carlo analysis conducted by Orbital. The atmospheric data used for the SepSim program were the reference atmosphere data for all 12 months of the year, with the Vandenberg wind profiles added. The SepSim program randomly selected one month for each Monte Carlo analysis.

The Hyper-X launch-vehicle flight-control model used in SepSim was based on descriptions supplied by Boeing. The guidance system model was provided by Honeywell. The error states in the guidance system model were linear and were held constant during each run. These included positional and velocity errors as well as tilt and azimuth errors. Misalignments of the guidance system also were simulated. The error states and misalignments resulted in variable feedback errors in angle of attack, Mach number, dynamic pressure, velocity, bank angle, pitch angle, and body rates.

The Hyper-X launch-vehicle control surface dynamics were modeled as a combination of two elements, the actuators and the freeplay. The second-order model was initially based on Boeing specifications and was then revised using a high-fidelity math model developed by Moog, manufacturer of the actuators. The Moog math model was further refined with the addition of data from acceptance testing, actuation, and hysteresis testing, and aircraft-in-the-loop tests at Dryden.

The final element in the separation sequence, and the one that set the whole process in motion, was that of the explosive bolts and ejector pistons. The timing of the explosive bolts was modeled from a series of tests run by Orbital Sciences. The ejector pistons, which pushed the X-43A away from the adapter, were adapted from B-1B bomb ejector racks. These pushed bombs through the turbulent airflow around the bomb bay, so that weapons did not strike the aircraft, or became caught in the airflow and followed along with the aircraft. Orbital did numerous firing tests of the cartridges in an effort to understand the variability in pressure they generated to drive the pistons, cartridges' timing, and force profile.[12]

Running concurrently were ground tests of the pistons, to test the effects of any side loads on the X-43A and Hyper-X launch vehicle resulting from the separation angle. The tests were done at Orbital's Chandler, Arizona, facility, using concrete slabs weighing as much as the X-43A and the burned-out booster. These were mounted on air bearings to minimize friction and better represent the forces acting on the two masses. The separation pistons were mounted between the two concrete slabs. When the cartridges were fired, any differences in the force from the pistons would cause lateral motion between the two slabs. Two tests were performed, and neither showed any yaw attributable to uneven piston forces. Such tests were not without risk, however. On one, the restraining system on the 3000-pound slab simulating the X-43A did not work or was not engaged, and it went sliding across the laboratory floor.

These tests were followed by tests of a single piston that was subjected to side loads. This simulated the forces on the piston should the two vehicles be at some yaw or pitch angle at separation. The tests at Dryden were done at 500-pound increments from 500 to 2000 pounds. The data indicated that side loads would not affect the separation. Even though the higher side loads did damage the piston and cylinder, the data indicated that the pistons would perform as designed, even with the damage to the pistons and with side loads much higher than those expected in the actual separation.

The final separation test was done on September 16, 1999. The test was made using actual hardware—the second X-43A airframe (ballasted to its flight weight), the first adapter, and flight explosive bolts. The entire short stack was fitted with pyrotechnics, as it would be on the actual launch. In addition to gaining data on the separation, the test also would determine whether the shock of the explosive bolts and pistons firing would affect onboard instrumentation and other systems. When the separation was initiated, the X-43A showed no signs of yaw caused by the pistons. The vehicle was supported by a crane with a long cable that would have minimal effect on the X-43A's path. The data showed that no onboard systems were affected by the shock of the pyrotechnics going off. The model developed from the separation tests was cross-checked with the data produced during the original test program of the B-1B bomb ejector racks, then fed into the simulation.[13]

With all of the models, variables, and uncertainties now assembled, the final step before Monte Carlo analysis could be done was to validate the database. This was done on three levels. For the purpose of checking the individual models, the input variables, implementation, and simulation results were reviewed by the individuals who had developed the original models. The next level was the modular checks, which were done by verifying the results with an independent check program called Simulink. The integrated checks, the highest-level verification, were done by comparing the SepSim results with those of another independent program, called RVSim, which had been written at Dryden. When the SepSim and the RVSim results for five runs were compared, there was a nearly perfect overlay of the output.

The SepSim Monte Carlo analysis of the X-43A separation maneuver began with the command to fire the four explosive bolts attaching the X-43A to the adapter and ended 2.5 seconds later. At this point in the separation, the X-43A was clear of any aerodynamic influences of the adapter or booster and was ready to begin the cowl-open portion of the flight. The separation was considered successful if the two vehicles separated cleanly, there was no recontact, and the X-43A was able to attain the required flight conditions for scramjet ignition. To check for any recontact between the two vehicles, the positional data from each of the Monte Carlo runs were processed by the DIVISION Mockup software. This was programmed with three-dimensional models of the X-43A, adapter, and Hyper-X launch vehicle. The program then checked to see if any contact between them had occurred. If none had, the program would be run again to determine whether any of the vehicles had come within 1- or 2-inch "shells" around each of the computer models.

The Monte Carlo analysis of the X-43A separation maneuver involved 2000 individual runs. Of this, seven runs did not complete in 2.5 seconds. Eleven runs exceeded ± 10 degrees angle of attack or sideslip during the 2.5-second period of the simulation. Eight runs did not meet the angle-of-attack and sideslip criteria at 2.5 seconds. These 26 runs were classified as failures, but they amounted to just 1.3% of the total number of runs. There were no cases of the two vehicles colliding after separation. There was a single run in which the X-43A came within 1 inch of the adapter, and 54 runs in which the distance was within 2 inches. Analysis of the variables' means and standard deviations indicated that 2000 cases was statistically significant and that the Monte Carlo runs indicated a high probability of the X-43A successfully separating and meeting the required cowl-opening flight conditions.[14]

Well before the Monte Carlo analyses were completed, however, the data made clear that modifications would have to be made in the separation sequence. As several engineers had feared, the drop jaw did create a force on the X-43A fuselage/nozzle that caused the vehicle to pitch down, resulting in a loss of control. Several alternative scenarios, including delaying the drop-jaw activation until the pistons were at half-stroke or full stroke, were proposed. The simulations showed that these had similar problems. As a result, use of the drop jaw was abandoned. The first two adapters already had been delivered, however. Rather than rebuilding them, the mechanism was deactivated so that the drop jaw remained fixed in place.

The simulations did suggest a modified separation procedure. If the X-43A's all-moving horizontal tails were set at 6 degrees during the separation, the vehicle would remain controllable. The revised procedure was not approved by management until a later series of Monte Carlo simulations were completed.

In its final form, the X-43A separation began when the Pegasus inertial navigation unit sensed that the stack's axial acceleration had dropped to zero or a negative value for a period of 0.2 seconds (200 milliseconds). The booster's flight computer then signaled the X-43A to initiate the separation sequence. Over the next 3 seconds, several actions took place within the short stack. These included switching the vehicle's nitrogen purge system from tanks in the adapter to tanks within the X-43A. When this is completed, the

X-43A signaled the booster to initiate the separation. The ordinance train driver then ignited the four explosive bolts and the pyrotechnics that drove the two pistons. After a delay of 0.004 or 0.005 seconds (4 or 5 milliseconds) the pyrotechnics fired, and 0.025 seconds (25 milliseconds) later the pistons started to move. The pistons traveled nine inches in a period of one-tenth of a second, with a force of 22,000 pounds. Even in the face of a dynamic pressure on the order of 1000 pounds per square foot, this was sufficient to produce a relative velocity between the two vehicles of 13 feet per second. The simulations indicated that the entire sequence would be complete in less than 0.25 seconds.[15]

The Hyper-X computational-fluid-dynamics simulations and Monte Carlo analyses represented the height of computing capability in the final decade of the 20th century. These included the Cray C-90 and Origin 2000 computers, the NAVO Major Shared Resource Center Cray SV1, and an SGI Indigo workstation.[16]

Despite this, neither the SAMcfd nor the OVERFLOW programs could produce more than steady-state approximations of a very dynamic flowfield. Even after all of the work that had been done, after all of the simulations and analyses and ground tests, project engineers still viewed separation as a major uncertainty. There were *only* simulations and analyses and ground tests. There was still the unknown of how they would work in real air, at a dynamic pressure of a half-ton per square foot. The only way they would know if it would work was to fly the vehicle.

BUILDING THE X-43A HYPER-X RESEARCH VEHICLE

The X-43A was the fastest airbreathing vehicle ever to fly. Only the space shuttle had flown faster, and it made a gliding reentry, not a powered flight. The X-43A vehicle is a lifting body with aft-mounted control surfaces comprising all-moving horizontal tails and twin vertical fins and rudders. The fuselage is 144 inches long, has a wing span of 60 inches, and is 28 inches tall from the top of the fins to the underside of the scramjet engine. Its total weight is about 3000 pounds.

The X-43A was the sleekest appearing of the X-planes, with its long but shallow fuselage and sweeping lines. Ironically, its construction was conventional. The main fuselage was a long, shallow box. It was gently curved on the top, with a sloping inlet ramp, a flat area for the engine, and an exhaust half-nozzle on the underside. The center section is formed by two longerons running fore and aft and divided by several bulkheads. These areas held, from front to back, the battery, flight management unit (FMU), gaseous-hydrogen fuel tanks, the water-glycol coolant system, the S- and C-band transponders, and the actuators and controllers for the fins, horizontal tails, and scramjet engine cowl. The aft bulkhead had connections for the external power supply.

A view of the center section of the X-43A #1. This contained the hydrogen, silane, water, and nitrogen tanks, and the data system. The silver box at the left (forward) side of the photo is the flight management unit. (NASA photo EC01-0025-11.)

On either side of this center section were several bulkheads that form the X-43A's chines. The left chine had the instrument stack and the nitrogen purge system, while on the right side was the silane system, used to ignite the hydrogen/air mix in the scramjet. The longerons and bulkheads were

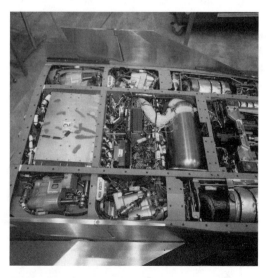

The aft end of the X-43A #1. This section contains the actuators and controllers in the large box, the S-band and C-band beacons just forward of this, and the cylindrical coolant tank. In the right chine is the silane tank, and in the left chine is the nitrogen purge system. At the rear of the fuselage are the power and fluid connectors to the adapter. (NASA photo EC01-0025-16.)

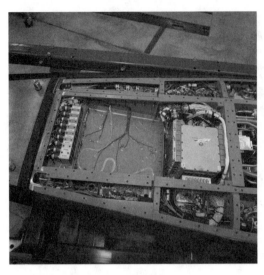

The forward section of the X-43A #1. The flight management unit is visible. The small silver cylinders on the forward bulkhead are the flush air data sensors. Forward of this is the tungsten nose, which serves as ballast. (NASA photo EC01-0025-12.)

made of various steel alloys, as well as aluminum and titanium. These were used primarily to ensure structural rigidity. The aft bulkhead was fabricated from titanium to protect against intense heat. The outer skin was steel and aluminum.[17]

One unusual design feature of the X-43A was its ballast section. This ballast was attached to the front of the main fuselage and was a huge wedge-shaped

The leading edge and tungsten ballast of the X-43A #1. The nose section was a heavy slab of tungsten alloy, with carbon–carbon leading edges to provide heat protection. The lower surface of the nose serves as the forward part of the inlet ramp, which slows and compresses the incoming air before it enters the scramjet. (NASA photo EC01-0126-25.)

slab of a tungsten alloy called Densalloy 180. It was probably the largest single piece of tungsten ever made. The ballast section had a total weight of about 865 pounds. Although the tungsten-nose section also served to simplify the heat protection in this area, its primary role was to shift the vehicle's center of gravity forward. This shift produced nearly neutral longitudinal-stability characteristics.

Manufacturing the ballast section was very difficult. Several blocks of tungsten were sintered together in a large furnace. Care had to be taken during the process to avoid slumping of the individual sections.[18] A serious problem that did appear in the manufacturing process was that of voids. When the ballast section for the first X-43A was delivered to MicroCraft in the spring of 1998, an inspection found it to be flawed. A total of 14 voids were discovered, requiring an estimated remanufacturing time of six weeks. This was accomplished successfully, with bond joints ultimately produced within specifications. In contrast, when the second ballast section was delivered, only a single void was found, near the nose-airframe joint.[19]

This was not the only fabrication problem arising from use of exotic metals. The fins and horizontal tails were fabricated from Haynes alloy, a very hard, high-temperature nickel steel. Normally, such hot structures are solid or nearly solid. With the X-43A, center-of-gravity issues prevented such construction. Instead, they were made with lightweight, machined-out internal structures with welded-on outer skins. The alloy's hardness made both the machining and welding processes difficult. In particular, the welding had to be done at such high temperatures that the fin skin was distorted. As a result, the very stringent waviness requirements in the design specifications were exceeded. A series of welding experiments had to be undertaken at ATK General Applied Science Laboratory and Boeing to solve the problem. In effect, a full-fledged welding research program was required to develop the procedures needed to create fins that would meet design specifications.

Several other problems arose because of the type of heat protection required for the X-43A and its effect on the vehicle's outer mold line. Normally the outer mold line of an aircraft is created by its outer skin. With the SR-71, for example, the aircraft's titanium and composite skin provided the necessary heat protection at Mach 3 flight conditions. The X-43A, in contrast, was completely covered with heat-resistant carbon–carbon material and thermal protection tiles. Without these, the vehicle's aluminum and steel skin and its internal structure would be unable to withstand the thermal environment encountered during flight.

The leading edges of the X-43A's ballast section were carbon–carbon. On the Mach 7 vehicles, the leading edges of the horizontal tails had carbon–carbon inserts, but the vertical fins did not. In contrast, on the Mach 10 vehicle both the horizontal tails and fins had carbon–carbon inserts on their leading edges. These represented a significant manufacturing problem because of the very small radius of curvature on the leading edges, which were needed to reduce aerodynamic drag at hypersonic speeds. The radii were 0.030 inches for the Mach 7 vehicles, and 0.050 inches for the Mach 10 vehicle.

These small radii posed challenges both in the fabrication of the carbon-carbon material and in applying a surface coating of silicon–carbide. As with the fabrication of the fins and horizontal tails, several attempts were required before procedures were developed to successfully produce such thin edges.

The upper and lower surfaces of the X-43A were covered with alumina-enhanced thermal-barrier (AETB) ceramic tiles. These were sized for Mach 10 heating rates and were about 0.5-inch thick. Exceptions were in places where an increased thickness was needed to give the surface the proper aerodynamic shape. The AETB tiles were attached to the X-43A using the same methods as used on the shuttle. Thin tiles were adversely affected by flexing of the underlying surface. Because the X-43A had such a rigid structure as a result of the stack stiffness issue, this was not a concern. Indeed, the X-43A, unlike the space shuttle, had no need for gaps between the tile edges to allow for airframe flexing.

On the shuttle, each tile was individually machined and then attached to the vehicle's outer skin. For the X-43A, the process was reversed. The thermal protective material was first added to each vehicle, and then the tiles were machined to form the shape of the final outer mold line. This was done using a large, three-axis numerically controlled milling machine that required a minimum number of setups. After the surface contour work was completed, the finished outer mold line was checked to ensure that it met specifications. A protective coating was then applied to the finished tiles. This coating cured at room temperature and gave the vehicle its black surface coloration.

The procedure of applying the tiles, then machining to the mold line, was judged to have simplified the manufacturing of the X-43A's thermal protective system and resulted in a very high-quality outer mold line. The procedure was made possible by the X-43A's small size. The weight, size, and more complex shape of a full-size aircraft or spacecraft would create obstacles in an attempt to use this procedure.[20]

The size of the diminutive X-43A offers an example of a paradox in design and construction. The small size made one-piece machining of the outer mold line possible, resulting in a high-quality mold line. At the same time, the vehicle's limited dimensions resulted in significant complications in packaging the vehicle systems within the airframe.

The X-43A's interior was tightly packed with electronic components, high-pressure tanks, pipes, wire bundles, and other equipment. These were either off-the-shelf systems or modifications of such existing systems. Unmanned research vehicles were typically much smaller than conventional manned aircraft, yet they had to also contain not only all of the required aircraft systems, but also the additional systems needed to replace a pilot. Corpening later noted that,

> One of the things we ran into through the fabrication stage is the challenge of size, if you will. I heard Lowell Keel [the X-43A project manager at MicroCraft] state at a Las Vegas conference that if we would have had about another foot and a half on this vehicle, life would have been a lot easier.

He added that, in another way, this volume limitation proved an advantage in program management,

> ... because you avoided endless design iterations. If you were constrained to 12 feet, that's it—game over. This is the shape of the vehicle; you guys have got to package it. If it was allowed to grow, you get the possibility of, "wow, you know, if we just had an extra 6 inches here, man, the system would be just everything we wanted." And all of a sudden, we've got to go through another design iteration for a 13-foot vehicle and all the aerodynamics and all that stuff has to be redone, and on and on. And there's a very real possibility now you're a year into your program, and you still don't have a design because you keep iterating; it's called "requirements creep." So I think it was very, very smart—even though it was a tremendous challenge to package everything—it was very smart saying, "it's 12 feet, that's it."[21]

The task of packaging the vehicle subsystems was complicated by the flight conditions in which the X-43A would operate. All of its systems had to be qualified to operate at altitudes of about 100,000 feet. The systems would be operating in a low-atmospheric-pressure environment rather than in the true vacuum of space. Paradoxically, this made the task of qualifying the systems in some ways more difficult than if they were being built to operate in space. This was especially true for the electrical and electronic subsystems. To accomplish all of this, the project partners build several simple mockups, but CAD-CAM models were the means by which the interior layout was developed. This allowed the designers and engineers to size, insert, rotate, even relocate parts within the innards of the X-43A.

To provide the necessary reliability, the X-43A needed large, aerospace-quality connectors and fittings, but their size took up the limited internal volume. Most of the problems with vehicle integration were the result of this. Resolving the issue required several iterations of equipment layout, custom brackets, connector modifications, and the use of a few nonstandard/high-density Deutsch connectors.[22]

All of the internal systems faced what Corpening called "this challenge of size." One example was the tanks that contained the water–glycol mix that cooled the scramjet's leading edge and cowling during boost and the free-flight engine run. This water–glycol mix was sprayed onto the engine cowling and then was carried away by the airflow, which meant the mixture could not be recirculated for cooling. The cowling had particularly demanding requirements, as warping from uneven cooling could prevent the cowling door from moving freely.

The tanks were mounted in both the adapter (to supply the water–glycol mix for ascent) and the X-43A vehicle itself (for the free flight). The connections between the tanks required fittings and couplings that competed for space in the aft fuselage. The volume of the tanks also was limited, so that the amount of the water–glycol mix needed had to be carefully calculated. This was done using thermal and stress analysis.

While, as Corpening noted, "you think a water tank, you can't hardly get a simpler system than that." He continued:

> [T]his water tank had to expel its water under various conditions—gravity, push forces, all these kinds of things. And the water tank volume could only be so big, and we had certain flow-rate requirements.... 95% of the water had to get out of this tank, guaranteed. So inside this simple water tank is a very complex set of bladders that essentially fold down in on themselves. And this had to be done in a very repeatable manner and very reliable manner.[23]

There were similar problems with the hydrogen and silane system. The high pressures in the system required careful system integration and vibration isolation. Highly compact/high-pressure pilot-operated valves were required, but their use was problematic because of the high pressures required to seat them properly. Several cycles of valve tests and design modifications had to be undertaken before these were qualified and considered reliable.

Safety considerations also had to be addressed in the design of the fuel system and ground-support systems. Silane is a pyrophoric gas, meaning it ignites on contact with air. The volatile nature of silane meant that special care had to be taken in handling the gas during fueling of the vehicle. Special vent and purging systems had to be built into the fueling system, while vent stacks were attached to direct vapors away from engineers and technicians working in the immediate vicinity. As a result, the ground support and servicing equipment became far more complex than originally planned.

One unusual aspect of the use of a hydrogen and silane mixture as an igniter was questions about possible effects that the high storage pressure would have on the gases. Hydrogen and silane mixtures had long been used as an igniter in scramjet ground tests but were kept at pressures of only about 1800 pounds per square inch (psi). This amount of pressure would not be suitable for the Hyper-X project.

Corpening observed:

> Because we needed a certain amount of hydrogen and silane, and only a certain amount of volume was available for that in the hydrogen and silane tanks, we had to up the pressure. At one point we thought we might have to go all the way up to 6500 psi in pressure in the hydrogen and silane tanks. It turned out we could back off to 4500 psi of pressure. But nobody knew the thermodynamic properties of hydrogen and silane at 4500 psi because nobody had ever used it there.
>
> So we were sitting there going, "geez, we don't think there should be any issue, but maybe it gets really strange at these high pressures. Maybe it becomes unstable. Maybe silane reacts somehow with the hydrogen. Maybe it stratifies." All these questions, we didn't have answers to. So we had to go out to a testing laboratory, and they had to develop a database on hydrogen and silane gas from 2000 [psi] up to about 6500 psi, to make sure it was safe. It turned out it was.[23]

For the X-43A flights to have any value, the vehicle's data had to be successfully telemetered to ground tracking stations and the receiving aircraft. This required that a range of data-collection subsystems be packaged into the airframe. The number of data channels on the X-43A was unprecedented for so small a research vehicle, a level of instrumentation necessary to produce enough data to qualify the design tools developed in wind-tunnel tests.

The role of wind-tunnel models such as this X-43A extended beyond determining the vehicle's free-flight aerodynamic characteristics. The Hyper-X project required tests of the complete stack from launch through the Mach 7 or 10 burnout and the complex flowfields of the separation. (NASA photo EC98-44385-01.)

These included pressure transducers, strain gauges, thermocouples, resistance temperature detectors, analog measurements from electrolytic oxygen sensors, inductive current sensors, and voltage dividers, as well as serial data from the FMU, which is relayed via a 1553 data bus interface. All told, a total of 1125 unique parameters are relayed from the X-43A's instrumentation, of which 788 are from the flight management unit.[24] In contrast, the X-15 telemetry system had 90 channels of data, which were transmitted to the ground stations. This was recorded on magnetic tapes, processed and then was converted to paper strip charts.[25]

As with other systems, the X-43A data subsystems were built from off-the-shelf equipment. The difficulty came in connecting the measuring devices with the recording system. The network of wire and tube bundles required for these connections posed a major packaging problem. Although this did not require extreme efforts, care did have to be paid to routing the bundles within the vehicle. This could only be done during the actual construction of each X-43A vehicle.

The large amount of electronic equipment being packaged within a relatively small volume raised another set of problems. When initial testing of the instrumentation and telemetry system was made, engineers discovered that the heat buildup within the vehicle had not been correctly allowed for. The telemetry transmitters had heating rates equivalent to those of small lights. In designing the X-43A, engineers had assumed that the vehicle's structure would act as a heat sink and cool the electronic systems. Testing soon proved those assumptions incorrect.[26]

The flight management unit was one source of the difficulty. This was a small box located between the battery and the hydrogen system in the forward part of the X-43A's interior. The unit integrated the functions of navigation, flight-control sensor, and mission computer into a single package. It handled such functions as control surface calibration updates, navigation and guidance updates, scramjet fuel schedule, igniter subsystem controller, and unstart logic.[27] To do all of this, the FMU had to operate (and produce heat) throughout the prelaunch phase.

As a result, the original calculations for the structure's heat-sink capability were no longer valid. Rather than passive cooling, an active cooling system would be required. The original role of the nitrogen gas system was only to purge the X-43A's interior of oxygen buildup, preventing a fire or explosion in the event of a hydrogen leak. With the FMU operating for a longer period than expected, the nitrogen gas had to provide cooling as well, but this demand now exceeded the capability of the amount of nitrogen that could be carried in the stack.

To solve the nitrogen supply problem, modifications had to be made to the B-52B launch plane, the adapter, and the X-43A. The B-52B was fitted with a rack of high-pressure nitrogen bottles. The adapter also had to be fitted with added tankage and purge lines to transfer the nitrogen from the B-52B into the adapter and then into the X-43A. These supplies of nitrogen would be used to both cool and purge oxygen from the research vehicle during the flight out to the launch point. Once the stack was released, nitrogen was supplied from the adapter to the X-43A during the boost phase. Once the X-43A separated from the Hyper-X launch vehicle, its internal nitrogen supply would assume the cooling and purging tasks.[28]

The problems did not end once the systems were packaged inside the vehicle. Packaging so many different systems, with different voltages, in such close proximity created new difficulties. To save space, all five actuator controllers for the control surfaces and cowl door were packaged in a single box at the rear of the vehicle. Corpening noted that, "the electronics for those actuators are all located in a box that's about the size of a squished-down breadbox, or a glove compartment in your car." As with the other electrical systems, the actuators and related equipment used standard connectors. Although fine for a manned aircraft, these connectors were huge compared to the scale of the X-43A.

The size of the connectors was not the worst of it. Corpening noted that another problem that was "really quite scary" was

> ...the electromechanical actuator system for the research vehicle. Moog, who did the design, did a wonderful job of packaging these [five] little actuator controllers. The problem was the different voltages that were used in the different components. Within there you have all of the instrumentation and controlling voltages—I believe it was 28 volts—right next to the voltage used to power these powerful little motors at 150 volts. And those two [voltages] are running around this little tiny box together, and they interfered with each other. And you got what's called electromagnetic interference, which was causing some chattering on the actuator motors because these electronics were so close together.

The result was significant crosstalk between the adjoining actuator controllers in the original design. As with other packaging issues, several design iterations were required before the cross-talk was finally eliminated. This was among the final issues to be settled before the first flight could be made. Corpening recalled:

> Moog had never packaged them that close together. We didn't find this out until we were within months of flight. Moog put the full-court press on. They went in and put some metal sheathing in there and rearranged things a little bit. And, it turned out, solved the problem. But we did not have a qualified actuator unit until about two months before flight. So we were headed directly to flight before the unit had actually passed all of its qualification tests. That was a little hairy. You're really hanging out there on that.[29]

The X-43A also was subject to requirements not mandated in earlier aerospace projects. One of these was the requirement to prepare environmental impact reports. When a recovery on San Nicolas Island was being considered, several issues were raised during the report review process. These went away when the recovery option was dropped.[30]

The impact area finally selected was well off the coast. Paul Reukauf later noted, "It turned out that splashing down way out to sea where marine mammals, shipping, and people don't go was just a lot easier problem [to resolve]."[31]

Avoiding environmentally sensitive recovery areas did not completely eliminate design complications, however. The X-43A would hit the water at the end of its flight at near-transonic speeds. Such a high-velocity impact would normally be expected to destroy a vehicle, leaving only floating debris. This was not an option with the X-43A, which contained volatile materials. Reukauf noted that the U.S. Navy

> ... also made us essentially guarantee that when the vehicle hit the water it wouldn't come apart—that it would sink to the bottom and all the pieces would stay there with it. Their concern was [that] pieces would start washing up on the shore or be picked up in the channel washing towards the mainland and someone on a boat or someone on the shore would pick up a hydrogen tank, or a silane tank, and drill a hole in it to see what was inside of it and hurt themselves.[31]

MACH 7 SCRAMJET ENGINE DEVELOPMENT AND TESTING

While the Hyper-X launch-vehicle booster and X-43A research vehicle were being designed and built, ground tests of the scramjet engine were underway. The Hyper-X flight mission planning done at Langley was based on previous hypersonic flight-test studies, including those with the Hypersonic Flight Experiment and Hypersonic Systems Technology Program. The plan that emerged had to satisfy research requirements without exceeding the project's schedule and budget constraints.

The initial effort at Langley called for performing an integrated vehicle/scramjet design study to define the airframe-integrated engine flowpath. This would allow detailed flowpath analysis, such as powered tip-to-tail computational-fluid-dynamics studies and design and fabrication of the subscale ground-test engines. Although a detailed scramjet database existed after previous research, the flight-test engine had to be specifically tailored to the X-43A's small size in order to produce enough thrust to accelerate the vehicle at Mach 7. The computational-fluid-dynamics flowpath studies and engine wind-tunnel tests began in the spring of 1996. These were designed to refine the scramjet design and to evaluate its operating characteristics so that autonomous engine controls could be developed.

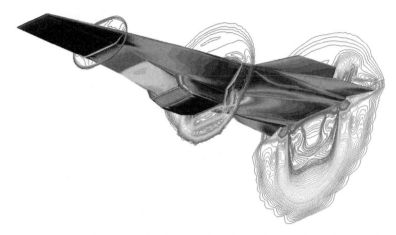

Computational-fluid-dynamics simulations played a critical role in the Hyper-X project. This included the stack flight characteristics, the separation maneuver, the X-43A's free-flight behavior, and the operation and efficiency of the scramjet. (NASA photo ED97-43968-1.)

The first step was to use a computational-fluid-dynamics program called SCRAM3L—an analytical three-stream, finite-rate chemical kinetics code— to determine the minimum acceptable airframe/engine length. SCRAM3L determined the reaction efficiency of progressively smaller scramjet designs. The program indicated that a 12-foot vehicle could be built with only a 5% loss in combustion efficiency. Below this size, however, the vehicle design became problematic.

The next task was refining the engine flowpath for the 12-foot length. This was aimed at regaining losses resulting from the viscous dominated flow, which was caused by high shear forces at low unit Reynolds numbers as well as overconcentration caused by relative boundary-layer displacement thickness. The SRGULL hybrid analytical-numerical computer program was used in the design efforts.

SRGULL was developed at Langley and utilized a series of codes to predict flow phenomena such as inlet mass capture and kinetic energy efficiency; boundary-layer shear, heat flux, and transition; and isolator performance, combustor distortion, nozzle expansion, and divergence losses. The code used a two-dimensional Euler calculation on the forebody and inlet, combined with an integral boundary-layer solution, to predict the forebody/inlet drag and the flow properties of the air entering the engine. The isolator/combustion solution is accomplished with a one-dimensional multiple-step, equilibrium chemistry cycle analysis. Finally, the nozzle characteristics were determined using the two-dimensional Euler and boundary-layer codes with a frozen ratio of specific heats. To model the finite-rate chemistry, mixing, and three-dimensional effects required use of parameters calibrated to computational-fluid-dynamics solutions and ground-test data.

The primary input for the SRGULL codes were engine geometry, boundary conditions, initial conditions, and several empirical parameters to correct known limitations in the analysis. The SRGULL program also could accurately predict inlet unstart, propulsion lift and pitching moments, thermal and pressure loads, and fuel temperatures for regeneratively cooled engines. The SRGULL could provide an accurate assessment of any ramjet, scramjet, rocket-based combined cycle, or ducted rocket, for speeds between Mach 2 and 25. Perhaps most remarkable of all, whereas classic computational-fluid-dynamics codes required weeks or even months to generate solutions, SRGULL could do the same in a few minutes, while running on a personal computer.[32]

The ground-engine tests for the Mach 7 missions were done in a series of steps, with five different very small, subscale engine models in three different wind tunnels. The plan was to use boilerplate engines in the initial tests, which would permit rapid closure of the most critical issues. Once these boilerplate tests were completed, an actual flight engine would be wind-tunnel tested. This approach avoided any impact on the schedule or hardware for the first X-43A flight.

The initial dual-fuel experimental parametric engine design to be wind-tunnel tested was called the DFX, so named in reference to the original McDonnell Douglas Aerospace DF-9 study contract. The DFX engine was, in turn, derived from modified National Aerospace Plane engine hardware.

A scramjet undergoing wind-tunnel testing at the Langley Research Center. One advantage of the X-43A's small size was that the actual engine could be tested, eliminating any scale effects or other possible differences caused by using a model. (NASA photo ED04-0082-2.)

This was done to allow a quick performance and operability evaluation of the Mach 7 flowpath design. The DFX scramjet had the same height and length of the X-43A engine internal flowpath, with the correct forebody, cowl, and sidewall leading-edge radii. The engine had only 44% of the actual X-43A engine's width, and the forebody and afterbody were truncated. The X-43A scramjet design was considered a quasi-two-dimensional configuration, so that the reduced width still provided a good representation of the complete engine. The only significant issue from the reduced engine width was corner effects.

The DFX scramjet was designed to serve as a test article to quickly and cheaply evaluate flowpath modifications. For this reason, it was fabricated from copper and used heat-sink cooling. (The X-43A scramjet's active cooling system had a water-glycol mix.) The lack of a cooling system limited the engine to about a 30-second test time at dynamic pressures of about 500 pounds per square foot (psf). It was not possible to test the design at the actual 1000 psf dynamic pressures the X-43A engine would experience. Another difference between the DFX and X-43A scramjet was the cowl design. The DFX had a cowl that rotated about the cowling's leading edge. This made flowpath changes easy to accomplish. The X-43A cowl design had a forward cowl flap.

The DFX tests were done in Langley's Arc-Heated Scramjet Test Facility (AHSTF). This wind tunnel uses an electrical arc heater capable of 3000 Btu/pound. The hot air is mixed with ambient air to produce the required high-enthalpy test gas. The AHSTF simulation was not able to fully reproduce Hyper-X flight conditions because of power limitations. The Mach 7 tests were made at a dynamic of 500 psf, while the Mach 5 simulations were at 800 psf. (The Mach 5 dual-mode test was still being planned for at this point.) The AHSTF also could not produce "clean air" because of arc heating. The primary contaminate was nitric oxide, and this potentially could cause problems with the accuracy of the data.

The AHSTF data system could collect about 650 channels of data. These included surface temperatures and pressures, a six-component force balance, pressure and temperature probe, and gas sampling. The AHSTF provided the data at low cost, but required the use of reduced-width engine designs. The full-width scramjet would not fit in the tunnel.

The DFX engine was tested more than 250 times in four different configurations. The process successfully accomplished the goal of testing the initial flowpath. The engine was tested at a range of Mach numbers and sideslip angles around the nominal values of the flight plan. The AHSTF tests verified the predicted engine forces and moments as well as the inlet and combustor component performances. The tests also determined several operability characteristics, including ignition requirements, flameholding limits, and inlet-combustor interaction limits.

By the spring of 1997, the final flowpath lines of the Mach 7 engine had been completed. Overall, the DFX engine tests provided the data necessary to anchor the final engine flowpath lines and the preliminary Mach 7 force, moment, and operability database for use in developing both the engine and vehicle control laws.

The next step in the Mach 7 engine ground tests involved the Hyper-X engine model (HXEM). As with the DFX, the HXEM's sidewalls were moved inward, and it initially also featured the truncated forebody and aftbody, changes that allowed it to be tested in the AHSTF. Otherwise, the HXEM was the same height and length as the flight engine. The HXEM also could be fitted with several features that would be on the flight engine, including the active cooling system, which allowed testing at the flight dynamic pressures, and the articulated, two-position inlet cowl.

The HXEM was initially tested in the AHSTF, and, like the DFX tests, this was done at the reduced 500-psf dynamic pressure and with the nitric-oxide contamination. Effects caused by the test facility and the test gas, rather than from the engine design, could be identified. The HXEM was then modified as a full flowpath simulator, for testing in Langley's 8-foot High Temperature Tunnel (HTT).

The HTT was used for most of the Mach 7 engine flowpath and control system verification tests. It had been built in the 1960s and had been used to conduct aerothermal loads and aerothermostructural testing and high-enthalpy aerodynamic research. Methane was mixed with air in the tunnel and then burned to produce the high-temperature test gas. This was then expanded through an 8-foot-high exit-diameter hypersonic nozzle and into the 12.5-foot-long test section. The combustion process generated contaminates, primarily water vapor and carbon dioxide. These contaminates had to be allowed for in assessing scramjet performance.

The scramjet engine model was mounted on a hydraulic elevator system, which included a three-component force measurement system. Initially, the engine model was retracted, protecting it from damage during the startup dynamic loads. Once the steady-state hypersonic flow had stabilized, the model was raised into the hypersonic flow, a process that took about 1.5 seconds. The test could then begin. The HTT data system could measure about 1000 channels of electrically scanned pressures and 500 channels of strain gauge measurements.

The HTT was literally a perfect fit for the Hyper-X engine. Because of the test-section's length, a complete, full-scale and width X-43A inlet ramp, engine, and nozzle could be fitted on the elevator. Researchers and engineers could test what they would fly. Had the airframe been larger it would not have fit, and subscale tests would have had to be made. Additionally, a full-duration test burn of the X-43A scramjet could be conducted in the HTT, and when the engine was raised into the hypersonic airflow, the shock waves from the Mach 7 airflow were visible. Once the burn was completed, the engine would be lowered, to protect it from damage caused by the shutdown dynamic pressure, and the airflow in the HTT terminated.

The initial version of the Hyper-X engine model tested in the HTT was called the full flowpath simulator (HXEM/FFS). This test model had the partial width and was fitted with the truncated forebody and aftbody, as with the Langley Arc-Heated Scramjet Test Facility tests. It now had the full flowpath and was configured for boundary-layer diversion testing. A duct was fitted to the aft end of the forebody, and a duct in the fuselage vented the boundary-layer airflow. This configuration allowed the effects of partial boundary-layer ingestion by the truncated forebody engine to be measured. The tests were done at a dynamic pressure of 650 psf and at the full flight conditions of 1000 psf.

The HXEM/FFS was then modified with a full forebody, for tests of the full boundary-layer ingestion. As with the partial boundary-layer diversion testing, this was done at dynamic pressures of 650 and 1000 psf. Comparing the data from the series of tests showed the effects of configuration differences between a partial-width/truncated flowpath engine and a partial-width/full flowpath design, facility effects and test gas, pressure, and boundary layer. Despite the truncated vs full forebody and the partial vs full boundary-layer ingestion, the engine model remained identical.

The final step in the High Temperature Tunnel testing was to use an actual flight engine. This would complete the flowpath and control system verification effort. The Hyper-X flight engine/vehicle flowpath simulator (HXFE/VFS) was the first production engine built by ATK General Applied Science Laboratory. (The second scramjet would be flown on the first Mach 7 launch.) The HXFE/VFS was to undergo what amounted to a ground simulation of the Mach 7 flight profile. The flight engine was attached to a duplicate of the X-43A's underside, which was positioned upside down on the HTT's elevator.

These wind-tunnel test series demonstrated a wide range of scramjet operations in simulated flight. These included the inlet starting with the full-width/full-length vehicle with the boundary-layer trips, wall roughness and temperature, and cowl actuation. The wind-tunnel tests also provided data on the fuel-control-system operation and demonstrated engine operations during the fuel sequence without causing an unstart of the inlet. Beyond this information, the flight-engine tests also provided limited aerodynamic force and moment incremental data from the cowl inlet flap opening and closing and the powered portion of the simulated flight.

Vehicle force and moment data would not be produced by this series of tests, however, as the engine extended beyond the HTT's high-quality core flow. Interference effects caused by the large mounting strut were another problem; the strut provided support and connections for the fuel, nitrogen purge, and instrumentation. Because the flight-engine's flowpath *was* within the core flow, however, the tests should provide good-quality flowpath force increments.[33]

Tests in the Hypersonic Pulse Facility (HYPULSE) were another element of the Mach 7 scramjet test effort. Unlike the other wind tunnels, the HYPULSE did not provide continuous airflow. Instead, it was a "shock tunnel," producing a single wave at speeds between Mach 5 and 10. The steady test period lasted only 3 milliseconds (0.003 seconds). This shock wave was generated by the rupturing of a double diaphragm separating the high-pressure cold helium driver from the lower-pressure shock-tube gas. The primary contaminate in the airflow was water vapor. Despite the high velocity of the pulse, the duration of the test was so short that the engine was at nearly room temperature when the test was completed. The HYPULSE was operated under contract with NASA by ATK General Applied Science Laboratory, and was located at their facility.

The HYPULSE data system included piezoelectric quartz-crystal pressure transducers and thin-film thermocouple heat-flux gauges readings from which go to digital oscilloscopes. Also included was an optical system featuring a four-frame sequential schlieren system, a laser holographic interferometer, a laser-based fuel plume planar imaging system, and path-integrated water-vapor measurements. The airflow inside the engine's isolator and combustor sections was observed through windows.

The HYPULSE scramjet model (HSM) engine was used for the tests. This had a full-scale-height/reduced-width copy of the X-43A engine flowpath. The HSM had an internal width of about 6.6 inches and an overall length of about 70 inches. The flowpath for these tests was the Mach 7 Keel Line 6 (M7-KL6). As with the Hyper-X engine model, the forebody and nozzle were truncated to fit in the HYPULSE tunnel. The Mach 7 test runs of the HSM engine were limited compared to those of the other models. Only one series of Mach 7 tests was run, between November 16, 1998, and January 26, 1999. This consisted of 16 calibration runs, three unfueled (or "tare") runs, 18 fueled runs using 5% silane in the hydrogen fuel mix, and six hydrogen fuel-only runs. These served both as a facility shakedown and for calibration.

The goal of the initial Mach 7 HYPULSE tests was to validate testing of the HYPULSE scramjet model in a short-duration shock tunnel rather than in the long-duration airflow tunnels used with the other engine models. This was necessary to identify potential facility effects. The HSM was primarily for Mach 10 tests. Because it was not possible to produce a continuous Mach 10 airflow in any available wind tunnels, the HYPULSE shock tunnel had to be used. This facility, however, could only produce stable airflow lasting a few milliseconds. It was necessary to ensure that these single-data-point tests corresponded to results from conventional tunnels.[34]

In all, a total of 710 engine tests were performed in support of the Mach 7 testing effort. These began in late 1996 and continued into the early part of

1999 and were an integrated, evolutionary, and multidimensional program that reflected the unknowns of scramjet technology. The use of different engine models and wind tunnels allowed engineers to refine their design step by step, while isolating and measuring the effects on the engines of scale, dynamic pressure, and test gas differences. These were the result of test techniques and facility limitations and were dealt with through design and analysis of the vehicle/engine design, selection of flight-test conditions, and the fuel/silane schedule. The SRGULL codes were used to analyze test results produced with the different wind tunnels and engines, determine combustion efficiency, quantify the test methodologies' effect on the combustor performance, and predict the scramjet's performance in flight.

UNCHARTED TERRITORY—HYPER-X SCRAMJET AT MACH 10

The designs of the Mach 7 and 10 scramjets were almost identical. At Mach 7 speeds, the engine would have excess thrust, compared to the amount of drag. At Mach 10, the margin between the amount of thrust, and the much higher amount of drag at that speed, would be small. To sustain cruise flight, the scramjet would have to produce a thrust *equal* to the vehicle drag. The Mach 10 scramjet ground testing would be more difficult because of the limitations of wind-tunnel testing at that speed.

Balancing this difficulty was the existence of a large experimental aerodynamic database, which allowed potential engine designs to be evaluated based on trimmed net axial forces. The engineers still faced a large number of design variables with which they had to deal. The task required a two-stage analytical approach that would define the initial flowpath and fuel-injection system.

As with the Mach 7 engine work, the first step was to use SRGULL codes. The results then were supplemented using information on three-dimensional spillages, kinetic energy efficiency penalty, combustion efficiency, and base pressure. Additionally, flight conditions were included in the analysis: Mach number, angle of attack, and dynamic pressure, as well as five geometry variables. Once the database was complete, additional constraints were imposed: combustor entrance pressure, the angle of attack based on forebody shock positions, combustor geometry, and the similarities with the Mach 7 engine design. This process resulted in establishment of a preliminary Mach 10 engine flowpath and an understanding of the vehicle's sensitivities to major design variables.

The second stage of the initial Mach 10 engine design effort dealt with the fuel injectors and combustor design variables. The GASP software was used to model the forebody and inlet, and the SHIP program to model the fuel injectors, combustor, and nozzle. The calculated propulsion forces and moments were combined with the vehicle's aerodynamic database, and design decisions were made based on the trimmed net axial forces. This was done instead of using a component performance metric, such as fuel mixing efficiency. A thermal analysis was performed on the thrust-optimized design to confirm that the engine could withstand exposure to Mach 10 enthalpy airflow both with and without the hydrogen fuel.

The result of this analysis was a completely defined Mach 10 flowpath and fuel-injection system. The design was then incorporated into a wind-tunnel engine, and initial testing of it began.[35]

The HYPULSE scramjet-model boilerplate engine of the initial Mach 10 testing used the M7-KL6 flowpath configuration (the same flowpath used for the HSM Mach 7 HYPULSE tests). The HSM Mach 10 HYPULSE tests ran from January 27 to February 17, 1999, a much shorter test series than conducted previously both in terms of time and number of runs. There were four Mach 10 calibration runs, two tare runs, five fueled runs using the 5% silane in the hydrogen fuel mix, and a single hydrogen run.

The HSM flowpath was then modified during the spring of 1999 to the M10-KL6 flowpath. This configuration was tested between July 1999 and March 2000. The major change was to the silane ratio in the fueled runs, which was cut to a 2% ratio and used for the majority of the subsequent HSM wind-tunnel tests. This was followed between May and October of 2000 by a second series of Mach 10 scramjet tests, also with the M10-KL6 flowpath. The two test series involved a total of 8 tare runs, 26 silane–hydrogen runs, and 31 hydrogen-only runs.

After analyzing both the wind-tunnel data and the concurrent computational-fluid-dynamics analysis, engineers found that the HSM engine was not providing an adequate representation of the flow structure entering the combustor. This was because of the leading-edge shock of the HSM forebody not matching that of the X-43A. The inlet shock train of the HSM was, as a result, misplaced at the inlet isolator section at the start of the combustor. Although the integrated, flux average properties at the cowl leading edge and in the inlet isolator were in good agreement with the flight profile and the HSM test conditions, more complete computational-fluid-dynamics analysis showed that the flow profiles were not. To better reproduce the X-43A shock positions predicted by computational-fluid-dynamics analysis, the cowl on the HSM was moved aft by several inches. The experience showed that at hypersonic speeds the shock-dominated flow entering a scramjet needed to be reproduced accurately in ground tests.[36]

Engineers also found that the silane–hydrogen fuel mix was more robust for all test conditions. The data also showed that fuel composition, too, had an effect on operations. Although use of silane as an ignition source was a feature of the engine design, Hyper-X program managers wanted hydrogen-only ignition to be as robust as possible, and the design was subsequently modified to maximize the efficiency of hydrogen-only ignition. This resulted in the final Mach 10 scramjet design.

As with the Mach 7 tests, computational-fluid-dynamics analysis was conducted on the wind-tunnel data. The process was built around a consistent data-analysis methodology with a simplified two-dimensional approach. GASP code was used to model the forebody and inlet sections. This was possible because wind-tunnel tests used a modified forebody that minimized the three-dimensional effects. The blunt-leading-edge effects were included, and an elliptical solution was used for the inlet to capture any shock-induced boundary-layer separation.

SHIP code was used to model the flow from the combustor entrance to the model's end. The modeling included the fuel mixing process and the mixing efficiency η_m. An elegant analysis technique was developed to produce a reaction efficiency model from experimental wind-tunnel measurements. In the Mach 10 engine, the amount of reaction was controlled by a reaction efficiency η_r profile or variations with the combustor length. Combustion efficiency η_c therefore was defined as $\eta_c = \eta_m * \eta_r$. With the combustion efficiency for each test based on the test conditions, the pressure rise, and the computational-fluid-dynamics-predicted mixing efficiency, a reaction efficiency model could be developed using the experimental results.

This approach had the advantages of being fast, robust, and could be easily modified to accommodate the thermodynamic properties of the fuel and combustion products. Use of silane simplified combustor analysis. The discrete comparison with the pressure levels in the combustor was used to determine the reaction efficiency profile, while the reaction efficiency at the combustor exit was determined by matching the integrated internal nozzle pressure force.

Analysis of the tunnel data indicated that the Mach 10 engine's reaction efficiency was sensitive to combustor entrance pressure and velocity. This indicated that there would be a fairly significant performance decline at high inflow velocity and low pressure, which was expected given the small scale of the X-43A vehicle and the ranges of the design space.[37]

NOTES

[1] Corpening, Griff history interview, Dec. 20, 2004, NASA Dryden Flight Research Center History Office, p. 42.

[2] Joyce, Phillip J., John B. Pomry, and Laurie Grindle, "The Hyper-X Launch Vehicle: Challenges and Design Considerations for Hypersonic Flight Testing," AIAA Paper 2005-3333, pp. 2–4.

[3] Corpening history interview, p. 42.

[4] Reubush, David E., "Hyper-X Stage Separation—Background and Status," AIAA Paper 99-4818, p. 3, 4, and Corpening interview, pp. 37, 38.

[5] Reubush, "Hyper-X Stage Separation—Background and Status," p. 4, and Pieter G. Buning, Tin-Chee Wong, Arthur D. Dilley, and Jenn L. Pao, "Prediction of Hyper-X Stage Separation Aerodynamics Using CFD," AIAA Paper 2000-4009, pp. 3, 4.

[6] *Aerospace Project Highlights*, Aug. 15, 1997, NASA Dryden Flight Research Center History Office.

[7] Ibid, Nov. 14, 1997, Nov. 17, 1997, Nov. 28, 1997.

[8] Ibid, Jan. 23, 1998.

[9] Buning et al., "Prediction of Hyper-X Stage Separation Aerodynamics Using CFD," pp. 4–6.

[10] Reubush, David E., John G. Martin, Jeffrey S. Roberson, David M. Bose, and Brian K. Strovers, "Hyper-X Stage Separation—Simulation Development and Results," AIAA Paper 2001-1802, pp. 2, 3.

[11] Corpening history interview, pp. 20, 21.

[12] Reubush et al., "Hyper-X Stage Separation—Simulation Development and Results," pp. 2, 3.

[13] Reubush "Hyper-X Stage Separation—Background and Status," pp. 4, 5, Reubush et al., "Hyper-X Stage Separation—Simulation Development and Results," pp. 2, 3, and Corpening interview, pp. 17, 18.

[14] Reubush et al., "Hyper-X Stage Separation—Simulation Development and Results," pp. 3, 4.

[15] Ibid, p. 2, and Reubush, "Hyper-X Stage Separation—Background and Status," pp. 2–4.

[16] Buning et al., "Prediction of Hyper-X Stage Separation Aerodynamics Using CFD," p. 4.

[17] Harsha, Philip T., Lowell C. Keel, Anthony Castroiovanni, and Robert T. Sherrill, "X-43A Vehicle Design and Manufacture," AIAA Paper 2005-3334, pp. 2, 3.

[18] Ibid, pp. 5, 7.

[19] *Aerospace Project Highlights*, May 1, 1998, June 5, 1998, and Oct. 5, 1998, NASA Dryden Flight Research Center History Office.

[20] Harsha et al., "X-43A Vehicle Design and Manufacture," pp. 3, 5. It is hard to imagine a milling machine large and powerful enough to move a space shuttle into the different positions needed to grind the tiles.

[21] Corpening history interview, pp. 22, 32, 33.

[22] Harsha et al., "X-43A Vehicle Design and Manufacture," pp. 6–8.

[23] Ibid, pp. 5, 6, and Corpening history interview, pp. 22, 23, 25, 26, 33, 34.

[24] Marshall, Laurie A., Catherine Bahm, Griffin P. Corpening, and Robert Sherrill, "Overview with Results and Lessons Learned of the X-43A Mach 10 Flight," AIAA Paper 2005-3336, p. 6.

[25] Jenkins, Dennis R., and Tony R. Landis, *Hypersonic The Story of the North American X-15*, Specialty Press, North Branch, MN, 2002, p. 55.

[26] Harsha et al., "X-43A Vehicle Design and Manufacture," pp. 6–8.

[27] Marshall, Laurie A., Catherine Bahm, Griffin P. Corpening, and Robert Sherrill, "Overview with Results and Lessons Learned of the X-43A Mach 10 Flight," AIAA Paper 2005-3336, pp. 5, 8.

[28] Harsha et al., "X-43A Vehicle Design and Manufacture," pp. 5, 6.

[29] Ibid, p. 6, and Corpening history interview, pp. 26, 27.

[30] *Aerospace Project Highlights*, Aug. 28, 1998, p. 2, NASA Dryden Flight Research Center History Office.

[31] Reukauf, Paul, history interview, Feb. 17, 2005, NASA Dryden Flight Research Center History Office, pp. 33, 34.

[32] Ferlemann, Shelly M., Charles R. McClinton, Ken E. Rock, and Randy T. Voland, "Hyper-X Mach 7 Scramjet Design, Ground Test and Flight Results," AIAA Paper 2005-3322, pp. 2, 3.

[33] Ibid, pp. 3–5, and R. T. Voland, K. E. Rock, L. D. Huebner, D. W. Witte, K. E. Fisher, and C. E. McClinton, "Hyper-X Engine Design and Ground Test Program," AIAA Paper 98-1532, pp. 3–6.

[34] Rogers, R. C., A. T. Shih, and N. E. Hass, "Scramjet Development Tests Supporting the Mach 10 Flight of the X-43," AIAA Paper 2005-3351, pp. 2, 3.

[35] Ferlemann, Paul G., "Comparison of HYPER-X Mach 10 Scramjet Preflight Predictions and Flight Data," AIAA Paper 2005-3352, pp. 1, 2.

[36] Rogers et al., "Scramjet Development Tests Supporting the Mach 10 Flight of the X-43," p. 5. The May to October 2000 tests were followed by a separate series of Mach 15 tests of the M10-KL6 flowpath. These were apparently independent of the X-43A effort.

[37] Ferlemann, "Comparison of HYPER-X Mach 10 Scramjet Preflight Predictions and Flight Data," p. 2.

Chapter 4

X-43A CHECKOUT AND EMERGENCY PROCEDURES TRAINING

The last of the lonely places is the sky, a trackless void where nothing lives or grows, and above it, space itself. Man may have been destined to walk upon ice or sand, or climb the mountains or take craft upon the sea. But surely he was never meant to fly? But he does, and finding out how to do it was his last great adventure.

Frederick Forsyth, British novelist 1938

The delivery of finished flight hardware to Dryden represented a major milestone for the Hyper-X project. The design work, wind-tunnel research, computer analysis, and fabrication were now complete. Project engineers and researchers now had actual flight vehicles to work with. All of the earlier efforts now had physical form. On another level, however, delivery represented only a single step in the march to the first flight. Much work had yet to be done before that journey would be complete.

The first X-43A arrives at Dryden in a shipping container and jig. Heavy lifting is still required. (NASA photo EC99-45208-6.)

The vehicles that comprised the stack still faced a long and complex series of testing and checkout procedures. Flaws in their design and systems still had to be identified. Fixes had to be developed and then verified in a series of reviews before being approved and finally incorporated into the vehicles. It was a long and difficult process, one that had begun even before the X-43A design was complete.

NASA engineer Yohan Lin was among those involved in the checkout of the three X-43As. He was assigned to the X-43A flight systems group when he started as a full-time Dryden employee in March 1997; work on the project was his first job after college. (Lin had worked at Dryden as a co-op on the F-16XL supersonic laminar flow project while still a student. This is a common means of acquiring experience before graduation. A significant number of employees at Dryden, and other NASA centers, were originally co-ops.) Lin recalled later,

> When I started out my duties were to come up with various types of tests to verify and validate the research vehicle. I had to write test plans and work the details to formulate the test procedures. So, as we got the vehicle and learned more about it and read up on all the documentation, I generated the procedures and worked them out. I was also responsible for conducting the tests. In addition to that I was responsible for the vehicle integration to the adapter and the launch vehicle.[1]

The initial difficulty facing the flight systems group was that they were designing checkout tests as the X-43A was itself being designed. They did not have an existing piece of hardware to use as the basis for developing their plans. As a result, the group had to begin planned testing at a very simple level. The engineers knew the basic design and knew what they had to accommodate. In some cases, the vehicle had to be physically supported in certain configurations. As a result, some components or wiring were not easily accessible. Engineers had to write into the procedures how to get around these difficulties and test certain functions. They also had to develop specialized test equipment. Lin noted, "We knew most of that up front but there were things and detailed steps that we had to incorporate into the procedures after we got the vehicle."

Once the initial release of the test procedures and requirements documentation was written, it was reviewed and "debugged." This was done by submitting the test plans to peer reviewers, including the contractor teams. Lin recalled that "...we'd catch as much as 75 to 85% of the errors. The rest pretty much works itself out as the test is conducted." Subsequent releases would go through an internal review, he said, in a "pretty smooth and well greased" procedure.[1]

The first X-43A scramjet engine after its delivery to Dryden. The engine was developed based on data from the NASP project and was intended to demonstrate the ability of a scramjet to operate in flight. (NASA photo EC99-45291-04.)

STEP BY STEP

Once the procedures were established, checking out the X-43A involved a long, complicated, and step-by-step process. The situation was made even more demanding by the hypersonic environment in which the research vehicle would operate. The various tests the vehicle underwent were very specific as to their nature and goals.

POSTDELIVERY FUNCTION TEST

Once the research vehicle arrived at Dryden, engineers and technicians went through a variety of tests of basic vehicle functions to ensure that the different subsystems were integrated properly and working. For example, the flight management unit (FMU) was checked to verify that its logic was working as designed. The computer's built-in test functions were checked, as were the inhibits, switches, valves, and relays. The heaters were checked to make sure they turned on and off. Checks of the power system were made to see that it delivered current to the correct subsystems.

All of this was extremely basic—the switch is turned, and the system comes on. Lin said later, "If it doesn't work, then basically that could mean either the wire was loose or something happened in shipment or it wasn't put together right." Beyond this, the tests become more specific.

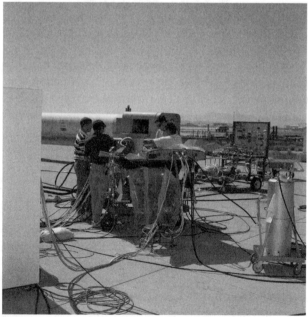

Ground testing of the X-43A #1 began in 2000. Although a specially prepared hangar was used for much of the ground checkout and testing, some was done in the open air. (NASA photos EC00-0265-01 and -02.)

FAILURE MODE AND EFFECTS TEST

These were done to induce nominal and off-nominal conditions between related subsystems. In an example, to test the communication of the FMU with the other subsystems through the bus communication systems, engineers would deliberately disconnect the bus and monitor the FMU reaction. Different uploads also were made via the communications link. Engineers were trying to see if anything would happen to the FMU if the upload were interrupted in midstream. The objective was to make sure that the subsystems reacted as they were designed to for a specific condition. If an off-nominal condition produced an unexpected result, engineers would have to go back and determine what might have been missed in the subsystem design. The testing identified errors that slipped through the design phase.

HARDWARE-IN-THE-LOOP TEST

The standard configuration for this type of test would be with the vehicle hardware connected to a simulator. With the X-43A the test involved just the FMU with the simulation bench, reproducing the trajectory for the flight experiment by sending the FMU simulated forces and moment data that told the computer the vehicle was "flying."

The goal of the hardware-in-the-loop test was to verify the flight-control and propulsion algorithms loaded into the FMU. As an example, the simulated flight results would determine if the propulsion control laws had the correct timing, the computer commands to open the valves were occurring at the correct time, and the flight control laws sent the correct servo commands at the right time and with the right magnitude.

AIRCRAFT-IN-THE-LOOP TEST

This was the next level up from the hardware-in-the-loop test. As before, the FMU was fed simulated force-and-moment sensor data, but for this test engineers connected the actuators that move the control surfaces. The simulation was used to prove that the actuators were active and responding correctly to the FMU's command. Engineers wanted to ensure that the complete system was operating correctly. If the rudders were supposed to move 5 degrees to the right, the test would show that they would not be commanded to go over or under the 5 degrees.

FREQUENCY-RESPONSE RAMP TEST

These would allow engineers to understand how the actuation system behaved as an installed system. One element of the testing was to determine whether differences existed between how the actuators moved when they were mounted in the vehicle vs when they were tested as independent components on a bench. In the X-43A, the actuators were connected to linkages, which added inertia and weight. The actuators' performance could be significantly different because of the influence of other components. The presence of a differential was determined by measuring the actuators' frequency response.

Inputs such as sinusoidal waves were fed to the actuator system to see how quickly they responded to a command. Engineers then increased the rate of the commands so that the actuators would move faster and faster. Lin recalled:

> We want to see how well the actuator can keep up its performance. It will come up to a certain limit. And we want to know and characterize that limit so that we understand the system as it is installed. What we do with the information is put it into our actuator models for the simulations so that we can have an accurate representation of the true hardware dynamics.
>
> Here is basically a command at different frequencies—we start from a slow frequency to a very high frequency command, at a constant amplitude or magnitude... . There will come a time when the commands are so quick, [the actuator's] response cannot keep up. So it would be out of phase with the command. For example, if you are commanding [the actuator] to the high position, it might still be at the low position because the command is going so fast that it cannot match the pace. We need to understand that because if we design flight maneuvers that are too quick for the actuator to keep up, we might not be able to have the vehicle perform the way it has to in order to fulfill the objectives.[2]

UNLOADED SURFACE CALIBRATIONS

These tests measured the relationship between the command voltages and the movements of the control surfaces. The amount of control surface movement is determined by the amount of voltage sent to the actuators. For the unloaded surface calibrations test, the control surfaces do not have hydraulic jacks or rams attached to simulate aerodynamic and other external forces acting on the surfaces (Thus the term "unloaded.") This test provided the basic standard calibration of the surfaces' responses to commands. Lin explained:

> We want to make sure that the angle commanded is actually what the system is giving us. Now, let's just say that you want to command the surface 5 degrees. You need to provide that equivalent in voltage terms in order to get the actuator and surface to move and arrive at that 5 degrees. So we need to map that relationship between voltage and angle.

Once the unloaded surface calibrations tests were completed, the engineers had a calibration curve of the voltages required for specific amounts of control surface movement. This curve was then loaded into the FMU and would be used to translate the unit's guidance commands into control surface movements.

COWL-DOOR CALIBRATION AND FREEPLAY TEST

The movements of the cowl-door actuator had to be calibrated in the same fashion as the control surfaces, so that the FMU could be programmed as to the amount of voltage needed to open the cowl door. For the freeplay test, what is being measured is the free-floating angle of the cowl door.

The actuation systems and the linkages in both the control surfaces and the cowl door had freeplay or backlash in them, and engineers need to measure its amount. This was created when gears inside the actuation system were not loaded and did not make full contact with each other. As a result, there would be a delay before a movement occurred as the gear moved back and forth. This discrepancy had to be accounted for in the flight model programmed into the FMU, so that the unit's commands were representative of the actual hardware. Timing and engine performance could be adversely affected without these data.

COMPLIANCE TESTS

These measured the elastic deformation of the actuators and their linkages under loads. When the vehicle was in flight, it would experience aerodynamic loading on control surfaces. Even though an actuator might be at a steady-state deflection of 5 degrees, the surfaces would be pushed slightly because of the aerodynamic loading, so that the deflection might actually be different than indicated by the feedback system.

The elasticity of the linkages was another part of control system compliance. The tests characterized this behavior and were made to ensure that the actuator models were representative of the real flight hardware under real flight conditions. This was a critical issue, as the X-43A would be flying at speeds of Mach 7 or 10. At such speeds, a control surface deflection of even one-tenth of 1 degree would cause the vehicle to depart from the planned trajectory very quickly if compliance were not accounted for in the control laws.

Another potential source of compliance errors was the sensors used to measure the total surface deformation. On most actuation systems, feedback is measured at the actuator, but deformation not only occurs within the actuator but also outside the actuator in the control surface linkages. As a result, if the aerodynamic or other loads cause the linkages to go through compliance, the resulting errors might go undetected by the actuators' feedback system. This meant that the flight management unit would not receive feedback reflecting the actual surface compliance. It would only "see" what the actuator "sees."

In that event, the FMU received inputs that the surfaces were at one set of positions, when the surfaces actually were at different ones. As a result, the FMU might attempt to "correct" the flight path of the vehicle, resulting in erroneous commands. To prevent this, an offset had to be written into the control laws. This allowed for the compliance outside of the actuation system, in the linkages, how much "give" the surfaces had, and how much they deflected under load and how far off they were.

DYNAMIC HYSTERESIS

This was the damping caused by friction between surfaces that slide past one another. In the actuation system, the linear motion of the actuator is translated into rotational motion of the control surfaces via a crank arm or servo arm. There is friction on the bearing and on the surfaces that slip and slide past each other to cause the motion. This can create nonlinearities that need to be measured and analyzed to determine whether they would degrade the actuation system performance.[3]

INERT GAS TEST

This verified and validated the research-vehicle's propulsion control system. Lin said of the test:

> It is a very complicated test to set up. It involves pressurizing all the propulsion systems, the fuel system, and the igniter system as well as the purge systems with nitrogen gas. Our objective is to perform a simulated mission and make sure that the propulsion control algorithms open the fuel valve, the igniter valve, and the purge valves at scheduled times. We have to service all the fluid systems and then basically perform an aircraft-in-the-loop test with the flight control system and propulsion system. This is the full-up simulation, using the real flight hardware to move the valves and the control surfaces.

Because of the fire and explosion dangers to ground personnel posed by hydrogen gas and the silane, the inert gas test is done with nitrogen. This simulates the gases used in the X-43A and could be done in a normal hangar environment. Lin observed:

> You don't have the fire hazards and so forth associated with handling silane. It's a pyrophoric gas; it ignites upon contact with air. So that's not something you want to use if you don't need to. The minute that you release the gas into the air, it will just ignite immediately. And that's the reason why we use this [silane] gas to provide flame holding capabilities, because we need to combust the mixture of air and hydrogen fuel for the scramjet experiment. As long as there is air, it will keep on burning.

The aft end of X-43A #2 during preflight ground tests. Testing of the fluid systems required that high-pressure nitrogen be used instead of the flammable hydrogen and silane gases that posed serious risks to the check-out personnel. The fluid system checks also required extensive preparations, requiring a significant period of time. (NASA photo EC04-0001-06.)

SHORT STACK COOLING AND PURGE TEST

This test extends the checkout of the propulsion system to the interconnected water–glycol cooling and nitrogen purge systems inside the adapter and research vehicle. These systems operate during ascent, separation, and scramjet burn. During the flight out to the launch point, nitrogen gas is supplied from tanks inside the B-52B. At launch, the nitrogen purge to the research vehicle is provided by a supply in the adapter. Then, just before the X-43A separates, there is a handoff of the nitrogen purge to the research vehicle's supply. Lin noted:

> [B]asically what we want to do is cool the engine and purge the research vehicle compartments and make sure that everything stays cool and nothing melts down and you do not have any source of oxygen inside the compartments of the research vehicle. We need to make sure the handoff works properly and make sure that all the valves are working properly.

The cooling and the purge systems were serviced with nitrogen gas, whereas the test itself reproduced the sequence of events that the adapter and X-43A systems underwent during flight. The transfer of cooling and purge activities during the separation required a communication link between the adapter and X-43A systems. What engineers did to provide this link was to simulate the adapter communications to the X-43A. These signals exercise the valves of the research vehicle's cooling and purge systems. The separation logic prepares the X-43A vehicle to go into the preseparation mode. This initiates the control system and related systems and within 3 seconds opens the valves.

SYSTEM-TIMING TEST

This was the final step in the testing and was an end-to-end test of the amount of delay in the control and actuation systems. This involved first determining the amount of time required for the flight management unit to send a command to the actuator and then for the control surface to move to the desired position. This is the initial timing information engineers needed. Then, the test determines the length of time it took for the actuation system's feedback to measure the new position and for this data to reach the FMU computer. Lin explained the need for the tests:

> The reason why we do this is because we want to understand the time delays of our vehicle and add them to the simulation to make it more realistic, to see if any of these delays would affect our performance and prevent us from reaching our mission objectives ... with the system timing test we wanted to understand and make sure that these delays were accounted for and making sure that our models are correct to ensure that we meet our objectives for the experiment.[4]

The checkout and test procedures, on the initial level, indicate whether any components are broken. Beyond this, however, they entail a complicated and multilayer effort to understand the minute details of how each system works, independently as well as part of the complete vehicle. Special attention was given to the actuation systems and the propulsion systems. The tests are made in order to understand the components' specifics, so that the vehicle's function can be checked against the design and engineers can confirm that the design is able to meet the project goals.

Lin noted that,

> [I]f you don't account for those things and if your system is not designed to be very robust, you can fool yourself into thinking that you have a robust vehicle when it's not stable and you might not fulfill what you intended to do .... You need to be prepared and understand as much as you can and test as much as you can on the ground so that you have the most flight-like representation and you understand it in your models and in your simulations.

The duration and breadth of the X-43A testing was necessary because the vehicle comprised many new and complex technologies and would operate in a demanding hypersonic flight environment. In addition, the "one-shot" nature of the mission was an overriding factor driving the exhaustive test process.[5]

An aerospace vehicle, be it an F-18, an X-43A, or a spacecraft, is a machine. How it responds to a specific flight condition and the individual characteristics and minor variations between different vehicles are caused by physical forces. It is a machine; it does not think, and it does not react to praise or anger or desperate pleading. A machine cannot have a personality. But after his experiences on the X-43A project, Lin concluded otherwise:

> Ah, yes. You know, some people don't believe in hardware having personalities, but believe it or not, having conducted all this hardware and software testing, I can tell you that each research vehicle had its own set of quote, unquote, personalities. The first vehicle was basically our baby. It was a learning experience for us. We learned a lot. We, in going through the growing pains, had to swap out and replace a lot of different components and spares because, again, that's part of the learning process. Ship two went very smoothly, no problems. By that time we pretty much understood the systems fairly well and in terms of operations there were no significant problems.
>
> Vehicle 3 was by far the most difficult vehicle to test. It just basically did not want to fly. You know, it's like trying to push someone to go swim in the water and it just doesn't want to go, and is afraid, and thinks the water is going to be cold and so forth. Every step of the way there would be issues or things we had to address anomalies that we had not experienced in vehicle 2. Some were small, some were identifiable, and others just kind of came up and went away on their own.[6]

Packaging the subsystems within the vehicle's limited interior volume had posed difficulties during the design phase. This limitation also affected checkout procedures. The propulsion system checkout was the biggest issue for the engineers. The tight packaging of the subsystems made it very difficult to perform the inert-gas test. This was because all of the fluid systems had to be serviced, and if there were a leak, getting to the leak, whether it was in a valve or tubing, required removing a pallet of systems.

Additionally, the control systems that regulated the tanks, the tubing around and under the tanks, and the valves all, were installed upside down because of volume constraints. To service or repair these components, engineers had to disassemble components and move other tubing, which created not only further delays but also the potential for more leaks. Lin recalled, "[We] sometimes tore up a thermocouple wire or two or crimped a pressure tube because things were delicate and when you're tearing things apart you

The X-43A #2 with test cables attached. To check out the vehicle's systems required inputs that simulated the forces and moments they would experience in flight. Clear plastic sheets and foam padding were used to protect components and carbon–carbon leading edges during the testing. (NASA photo EC04-0001-19.)

just can't help it—accidents happen."[7] The work required to get all of the connections leak tight for a test took a week or more before test preparations even began. Then as many as five days could be required to service the system for the test. And once the test was completed, another two or three days were needed to deservice the vehicle.

Although the focus on testing and checkout tends to be on the vehicle, on the X-43A another source of difficulty was getting the different test simulations to work together. Inertial simulators by Honeywell were used for tests involving the flight management unit. These generated signals to the FMU, matching those it would receive in flight. It seemed a simple enough task, but of the problems they encountered Lin recalled that,

> Getting that inertial system simulator to sync up with our simulation bench and the vehicle was quite a challenge. That took us about a good part of half a year or so to try to determine and resolve most of the issues. And sometimes not everything would be perfectly resolved. But you have work-arounds and you basically live with it. Most of those challenges were due to lack of documentation. Some of it was just getting things to work together, syncing up the different systems because they come from different manufacturers. Sometimes, it's just a difficult task to do.[8]

Discrepancy Reports, Configuration Change Requests, System Test Reports, and Waivers—Alphabet of Configuration Control

The importance of configuration control was apparent to the National Advisory Committee for Aeronautics (NACA) from the very beginning. The very first NACA research aircraft were a pair of Curtiss JN4H Jenny trainers acquired in 1919, which were fitted with instrumentation for stability and control data. When the two aircraft were compared, they differed significantly in their configurations. One aircraft had a propeller that matched the design drawings, whereas the other's propeller was significantly warped. Additionally, the wings of the two Jennies were significantly different in camber from each other. This early experience made clear to NACA researchers that the aircraft blueprints, wind-tunnel models, and the "as-built" aircraft all must match as closely as possible. Otherwise, the three very different shapes would render meaningless the correlations among the aircraft's planned characteristics, the wind-tunnel data, and the flight data.[9]

As aircraft became more complex, the need for configuration control increased. By the start of the 21st century, this was no longer limited to the vehicle's external shape, but extended to its subsystem designs, software, control laws, and individual components. The potential results of a configuration control error in a vehicle with the performance demands of the X-43A were obvious. An analysis of the X-43A's stability that used an outdated actuator compliance model would be, at best, valueless. At worse, it could show problems where none existed or fail to show problems that might mean the loss of the vehicle. All changes and modifications to each element had to be documented to ensure that such errors did not slip through.

In March of 1996, Linda Soden had joined Dryden as an administrative secretary, supporting five project managers. She had been involved in the advocacy phase of the Hyper-X project, preparing the various presentations and proposals. She then moved to configuration control once the project began. She said later:

> I basically tracked hardware, software, and documentation changes on the vehicles, the ground support equipment, the launch vehicle. I tracked those changes from the time they were opened until they were closed and there were various different means of closing out the items and keeping track of all of the supporting documentation that showed what changes that were implemented into the system.
>
> The goal was no loose ends. In actuality [there were a] few loose ends. And it kept everybody on the same page and if anybody needed to know what changes had been made, that information was made available to them. I kept a hard-copy library of the configuration management records in the project office for everybody to review as required .... You have to be able to go both forwards and backwards in this system.[10]

The aft end of the first Hyper-X launch vehicle awaiting assembly. The nozzle, rocket casing, and the wing attachment structure are visible. (NASA photo EC99-45146-3.)

Another view of the partially assembled HXLV. The wing has been attached by this point, but the fins still have to be installed. (NASA photo EC99-45163-08.)

The aft end of the first HXLV with the fins attached. Like much else with the HXLV, the fins required changes to their thermal protection system, which caused small but significant changes to their shape. (NASA photo EC01-0019-14.)

Just as the tests the X-43A underwent were exact and rigorous, so too were the procedures by which the problems were reported, the corrective actions approved, the fixes made, and the configuration control process documented.

The configuration control process for the Hyper-X project at Dryden started when an unusual situation was observed by a member of the test team. This might have been an assembly error spotted during an inspection, an odd reading or event during a test, a software issue, or an outright test failure. The event was recorded on a discrepancy report (DR), which included a description of what occurred and the specific details. In some cases, the DR also included a proposed fix for the problem.

The DR was then submitted to the weekly configuration control board meeting. How the DR was dealt with varied based on the situation. In some cases, the problem was quickly determined not to be an issue, and it was closed on the spot. Often the DR was assigned to an engineer, who researched the problem and developed a solution. This ranged from a minor repair to the replacement of a defective part, a new software upload, or a full redesign of a component.

Once the fix was determined, a configuration change request (CCR) was written. If necessary, a work order authorizing the modifications was issued. Once the fix was completed, the test would be repeated, and, if everything passed, a system test report (STR) was written. The STR described the problem, the fix that solved it, how the fix was tested, and why engineers believed the problem was now fixed. The STR was then signed by the con-figuration-control-board chairperson as well as by the person who did the test and the person who witnessed the test. In all, the first X-43A had a total of 119 DRs, 384 CCRs, and more than a hundred STRs written against it.[10]

The goal of this process was to fully document every step, from the original discovery of a potential problem through development of the fix and its implementation, the testing process, and the final disposition. The rationale governing the process was to provide a means of reconstructing the event should a problem or failure later occur. This procedure is also required of NASA because it is a government agency and is therefore responsible to the American public for its activities. Practices and obligations expected of private-sector contractors were often different.

A separate process was the issuing of waivers. This was the decision by project management to change or ignore a design specification or perfor-mance requirement of a vehicle component or system. Issuing such waivers became a public issue following the loss of Space Shuttle *Columbia* in February 2003. During the investigation, it became known that some 1600 waivers had been issued by shuttle managers during the previous two decades. The perception was that this amounted to an easing of safety procedures. The reality involved in the process of issuing wavers was more complex.

Hyper-X project managers also faced the issue of waivers. The waiver pro-cess began when a design specification or performance requirement could not be met. The X-43A's tungsten nose section, for example, had a manufacturing requirement specifying the extent to which the surface could be rippled. This was not a trivial issue, as the X-43A's forward lower surface formed the inlet ramp for the scramjet. Potentially, if that surface were too rippled, the shock waves would not be properly formed and/or positioned to slow and compress the airflow entering the engine.

Before a waiver was issued, the consequences were analyzed. This occurred on several levels: First, although the specification had been violated, was the violation significant? Would, for example, a valve leak rate 1 or 2% higher than called for by specifications have any real impact on safety or mission success? Another issue was whether a specification could actually be met with the existing manufacturing techniques. Schedule and cost also entered into questions involving waivers; projects have finite limits on both time and money, as well as limits on how much these can be exceeded before there was the risk of cancellation.

The determining factor in whether or not a waiver was issued was whether a violation could be ignored, or if corrective action were needed. And if some corrective action were necessary, then what type of change was needed—a minor modification or a complete new design? To decide this, the engineers analyzed the consequences of each option and the level of risk posed by each.

Although the potential consequences were straightforward, risk was more ambiguous.

On the surface, risk seemed black and white, yes or no, safe or unsafe. The reality was that risk assessment is not anything remotely like what most people assumed it to be. Reliability and risk come only in shades of gray. As the Hyper-X project showed, sometimes a fix can transform a minor problem into a major problem, putting the project at risk. Lin, looking back on his X-43A experiences, recalled:

> Risk is not easy to quantify. And the reason why, to me, is because it's a subjective thing. One issue might be very risky to you and maybe moderately risky to me. So trying to put a metric to that and then have a buy-in from everybody is not easy. To have people grade what the value of that risk is and how much risk it carries in terms of dollars or lives, is sometimes very hard to say—"yeah, high risk, moderate risk, low risk" and so forth, depending on your view and where you're coming from, your background. It's sometimes very subjective and to get buy-in is hard.
>
> But in the end, you still won't know 100% and you probably never will. So, you've got to do your best to understand the risks to the extent you can and have people look at you and make sure that you're doing the right things and you've done the right things.[11]

In some ways, things have changed little in the century since the Wright brothers first flew at Kitty Hawk. Twenty-first-century engineers, faced with more complex machines, might take more time and do more extensive calculations, but exploring uncharted territory is essentially unchanged; many aspects of the endeavor—time, weather, circumstances—remain beyond the control of engineers and researchers.

All of this testing and analysis took time. In 1998, the first Mach 7 flight was scheduled to take place in early 2000.[12] When the year 2000 finally arrived, hardware was still undergoing checkout, and an actual flight date was still not within reach. As the checkout dragged on, managers would press project engineers for the soonest date on which the mission could be flown.

Reukauf said later, "We essentially got into the situation where we would project—given the best possible scenario, with no further problems—we could fly on a certain date." The date kept slipping, from a first flight in July of 2000 to a September 2000 flight, and then another estimate of December of 2000. Langley's center director, Jerry Creedon, finally forced the issue. He said during a meeting that the situation had become "ridiculous," complaining that he had been told the first X-43A would be flown on this date, then on this date, and then on this date. He ended by demanding to be given a firm date on which the X-43A was going to fly.

Reukauf continued:

> So, of all sudden, our management came back and said "We want to
> know a real date when you're going to fly, not the best possible date. We
> want you to be able to guarantee us a flight date." And so, we did exactly
> what anybody else would do. We looked at the work that was left and we
> essentially doubled the time we thought it would take to do it and we
> came up with a date like May or June [of 2001]. We thought, "that will
> shock them," and we went to them and they said okay and we said okay.
> I think at that point it was overkill. We then put ourselves into a situation
> where we were spending more time monitoring and adjusting the
> schedule than we were actually working.[13]

EMERGENCY PROCEDURES TRAINING

Just as the Hyper-X components were being tested and prepared, so too
were the engineers who would monitor the vehicle during the launch and free
flight. Today, the idea of ground controllers overseeing a research flight is
commonplace. In fact, this is a fairly recent development.

The pilots of the early rocket planes—the X-1 series, the D-558-II, and the
X-2—all lacked such monitoring and assistance from the ground. During launch
and landing phases, chase planes provided some support, but during speed and
altitude runs the rocket pilots were on their own. Data were recorded by onboard
instrumentation. Not until the rocket planes had landed and the film-recorded
data were processed and analyzed could potential hazards be identified. The X-1
research aircraft did have a limited telemetry capability, but data were recorded
for later analysis, not monitored in real time. The rocket planes were tracked
optically and by radar, but position data were not relayed to the pilots. Radio
transmissions were recorded on the ground, but there were no means by which
rocket pilots could be warned of potential problems in flight.

As a result, if an emergency occurred, ground personnel would have no
idea what was wrong, where the aircraft was, or if the pilot were alive or
dead. Pilots in the mid-1950s were flying at speeds of Mach 3 and altitudes
above 100,000 feet, but were using the same safety procedures propeller aircraft pilots had used more than two decades earlier.[14]

The situation changed with the arrival of the X-15 at Edwards Air Force
Base in 1959. With a top speed of Mach 6, and an altitude capability of over
60 miles, a new approach had to be developed. The aircraft was fitted with
instrumentation that transmitted data to a control room. The data were then
displayed on multichannel strip charts and a map display. Engineers monitored
the strip charts and aircraft position. If irregularities in the data or indications
of a malfunction were spotted, an engineer would notify NASA 1, who was
the only person talking directly to the X-15 pilot. He would then pass on any
warning or advice he felt was necessary.

This practice originated with the X-15, but very soon the same procedure was being used to monitor and control the Mercury spacecraft. The rows of controllers at their consoles would report to the flight director, while the capsule communicator (capcom, the later incarnation of NASA 1) talked to the astronauts. Over the decades, the strip charts and paper map in the original X-15 control room have given way to computer monitors and high-definition television screens. What has not changed is the basic concept of ground control and the demands placed upon the people in that room.

For the Hyper-X project emergency-procedures training was undertaken by primary as well as backup personnel, who were drawn from engineers who had worked on the project's various elements. Unlike the mission controllers at Johnson Space Center in Houston, controllers for the Hyper-X project did not work full time as controllers. Rather, their regular day-to-day activities were testing, checkout, analysis, and other engineering duties.

During emergency-procedures training scenarios, controllers experienced simulated stack and/or B-52B system failures. Their displays showed computer-generated telemetry data as if it were actually transmitted from the vehicle. Video was displayed on the wall screens showing the B-52B in flight. the scenarios were scripted in advance, with only the mission director knowing what was going to happen, why, and when. The simulation followed a standard format: the scenario began, and a problem appeared that controllers must identify, correctly assess, and resolve. Once the simulation was complete, a debriefing was held to explain what had actually happened and why, discuss any errors in procedures or questions raised by the simulation, and note any difficulties that occurred.

The emergency procedures training had several roles. These included the obvious roles of familiarizing the controllers with their duties, the procedures followed in the event of specific problems, how malfunctions were indicated on their displays, and to meld the individuals into a team. Just as the preflight testing of the vehicles served to find problems in their design, construction, and installation, the emergency procedures training had a similar function. They provided an opportunity for the personnel to try out both the standard and emergency checklists under realistic conditions. This was quick means of discovering shortcomings and suggesting changes. The debriefings allowed the controllers to discuss what occurred in the simulations and to raise questions or issues that the events highlighted.

The X-43A had significant differences from other unmanned research vehicles, and this was reflected in the training simulations. Other unmanned vehicles were capable of being remotely piloted, which meant that if certain types of failures occurred, a pilot on the ground could take over and fly the vehicle to a landing on the lakebed. In the event of a more severe malfunction, a parachute could be deployed, and the vehicle would descend to a soft landing. With the X-43A, neither of these options was viable. The vehicle and its flight were entirely preprogrammed and autonomous.

Once the Hyper-X launch vehicle was launched, it was on its own, with no manual backup options. As a result, the simulations were of the takeoff, the flight to the launch point, and the final countdown. They ended with the "launch, launch, launch" call. As the stack was controlled in flight by its onboard computers, the ground controllers did not have a role beyond the launch. In the event of a malfunction, range safety at Point Mugu's only option was to transmit the destruct signal.

Several examples of the emergency-procedures training scenarios used give an idea of the areas covered and the challenges controllers faced.

One scenario involved a C-band beacon transmitter problem. During the "flight" out to the launch point, the transmitter worked only intermittently. Then the red temperature warning light was illuminated on one of the controllers' consoles. The indicator briefly showed a drop in temperature, but went red again. Transmission dropouts from the beacon also occurred. The drop was aborted, and the B-52B crew was ordered to return to base. A manual vent of the high-pressure hydrogen, silane, and nitrogen gases was ordered, and the call was made to power down the X-43A. By this time, the C-band was back to operating within temperature limits. The decision to power down the vehicle was reversed, and it was kept at powered-up status. The controllers then purged the onboard high-pressure tanks. The nitrogen pressure indication dropped, and the beacon was powered down. The vent and purge was complete, ending the simulation.

During the debrief, the mission director explained that the C-band transmitter temp had climbed to 160 degrees and stayed there for 2 seconds and then gone down. The temperature went up a second time, this time to 190 degrees—outside operating limits—and the beacon would have to be replaced. An abort was called, and the fuel system was vented. The problem with the C-band beacon meant that it had to be shut down quickly. Engineers then discussed the protocol and procedures to be used should this situation actually occur. The whole atmosphere during the simulation was very low key, with the calls being made in very matter-of-fact tones.

The simulation was then reset, and the next scenario began. Again the B-52B was heading toward the launch point. Suddenly, four fire-warning indicators turned red. Controllers vented the silane and the hydrogen gas from the X-43A, but the temperature continued to rise. The chase-plane crew "reported" that the venting was taking place as it was supposed to. The fire-warning indicator, however, remained lit. The B-52B was ordered back to Edwards. The chase plane then reported no visible fire, and the venting concluded. The controllers then powered down the X-43A's onboard systems.

In the debriefing, the mission controller noted that the fire warning and the "vent, vent, vent" call were made on time. Because the fire apparently was still burning, the X-43A was powered down. The question was raised about whether or not to power down if the fire warning remained lit but no combustible fluids remained onboard. The temperature shot up from a normal reading to 900 degrees instantly, with no trace of electrical or other problems. The situation did not allow enough time for controllers to consult the emergency-procedures page in the checklist. A decision was made that they should vent if controllers saw a problem, as this would be required anyway. If the fire warning were caused by an instrument failure, then they would have to recycle. Under these conditions, it would be hard to make the launch. The controller also needed to specify which emergency-procedures page to go to when he made the "vent" call. The mission controller said the simulation was of an instrumentation failure, rather than a real fire.

Although some of the simulations were short, others were long and very suspenseful. One began at the launch minus 9-minute (L-9) point. The built-in test ("bit") check, the switch to internal power, and the go/no calls all were made successfully. At L-5, there was a successful bit check, the B-52B video was switched to the aft camera, and the go/no go calls were again made. The major milestone was the L-2 point, when the fin sweep was made. This was a check before launch of the fin actuation system (FAS), which moved the rudder and elevons. The FAS batteries had now been activated, and the simulated launch would now either have to be made or aborted, as the batteries would run out of power before the launch could be recycled. The simulation was still go at the L-1-minute and L-30-second mark. Then came the call, "abort, abort, abort." There were flight-management-unit and fin-actuation-system problems. The fin pins were put back in, which locked them for the return flight. The controllers did not recommend powering down the X-43A. The debriefing indicated that the abort was called only three to four seconds before launch. There were multiple problems with the navigation system, the flight management unit, and a bit error.

The simulations had an unusual effect on the participants. Every person in the control room knew that they were not participating in a real launch, that the B-52B was not flying over the Pacific Ocean, and that the stack was not under its wing. The preprogrammed data were computer generated, and the video was prerecorded. None of this is actually going on; none of the problems were real. At the same time, however, physical reactions were quite real during the simulation. Pulse and respiration rates increased, time seemed to speed up, and attention was sharply focused. When the abort was called in the final seconds, there was an almost physical shock.[15]

Other simulations involved the B-52B launch aircraft. Gordon Fullerton, the Dryden Flight Research Center chief pilot, recalled:

> Well, they [the controllers] did a lot of practice with simulated X-43 system failures, trying out their checklists and responses. We found a console in an adjacent control room…to sit [at] with one or two pilots and we threw in the real-life things that could happen in the B-52 to cause them to have to compensate. I made up some scripts that complicated their kind of tunnel vision on the experiment. And we also threw in some things to exercise the mission rules, like loss of hydraulics. We threw those in to make them think about how that interacted with the rocket and experiment.
>
> It seemed like we pre-cleared them with the other people who were bringing scripts for problems to insert on the [simulations] so that we didn't waste anybody's time by an impossible situation or blow another script by overriding it with an airplane problem.[16]

Several of the scenarios involved potential problems with the hooks holding the Hyper-X launch vehicle to the pylon. The stack was a heavy payload, and there was a strong possibility that high flight loads could cause the hooks to break, causing the stack to fall off, or requiring the stack to be jettisoned.

One scenario began at the L-9-minute mark. It ran for several minutes, then the front and right hook warning lights came on. Neither the left hook nor the pylon light was on. The B-52B crew continued with the launch, but was ready for an inadvertent drop. They wanted to attempt a launch, even with the hook lights on. The stack would have to be dropped if the hooks issue were not resolved. The controllers ran through the recycle checklist, and the simulation concluded.

In the debriefing, the mission controller said that the simulation was an Hyper-X launch-vehicle call with one or two hook lights at L-6 minutes. It took controllers 3 minutes to work the problem, however, so that there was not enough time to salvage the drop. But in such a situation, controllers might as well attempt a launch, as otherwise the stack would be dropped into the ocean. "Just go for it," was the advice, as there would be little to lose.

Whereas the preceding scenarios began in the final minutes before launch, another began before takeoff. In that simulation, an F-18 chase plane experienced a hydraulic failure, and ground aborted. This triggered discussion about mission rules regarding video coverage in the event of a ground abort; for purposes of the simulation, the videographer "switched" to the second F-18, and the mission proceeded.

The B-52B then took off, and immediately the crew reported high hook loads on the pylon. The aircraft flew straight and level at 200 knots, with the hook loads at 90%. The aircraft stayed in the local Edwards area rather than heading west toward the coast. The hooks were rated for a maximum time of

20 minutes at 90% hook loads, and so controllers once again had little time to deal with the problem. All four hooks were at 90%, but there was no movement of the stack or any damage. As the controllers analyzed the problem, they found that two hooks had high readings, while readings for the two others were low. No landing could be made with the hook readings above 70%. The B-52B headed for the Edwards drop zone for a possible jettison of the stack, while staying clear of towns and buildings.

The situation slowly became clearer. The forward right hook on the pylon adapter was at a 90% load, while the left aft hook load was near 90%. The clock also was counting down—at this point 12 minutes were left before the stack would have to be dropped. The B-52B crew began transferring fuel to the right wing, to balance the aircraft should a drop be necessary. The forward right hook load was now at 80%, the aft left hook at about 90%, and the other two hooks had load readings of 0%. There were now 8 minutes left. In addition, there was a great deal of confusion in the control room, as engineers knew the hook readings were not physically possible.

Now the situation changed, as a leak was detected in the nitrogen gas bottle. The tank pressure went down to 500 psi and then to 400 psi. The minimum pressure needed for the drop was 350 psi. Two minutes remained in the countdown. There was a change in plan, as a result of the nitrogen pressure drop; the crew would try a different drop method. Senior managers approved the jettison, as controllers had run out of time and no solution was available. The B-52B was over the east edge of lakebed and level at 10,000 feet. A clean drop was made over the PB-8 bombing range. Because of the loss of weight in the drop, three-quarters right aileron was needed to keep the B-52B's wings level. With the drop successfully completed, there was no need for a quick landing, and no postflight flyby would be made.

In the debriefing, the mission controller explained that one hook had broken on takeoff and the other three were left to carry the load. Controllers had taken a long time to determine whether the problem was an instrument failure rather than a real malfunction with the hooks. If the strip chart had been running, the situation of an instrument failure vs a real malfunction would have been clearer. A question was also raised by one of the controllers during the debriefing about who would be sent out to the impact point.

The simulation also showed problems with the procedures used by the controllers had it been real. There was no call made during the simulation to declare an in-flight emergency, as should have been done. The control room should have been locked down only after the B-52B had safely landed, not before, as was done in this simulation. In the event of a mishap, preserving all data and evident was the first step in the investigation. The practice was that nothing was to be removed from the control room except personal property. However, the B-52B still was flying, and it still needed to land. Also raised in the debriefing was the question of whether or not to vent the hydrogen and silane from the X-43A before jettisoning the stack. The controllers were told that venting would not have been ordered in a real accident, as the Hyper-X launch-vehicle's load of solid fuel posed a much greater danger than did the X-43A's onboard propellant. Controllers ultimately decided they would have wanted to keep the hydrogen and silane onboard.

The most serious issue uncovered in that simulation was the confusion over which hook was at a 0% load. Also of concern was that the B-52B pilot did not know the minimum nitrogen pressure needed for a drop. The debriefing also noted that the controllers went 1 minute long on the time limit for the damaged hook, but this was not as critical under a steady load as it would have been under dynamic loads. Fullerton also noted that if the hook problem had occurred just before launch, taking 5 more minutes to get a successful launch would have been worth the risk. The simulation was of a right rear hook breaking during takeoff. The controllers did identify the problem correctly, although it took more time than was ideal.

More routine B-52B problems were also simulated. Among those was a scenario that began with the B-52B at 1000 feet and climbing out after takeoff. At that point, the oil pressure gauge on the #7 engine began flickering. The chase-plane pilot confirmed that a large quantity of oil was visible on the engine nacelle. The oil pressure for the #7 engine dropped to between 0 to 5 psi and was shut down. Despite the loss of an engine, the B-52B pressed on to the launch point. At that juncture, the propulsion system controller reported a leak, followed by the call to "vent, vent, vent." Controllers then turned to the Emergency Procedures-1 checklist and confirmed a hydrogen and silane pressure drop. A manual vent was made of the gases, and the B-52B crew was ordered to fly back to Edwards.

A single debriefing covered the two events. The first was the oil loss on the #7 engine. The B-52B was too heavy to make a landing right way, and so the consensus by the controllers was that it would have been better to press on and see if the launch could still be made. Then the telemetry indicated one pressure measurement had increased and spiked while another had dropped. The first measurement broke the pressure limit, and so the controller ordered the venting. There was no fire or electrical problems. The launch director then contacted the tower to check winds. The team had correctly identified the problem and dealt with it.

The final exercise involved a simulation that began with the B-52B flying with eight good engines and a single F-18 chase plane behind it and located at a point 5 minutes short of when the aircraft were scheduled to cross the coastline. At this point, a red hydraulic warning light indicated that the #8 hydraulic pack was at 0 psi. A hydraulic pack was a turbine powered by engine-bleed air, and the turbine generated hydraulic pressure for various systems. After the failure, checks for air-bleed leaks were made by the B-52B crew. An attempt was made to restart the pack, but this failed, and the #8 hydraulic pack was shut down. As a result, the B-52B lost the use of half the spoilers on its right wing. (On the B-52B, roll control was not provided by conventional ailerons but by spoilers on each wing.) The formation continued to press on to the launch point.

Controllers reported good data coming from the X-43A and continued to run through the checklists despite the launch aircraft's problem. Then a high overcurrent reading in the flight management unit caused controllers to go to the Emergency Procedures-7 emergency checklist. The X-43A was powered down in response to the problem, and a "go" was given for manual vent. The cause of the problem was not with the flight management unit, but rather with the unit's battery. They went ahead with power-down process, and ordered a precautionary landing. The tower was contacted and warned about the B-52B problem.

The hydraulic pack failure meant that four of the seven wing spoilers would be inoperative for the drop. It was possible to correct this by using a crossover in the hydraulic system. However, Fullerton said during the debrief that he had not wanted to use the crossover, in case there was a leak in the hydraulic system. To compensate for the loss of the wing spoilers, he shifted the lateral center of gravity to the right, but not as far as normal, to avoid overstressing the B-52B's wing.

While the controllers' attention was on the B-52B problems, the X-43A suffered multiple failures. The 150-volt current reading went up while the voltage went down. The 20-volt current reading also went up. The battery went off line, and the power drained. The X-43A wing position measurement also was in error, causing the control surfaces to lock and become immobile. The temperatures continued to increase until the system was successfully powered down.[17]

The difficulties faced by controllers during the simulations were considerable. They had limited data; all they knew was what was displayed on their computer screen. Viewing that (simulated) data might suggest one course of action, but in reality some other action should have been taken. There also was the ambiguity of having to make an immediate decision based on potentially erroneous or misleading data. Lin later recalled:

> Sometimes you had to determine on the spot whether or not it's really a problem or if it was just an intermittent issue, where it wasn't really a problem. Those were also simulated. So you had simulated failures as well as what I would call "simulated intermittent." In these types of training sessions, you have to try to hone your skills to be able to decipher that spontaneously or in the fastest way possible. I thought that they were very good training exercises.
>
> Now, in addition to those control room trainings, our systems group went through a number of internal discussions about how we want to handle certain anomalies or problems and how the emergency procedures should be interpreted, and our functions in the control room.

And, he also noted,

> For this type of training they simulated different types of failures of different systems. Depending on the responsibility of your systems that you are monitoring, you need to respond according to the project mission rules and the protocol. Not only did we have to respond to the simulated problems, we also had to reflect on them and discuss in a group, and determine what the best action to take was.

In other cases, the failures would be very straightforward. If a specific valve failed to open, a specific set of events would happen, and a set procedure was used to correct them. These were not the focus of the simulations, however. Lin said:

> We have set procedures for those [straightforward failures]. But there would be simulated problems that would kind of be in between, where it could have been the determining factor but then again it might not have. Sometimes it was very shady; you could interpret it in different ways. Based on your interpretation of the readings, it could lead you to a very orderly type of emergency procedure shutdown, or you would have to come up with something right at that moment to troubleshoot the problem.
>
> Some of them were more probable because we knew that those systems were more at risk of failing. For example, pressures and thermocouples and oxygen sensors—they were more prone to intermittent problems and so forth. So those were the kinds of things that the one in charge of the simulation used. Some of them had to do with timing as we got closer and closer to launching the stack; he would put in failures at the very last second before it dropped. You had to call it in really quick. For those things it added to the element of surprise or excitement of the simulation.
>
> They provided an excellent way of working out things you never thought of. Overall they provide a near-real-live experience with group interaction. Whereas if you were just practicing on your own, or going through training with just your group, it's more isolated and you don't get the full effect. But here you're simulating that the vehicle is flying and so forth. It makes it a lot more realistic when you're using the environment, the actual control room that you're going to for the flight.[18]

The pressure and demands of control room activity create an exacting teamwork and discipline. The exchanges between the controllers have to be short but understandable. There is no time for chatter or explanations. To do this, there is a standardized set of phrases used during the simulation. One example of this was use of the phrase "in work" by a controller when a problem is being examined. Other phrases include "roger that," "understand," "copy that," and "I read you." Also there are words for differentiating the letter of the alphabet—Alpha, Bravo, Charlie—for "A," "B," and "C."

These terms, words, and phrases are much more than common slang to be picked up in an environment and passed along as new people come aboard. Their use, in part, is driven by the need for precision. When a group of people uses the same phrases, such as "in work" as opposed to, "Yeah, I'm looking at that," each team member knows exactly what is going on. Use of a standardized language within a culture leaves no room for misinterpretation. In the control room culture, this use of standardized phrases or words is part of learning the protocol and discipline associated with the job.[18]

What first began as several engineers monitoring a strip chart has become international aerospace practice. Watching the launch of the Mars Reconnaissance Orbiter on August 12, 2005, the author was struck by how similar the exchanges between the controllers were to those seen in the X-43A emergency procedures training. A more surprising example occurred during a Russian Soyuz flight to the International Space Station. The Russian checklist page and item designations used the same pattern as those of the X-43A checklists and emergency-procedures pages.

LAUNCH DAY

Since 1997, the Hyper-X team had been struggling to design, build, prepare, and test the fastest airplane in the world. With the beginning of the 21st century, it seemed that the X-43A was about to be a success. In late January 2001, Orbital Sciences personnel received the software required to finish their checkout of the Hyper-X launch vehicle. Once this was completed, final assembly took place. At the same time, an environmental test was completed, as was a checkout of the Navy test range systems at Point Mugu on the California coastline.

Before the X-43A could be launched, a series of reviews was required. One of these was the flight readiness review (FRR), and it was scheduled for the week of February 12, 2001.[19] This is a peer-review process that was part of established first-flight procedures at NASA. Griff Corpening recalled the atmosphere of the meeting:

> At our flight readiness review, which is the major technical review of the program, every one of the presenters final slide was essentially "we are go for flight." And we had been working, I think at that point, four years or so. We had done everything we could think of to understand the risk and to mitigate the risk within the constraints of the program schedule and budget. And I did my own polling. I would walk around and ask people if they were ready, and every person on the project was "go" for flight. We were confident we had done what we could think of to mitigate and understand the risk.[20]

The flight readiness review cleared the way for a March 15, 2001, taxi test with the stack attached to the B-52B. Dryden Chief Research Pilot Gordon Fullerton said later,

> [W]e went out and went down the runway at 100 knots mainly to bounce the rocket around on the hooks that hold it and the people in the control room are watching the strain gages on the hooks.
>
> So we're giving them a look at real-life loads other than just sitting still on the ramp. And it gives us a feeling for all the interfaces. The crew is onboard so they can check that the paths of data coming from the rocket are all working and show up on the screens. And so it's a good end-to-end test, and there were some dynamics.[21]

A second element of the review process was the Dryden independent review (DIR), something done on an as-needed basis. A DIR might be convened to examine a modification or a contractor's proposal or for a specific issue. It could be convened by anyone. Despite the confidence of the X-43A engineers, the DIR team members presented the project staff with a total of 80 requests for information. By early April 2001, a total of 58 of these requests had been answered, and 47 were considered closed. The other 11 were returned to project engineers with requests for more information.[22] Within a week, the total answered was 70 out of the 80 requests for information. Of these the DIR closed 57, with the other 13 sent back for more information.[23]

Running in parallel with the Dryden independent review was another review panel, the airworthiness and flight safety review board (AFSRB). This was a joint Dryden/Edwards management-level review conducted before a flight was approved. The Air Force became involved because its facilities were being used in the flight and it had shared responsibility.[24]

The AFSRB meeting was held on April 17 and gave provisional approval for the flight. This was dependent, however, on resolution of several issues. One of these was completion of an AFSRB review of the telemetry link. Tests had indicated the possibility that the ground stations would be unable to receive telemetry from the X-43A in flight. The DIR team also was conducting a review of contractor discrepancy reports, and the AFSRB an overall review of emergency procedures, go/no go items, and mission rules.[25]

The X-43A AFSRB follow-up meeting was held a week later, on April 24, at which approval was given for the flight to be made. A technical briefing—"Tech Brief" in flight-test parlance—was held the following day, and the captive-carry flight request was approved by both the Langley and Dryden Center directors. The captive-carry crew brief was scheduled for April 27, with the flight to be made the following day.[26]

A captive-carry flight is a full-up test of the launch aircraft, research vehicle, control room crew, tracking network, and all of the other elements of the mission. The launch aircraft flies the mission as planned, right up to the launch point. The only difference is that no launch is actually made.

The use of captive-carry flights for air-launched research aircraft dated back to 1946 and the original X-1 program. The practice continued through programs with the D-558-II, the second-generation X-1 aircraft, the X-2, the X-15, the various lifting-body aircraft, and the various unpiloted research vehicles such as HiMAT, as well as through the space shuttle approach and landing tests. Fullerton noted the advantages of a captive flight in preparation for the first free flight:

> The general idea is, again, to get in the air and find out under flight conditions that the instrumentation works right, the people are reading the data correctly we actually pulsed the controls to input some dynamics to the stack out there and again they could watch the loads so they knew what nominal loads were in case we had turbulence. They would know what was normal and have an idea where to draw the red lines. Everybody involved learned from it. Certainly a good test.

One important test done on the captive carry was to determine how the vehicle responded to the low temperatures at the launch altitude. Fullerton noted that, "Pilots are often surprised when you get really cold temperatures. Certain electronics and hydraulic systems tend to lock up or fail and we even had some of that."[27]

The April 28 captive-carry flight proved very successful, with few if any problems. Orbital Sciences personnel did a quick look at the Hyper-X launch-vehicle data from the captive carry, and all of the booster systems seemed to have worked correctly. The review of the X-43A and adapter data was to be made the following week.[28] By mid-May, the captive-carry data-review analysis was under way with the formal data review scheduled for May 11.

Final preparations for the launch were nearing conclusion. The final clean-up work on the X-43A's thermal protection system material was being completed. The X-43A and the adapter were prepared for flight, with a successful leak and functional check. The installation of the pyrotechnic charges in the X-43A/adapter coolant system also was finished. The DIR team had completed its actions and issued a memo confirming that to the Dryden Airworthiness Board.[29]

As May drew to a close, the carbon–carbon nose and wing leading edges were installed on the X-43A, and a battery current sensor that had failed during the captive-carry flight was replaced and successfully checked out. Regarding management issues, the X-43A tech brief was held on May 24, 2001, and all of the DIR requests for information were closed. The final steps were a DIR briefing and a "mini-tech" to discuss the last issues before the flight.[30]

Griff Corpening later described the mood in the final days before the first X-43A launch:

> We also knew that there were probably "unknown unknowns" out there. But we could not think of anything left to better investigate or uncover those unknown unknowns. And we were ready. We were going into the control room. We were confident that we had done due diligence. And in an emotional sense or a human sense, at least I did not have any doubt in my mind that we shouldn't launch and find out what we didn't know.
>
> It was briefed up to the NASA Administrator level that this is a high-risk endeavor. But I felt strongly—and I still do, even in hindsight—that we had done everything that we could think of on the ground, and it was time to go fly and find out what we knew and what we didn't know.
>
> Every person from Vince Rausch on down through Joel [Sitz], myself, Brad Neal and the entire team was go for flight. I can say with all honesty that there was nobody out there that was saying, "No, we shouldn't fly," that we ignored. Everybody felt we had done everything we could within the scope and direction we were given, and it was simply time to go out there and put the rubber to the road.

Asked if there were any second thoughts or unease about a potential problem with a particular system, he replied:

> No, no. We knew there were risks, certainly separation was a risk. We knew that actually flying a Pegasus booster on a trajectory that had never flown before was a risk. We knew that we had single-string systems all over the place, that if a component broke at the wrong time or a wire came loose, we would lose the mission. We knew those things. But we also knew that we had done all that we could do to mitigate those risks, and it was time.[31]

The flight was scheduled for Saturday, June 2, 2001.

NOTES

[1] Lin, Yohan, history interview, Aug. 12, 2005, NASA Dryden Flight Research Center History Office, pp. 2–4, 35.

[2] Ibid, pp. 4–10.

[3] Ibid, pp. 10–17.

[4] Ibid, pp. 17–24.

[5] Ibid, pp. 24–27.

[6] Ibid, pp. 27–29.

[7] Ibid, pp. 32–34.

[8] Ibid, pp. 32–34.

[9] Gorn, Michael H., *Expanding The Envelope: Flight Research at NACA and NASA*, Univ. of Kentucky Press, Lexington, KY, 2001, pp. 35–39. The differences between the

plans of the Jennies' wings and their wings as actually built were as much as three-quarters of an inch.

[10]Lin history interview, pp. 30, 31, and Linda Soden history interview, Aug. 25, 2005, NASA Dryden Flight Research Center History Office, pp. 1, 4, 5, 8, 9.

[11]Lin history interview, pp. 44, 46, 56, 58.

[12]Voland, R. T., K. E. Rock, L. D. Huebner, D. W. White, K. E. Fischer, and C. R. McClinton, "Hyper-X Engine Design and Ground Test Program," AIAA Paper 98-1532, p. 7.

[13]Reukauf, Paul, history interview Feb. 27, 2005, NASA Dryden Flight Research Center History Office, pp. 40, 41.

[14]Love, Betty (former NACA computer), and James Young (Air Force Flight Test Center Historian), telephone interviews, Oct. 24, 2006.

[15]Peebles, Curtis, X-43A notes, pp. 12–14. The simulations described were for the X-43A #3 flight, but were representative of the earlier training.

[16]Fullerton, Gordon C., history interview, Aug. 3, 2005, NASA Dryden Flight Research Center History Office, pp. 8–10.

[17]Peebles X-43A notes, pp. 14, 15, 19–22.

[18]Lin history interview, pp. 47–54.

[19]Aerospace Projects, Jan. 22, 2001, NASA Dryden Flight Research Center History Office, p. 1.

[20]Corpening, Griff, interview, Dec. 20, 2004, NASA Dryden Flight Research Center History Office, p. 28.

[21]Fullerton history interview, pp. 10, 11.

[22]Aerospace Projects, April 2, 2001, p. 1, and interview with Paul Reukauf, Nov. 3, 2006. The individuals who were on the DIR were referred to as the Dryden Independent Review Team (DIRT). The lesson learned from this is that care should be taken in the creation of acronyms.

[23]Aerospace Projects, April 9, 2001, pp. 1, 2.

[24]Puffer, Ray, interview, AFFTC History Office, Nov. 3, 2006.

[25]Aerospace Projects, April 23, 2001, pp. 2.

[26]Aerospace Projects, April 30, 2001, pp. 1, 2.

[27]Fullerton history interview, pp. 11, 12.

[28]Aerospace Projects, May 7, 2001, pp. 1.

[29]Aerospace Projects, May 14, 2001, pp. 1, 2.

[30]Aerospace Projects, May 29, 2001, p. 1, and June 4, 2001, pp.1, 2.

[31]Corpening history interview, pp. 29, 30.

Chapter 5

13.5 Seconds

Fate has ordained that the men who went to the Moon to explore in peace will
stay on the Moon to rest in peace. These brave men, Neil Armstrong and
Edwin Aldrin, know that there is no hope for their recovery. But they
also know that there is hope for mankind in their sacrifice.

"In the event of Moon disaster" contingency speech written by William Safire for President
Richard M. Nixon
July 18, 1969

You will fail. It is important to understand this certainty. As an aerospace
engineer, you will be building vehicles that fly under conditions never before
encountered. You will, despite all of the analysis and efforts put into the projects, still be voyaging into the unknown. You do not know what you will find.
In ancient times, much of the world was a blank. Mapmakers would mark
these unknown places with the words "Here There Be Dragons." Despite all
of the advances in the first century of heavier-than-air flight, you need to
understand that the dragons are still out there. You *will* fail.

That you will fail is certain. The causes of the failure you will experience,
however, will range from the overarching to the mundane. A failure might
come because, with existing knowledge and technology, the goal was
unattainable. It might occur because of changing social factors, national
needs, and aerospace policies. The failure might come as a result of a grave
mismatch between budget and tasks at hand, or a lack of necessary political
commitment. The failure might occur because an assumption was made that
should have been challenged, because a modification was made that was
better left undone, or a question went unasked, or some flaw went undetected.
And, perhaps worst of all, the failure might occur for reasons you will never
truly understand.

While you are being trained in the skills needed to successfully build an
aerospace vehicle, you might be less well prepared for events that can occur
in the wake of a failure. On the personal level, you will have to deal with
the emotional impact of having spent years working on a project, having
missed evenings, weekends, and holidays with family and friends, of having

overcome an endless series of problems and setbacks, only to see it all fail
within a matter of seemingly random and dispassionate seconds.

This wrenching but instructive experience will then be followed by a mishap
investigation, which can continue for months. During this time, the project is
no longer under the control of project personnel. The investigators are the ones
running things. You and the other project personnel have little input into what
is done in the course of the effort. You might also face uncertainty over the
project's future in the wake of the failure. As with the immediate aftermath,
this will take a toll on you and other project personnel.

The question is not if you will fail. Instead, the question is how you will
deal with that failure, and how you will overcome it.

JUNE 2, 2001

Launch day for the first X-43A had finally arrived, after some four years of
effort. The ground crew had been conducting final checks and preparations of
the stack throughout the night, making sure that the X-43A, the B-52B, the
Hyper-X launch vehicle, and everything else was ready. As dawn neared
on Saturday, June 2, 2001, a steady stream of cars began entering Edwards
Air Force Base as the engineers, pilots, ground personnel, controllers, and
various support personnel made their long drives from Lancaster, Palmdale,
Boron, North Edwards, Rosamond, California City, and the other communi-
ties scattered across the desert. For over 50 years, the personnel involved with
the X-1, D-558-II, X-2, X-15, the lifting-body programs, and other research
aircraft have made this trek under other star-filled night skies. And as on
those other nights, the arriving Hyper-X project staff did not know what
events the sunrise would bring.

The weekend launch date was unusual, but had been scheduled because of
the complexity of the test, the Mach 7 speed, and the long distance the flight
would cover. Even though flying at nearly 100,000 feet, the X-43A would
soon pass beyond the horizon of the ground tracking stations. As a result, the
X-43A flight required use of not only Dryden's tracking and control facilities,
but also the Naval Air Warfare Weapons Sea Range located off Point Mugu
and a pair of modified P-3 Orion patrol aircraft positioned further down range.
With both the ground stations and the airborne receivers, the
X-43A could be tracked from launch to splashdown. Further complicating
matters was that the launch also had to be coordinated with the Federal
Aviation Administration (FAA) to avoid conflicts with the stream of airliners
on transpacific flights arriving hourly in the Los Angeles area. The FAA designated a launch window; if the launch were delayed and could not be made
within the allotted time, it would be cancelled.[1]

A large press contingent also came out to Dryden Flight Research Center
for the event. A film crew from a German television channel had been on

The complete stack for the first flight on its trailer in the Hyper-X hangar. This building was specially modified to support the project. (NASA photo EC01-0019-18.)

hand for several days. They had been shooting film of the base and of the second X-43A undergoing checkout in its enclosure. As foreign nationals, they were escorted by Dryden personnel. With the takeoff time at hand, a group of reporters was taken to the runway to watch.

The B-52B crew consisted of Dana Purifoy (pilot), Frank Batteas (copilot), Matt Redifer (X-43A panel operator), and Brian Minnick of Orbital Sciences (HXLV panel operator). Accompanying the B-52B were two Dryden F-18 chase planes. Gordon Fullerton (pilot) and Lori Losey (videographer) were in F-18 NASA 846 and would fly off the B-52B's right wing, with James Smolka

The B-52B taking off on the first X-43A launch. On the Hyper-X project, the captive-carry and launch flights were escorted by two F-18 chase planes, which provided video and still photo support. (NASA photo EC01-0182-01.)

(pilot) and Jim Ross (still photographer) in F-18 NASA 852 to the left of the bomber. Each F-18 was to fly about 1000 to 1500 feet on both side of and 1000 feet below the B-52B, positioned to allow the drop, ignition, and initial flight of the HXLV to be photographed.

The B-52B taxied to the end of the runway, and final checks began. When clearance was given, Purifoy ran up the throttles, released the brakes, and the B-52B began its roll down the runway. The large converted bomber accelerated slowly at first, trailed by its usual large plume of black smoke. As it drew closer, the reporters and media escorts could hear a sound like that of an onrushing train. As the B-52B reached the press group, the roar of its eight 1950's vintage J57 jet engines drowned out the sound of the two F-18 chase planes flying overhead. The B-52B lifted off runway 22 at 12:28 p.m. and headed west toward the Pacific Ocean.

The reporters climbed back into the vans and headed back to the Dryden cafeteria. When they arrived, several large-screen television sets were showing the onboard camera shots from the B-52B, as well as chase-plane video from F-18 NASA 846. Occasionally, the video chase would move closer to provide visual checks on the stack. Now flying at the 20,000-foot drop altitude, the crew continued their preparations. The control-room crew monitored the telemetry data. As the launch approached, the fins on both the X-43A and the Hyper-X launch vehicle were cycled back and forth. With everything now in readiness, the final countdown began.

Linda Soden, who oversaw configuration control, was watching the launch from the visitors' gallery between Dryden's Blue and Gold control rooms. She recalled the mood as, "It was chaos ... anxieties, frustrations ... we're doing it. I don't believe there was anybody that did not have some sort of goose bumps from one cause or another."[2]

At the call of "launch, launch, launch," the hooks released, and the stack fell away. The delay between the release and the Hyper-X launch-vehicle ignition seemed endless. Finally, the booster lit, and a brilliant yellow-white flame erupted from the nozzle.

The booster accelerated and began to pull away from the chase planes. The booster then went out of control, and, instead of climbing upward, began a descending spiral toward the cloud deck below. In the cafeteria, the assembled spectators let out a low groan at the sight. The rocket continued to burn, leaving a corkscrew smoke trail behind it. Finally, the destruct signal was transmitted, and a bright orange flash enveloped the Hyper-X launch vehicle.[3]

Fullerton, who was flying F-18 NASA 846 recalled later:

> I did see kind of a pulse out of the exhaust, like a flash of something going back in the exhaust stream. And I was thinking that must just be kind of a discontinuity in the grain. It really was one of the fins breaking off the

The first HXLV accelerating away from the B-52B. Although everything appeared to be going well at this point, failure was only seconds away. (NASA photo EC01-0182-35.)

rocket, followed by the other fins, and then it very quickly became apparent it was all over. The rocket just started to go in all directions dynamically. And it was following an average ballistic path down toward the water. Lori Losey was with me with a video camera. Of course the rocket accelerated away from us but then as soon as it started to tumble we caught up to it and I made a left-hand, steep, hard turn, all the way around it, just flying a circle around it as it made its way down. And Lori did a great job of shooting, really, out of the top of canopy as we were making this high-G turn to keep the picture on. So we got great video all the way down.[4]

Lori Losey recalled that the video F-18 was positioned so that when the rocket ignited, it would be about even with the canopy rail. As the Hyper-X launch vehicle accelerated, the F-18 turned 20 degrees away from the stack.

The smoke trail from the HXLV as it falls toward the Pacific Ocean. (NASA photo EC01-0182-11.)

This was to prevent the canopy frame between the front and back seat from getting into the picture. She then had to follow the stack as it accelerated away, while looking through the camera viewfinder.

Losey recalled hearing Fullerton saying everything looked good, and then the Hyper-X launch vehicle went out of control. She was not aware of the F-18's maneuvers as it followed the tumbling booster down, as she had to keep the rocket centered in the viewfinder. Several times Fullerton asked if she still had the HXLV centered. Losey was able to keep the HXLV in the field of view, because of Fullerton's skilled piloting and her own skill with the video camera. When the destruct signal was transmitted, Losey recalled seeing several pieces come off the booster. The F-18 was able to follow the HXLV until it entered the low-lying cloud deck. The chase plane then descended

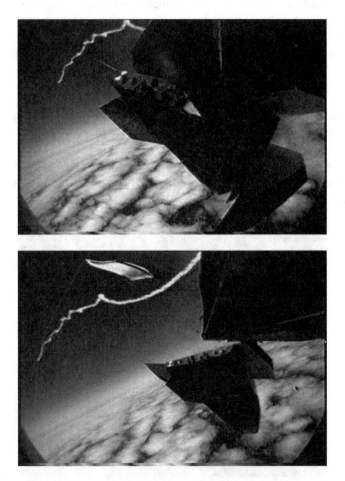

Two images from the adapter camera as X-43A #1 is torn off. Visible are the skin panel separation from the adapter and the spinning right horizontal tail. In the background are the HXLV's smoke trail and the smaller contrail from the B-52B. (NASA photos.)

through the clouds, in an attempt to get a global-positioning-system position on the impact point and to spot any floating debris. When they cleared the clouds, however, all that could be seen were ocean white caps.[5]

Jim Ross, who was the still photographer in F-18 NASA 852 flying to the left of B-52B, had a more worrisome view as the Hyper-X launch vehicle failed. He said later:

> We saw it drop and accelerate and I shot up most of the film that I had from that. And then what we saw was it kind of pitched to the left and kind of started to head towards our direction but it was just a momentary situation, and then we saw [it] start to pitch in kind of a spiral downward. And we just kind of maintained our position. I had the other camera that I'd been just shooting general shots of the bomber flying out with so I grabbed that camera and started to take shots of it. You could see the smoke trail on it as it headed toward the ocean.

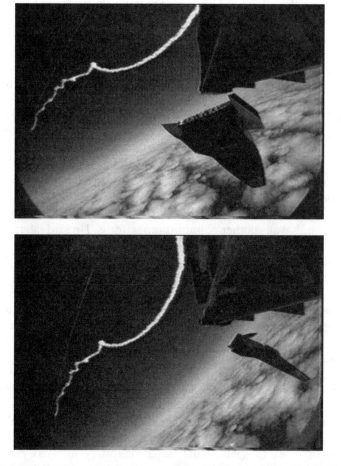

Two additional images from the adapter camera as X-43A #1 is torn off. (NASA photos.)

When Ross was asked about his reaction to seeing the Hyper-X launch vehicle coming toward his aircraft, he replied:

> I think mine was I wasn't sure where it was going. I think both Jim [Smolka] and I kind of had a slight hesitation as to what the thing was doing. But it was just a momentary thing because then it—we saw it start to do a downward process. And at the time it was still below us. So our thought process was that it probably was not going to pitch upward. It was going to go downward, which is what it ended up doing. I think we were both there for just a split second kind of wondering where we were going to need to go on this if this thing started to go crazy on us.[6]

The control-room personnel also witnessed the failure, on both the television screens and their computer monitors. Laurie Grindle, lead aerodynamics researcher at Dryden, recalled:

> So I basically had decided I am going to watch the drop, and I am going to watch some of the boost, and then when I can't see it anymore, I'll go back to looking at our actual data, and I knew that the other people I was working with were going to be watching it. I knew that the stuff that we really needed to watch wasn't going to happen until long after I couldn't see it anymore, physically, on the camera. So I chose to actually watch the video. Mark Davis, who is sitting next to me, was saying things like, "Oh! That doesn't look right, that doesn't look right." I am looking at the video, going, "No! It definitely doesn't look right." But he was making that evaluation from actually looking at the data, and I was actually looking at the video. And so, yeah, I didn't even know what to think. It's one of those things where I had never seen a launch, so I didn't know what to expect, but I knew that was not it. [7]

Griff Corpening was another control room witness. He said later:

> I remember the drop. As soon as the motor ignited, I think everybody was very excited, and we thought, "Okay, you know, we're on our way." And ... it was within seconds. I mean, it turned out to be about 13 seconds after drop; clearly the vehicle wasn't doing what we had thought it was going to do. And we continued to watch this thing spiral around. And obviously part of your brain is thinking, okay, it can recover—the illogical part. And the other part is going, we've just lost the mission.
>
> A couple of spots down was the Orbital chief engineer, Mike Pudoka. I remember just seeing out of my peripheral vision Mike's head slowly sinking down. And we knew it was over.
>
> You're certainly in a bit of a state of disbelief, having spent all this time and energy. We were all assuming maybe the pushover would be a problem, or we thought certainly separation was a high-risk problem. But this happened very early on. It turned out it was right before it flew

the transonic Mach 1 flight. And we were all a little stunned that it happened so quickly.[8]

Mishap Investigation Board

When any failure occurs involving a NASA vehicle, a rigorous investigation procedure is to be followed. This goes into effect immediately, even before a mishap investigation board (MIB) is established. The very first step in the investigation of the loss of the X-43A, as with any other accident, was that of securing the premises and data, as well as obtaining witness statements. This process was announced by the order to "lock the doors."

Corpening recalled: "we went immediately into an investigation mode. The control room was locked down. Nobody was allowed to take anything out of the control room, mainly because you don't want to lose any critical information that might help you understand what happened."[8] The different control rooms—not just the primary Blue Room and the Gold Room, but also the Telemetry and Radar Acquisition Processing System (TRAPS) Control Room and the structural analysis facility (SAF)—were considered accident sites. Notes, flight cards, computers, laptops, PDAs, and anything else were to be left exactly where they were.

Soden noted:

> We were told in advance, "Don't take personal effects in there if you can help it. Don't take your purse, don't take your keys, don't take anything that you want to have to leave behind in case of an emergency." So there wasn't any of that. But it was their notebooks, their flight cards, their flight plans, and their data that they were capturing, the strip charts, everything. You were told to get up, leave.
>
> And then, we were all herded downstairs and we kind of milled around a little bit. And everybody is in this state of confusion. We're all very disappointed. There were tears but, that's just part of it.
>
> We were all told to stay on-site and go collect our thoughts, go do this, go do that. And we were waiting for the B-52 to come back so that we could have a debrief. And that was held up in [Building] 4800 and, I believe, the large conference room. We had been told that the MIB, the Mishap Investigation Board—or men in black as we call them fondly—had already been selected. They were going to be out if they weren't already on their way and we would be debriefing with them on the following Monday. Now, this flight took place on a Saturday. So we had one day to get ready for our initial interviews with the MIB.[9]

There was a mass of materials from the accident. These included the data from onboard the B-52B launch aircraft, the video and still photos from the two chase F-18s, telemetry data from the stack, and the notes and written statements by the controllers, engineers, and technicians. There also were the data from the preflight testing and checkout of the Hyper-X launch vehicle, adapter, and X-43A. There was documentation from the modifications and reviews made during the checkout, the reports made, the configuration control records, and the waivers issued. All of these data had to be secured, organized, filed, and prepared for use by the MIB.

Soden again said:

> My involvement with that started on Monday, June 4, 2001, when we all regrouped here at Dryden. Joel [Sitz, X-43A project manager at Dryden] came up to me and said, "You get to build a database and you get to log and track all of the confiscated items." They set me up in [Building] 4840 in the vault and we had to catalog every single item that was confiscated. I am estimating there were 1200 items that had to controlled and maintained and then eventually distributed back to their owners.[10]

These were not the only data required for the investigation. The contractors each had their own documentation that had been generated during the manufacture, testing, and checkout of each component. Additionally, Pegasus accident and anomaly reports from earlier launches also were gathered for the insights these could provide. All of these data now awaited examination by the MIB. Evidence normally associated with an aircraft accident investigation was not available, however. The debris from the stack was under 1200 feet of water. No attempt was made to locate the wreckage and recover the flight hardware for examination.

The mishap investigation board for the X-43A was assigned responsibility for the X-43A investigation on June 5, 2001, based on verbal instruction of the NASA associate administrator for aerospace technology. The board's chairman was Robert W. Hughes, from Marshall Space Flight Center. Joseph J. Lackovick, Jr. (Kennedy Space Center) was executive secretary. Other members were Frank H. Bauer (Goddard Space Flight Center), Michael R. Hannan (Marshall Space Flight Center), Luat T. Nguyen (Langley Research Center), Victoria A. Regenie (Dryden Flight Research Center), Karen L. Spanyer (Marshall Space Flight Center), and Pamela F. Richardson (Aeronautics Mission Assurance). Chauncey Williams (Dryden Office of Chief Counsel) and Fred Johnsen (Dryden Office of Public Affairs) served as advisors.

With the mishap investigation board now established, its members faced a series of interrelated tasks. They had to coordinate the different facilities and support, make a series of X-43A familiarization tours, and undertake general data collection and fact finding.

The initial MIB meetings were held at Dryden from June 5 through June 23. Daily MIB meetings were held to review the flight data as they were being processed and interpreted. With this phase completed, the MIB members then went to the Orbital Sciences Corporation facility at Chandler, Arizona. Here, between June 23 and August 31, they reviewed Hyper-X launch-vehicle failure scenarios. The board then relocated to the Langley Research Center for the longest phase of their travels. They remained at Langley from September 10 through December 7, 2001, to support wind-tunnel testing. The final phase of their investigation was completed using teleconferences and e-mail.

During this phase, members not only collected data from the accident, but also conducted a new postflight analysis of different vehicle components. This included ordered testing of the stack software and hardware, evaluation of the fin actuation system (FAS) that moved the elevons and rudder of the HXLV, wind-tunnel testing of the stack aerodynamics, and a review of the HXLV analytical models, systems, subsystems, and processes.[11]

The investigation process was very demanding for board members. Corpening recalled that Hughes wanted the group to co-locate. As a result, they spent a month at Dryden, then several months at Orbital, followed by several more months at Langley. "They would be on site for several weeks," Corpening said, "then home for a weekend, back on site, through holidays, through birthdays, anniversaries, on and on. My hat is really off to their dedication and sacrifice."[12]

The fault-tree analysis technique was used by the board to determine why the vehicle was lost. This approach was selected for several reasons. The mishap-investigation-board members were familiar with the procedures it involved. The sheer complexity of the Hyper-X systems, the number of organizations involved in the project, and that a fault-tree analysis already had been conducted as part of the design of the Hyper-X systems all aided in this decision. Fault-tree analysis also had been used to perform the risk assessment for the program.[13]

The top level of the fault tree developed for the Hyper-X project had seven elements: loss of the B-52B flight safety (1.0), loss of X-43A stack (2.0), failure to drop/ignite (3.0), fail to reach desired separation point (4.0), unsuccessful separation of the X-43A (5.0), unsuccessful free flight (6.0), and ground operation stack damage (7.0).

Creating this fault tree involved a series of steps, based on the identification of potential faults or causes. The process worked from the top down. The initial fault-tree level was based on assessments of the physical, functional, engineering, and operational characteristics of the Hyper-X project. When the top-level faults were deemed to be credible, the lower-fault levels and subtier faults that might have contributed to the failure were developed, using potential scenarios for each of the specific high-level faults.

Technical evaluation of each lower-level fault served as the building block for the fault tree. The information derived from this analysis was combined with an assessment of the overall system environment of the Hyper-X. The results of each lower-level fault evaluation provided a determination of the potential for each of the individual faults to have contributed to the Hyper-X launch-vehicle failure. In constructing the fault tree, no assumptions were made about the potential cause of the accident. All possible failures were included.

For each fault tree, potential failure scenarios were used to establish a set of subtiers. This was further divided into branches, by specific anomalies that could result in each subtier failure scenario, and then down through one or more steps to the possible component failures or errors that were the root cause of the malfunction. Thus the fault-tree resembles its botanical counterpart— going from an individual leaf attached to a twig that was part of a small branch, which led to several larger branches, which finally merged into the trunk of the tree.

The use of the fault-tree analysis was not limited to identifying faults that directly contributed to the loss of the vehicle. Additionally, any contributing factors that could possibly have been used to prevent the loss would be identified. Finally, any other anomalies would be identified. These had no relationship to the accident, but could indicate design weaknesses in the systems. These might need modifications or redesigns to close off the possibility of another, independent failure. In all, there were a total of 613 elements in the different fault trees, and each of these elements had to be investigated, even if it was clear that they had no actual bearing on the failure.[14]

With the mishap investigation board's initial orientation and fact-finding now completed, the board moved to the analysis phase of their efforts. Of the seven elements in the top level of the Hyper-X fault tree, six of the seven branches were immediately eliminated as causes of the Hyper-X launch-vehicle failure. The B-52B had not been lost (level 1.0), the X-43A stack had not been lost (level 2.0), the stack had been successfully dropped, and the rocket ignited (level 3.0). The failure occurred after this point, but before the separation sequence and the X-43A free flight were attempted, which eliminated the levels 5.0 and 6.0. Finally, there was no evidence that damage from ground handling had caused the loss of the stack, which eliminated level 7.0. This left only failure to reach desired separation point (level 4.0).

The board members had to understand the data, the timeline of events, and the conditions. Fortunately, telemetry data allowed the precise sequence of events to be determined.

The Hyper-X launch-vehicle flight management system sensed the release from the B-52B at launch +0.03 (L +0.03) seconds. The sequencer then reset at L +0.18 seconds, and the autopilot was enabled L +0.38 seconds after the drop. Rocket ignition occurred at L +5.19 seconds. All of these events occurred as planned and at the proper times. The first anomaly appeared between L +6.23 and L +7.1 seconds, when a pyrotechnic gaseous nitrogen valve in the adapter opened. The regulator then malfunctioned and began an uncontrolled venting of the gas. This nitrogen was used to spray a mixture of water and glycol on the X-43A scramjet's leading edge to cool it during the boost.

At L +10.18 seconds, the Pegasus path-steering guidance was engaged as planned. Just over one-and-one-half seconds later, at about L +11.5 seconds, the vehicle began its pitch-up maneuver. At this point, the vehicle began experiencing a divergent oscillation in the roll axes at a 2.5-Hz frequency. The rudder and elevon deflections also began to increase at this time, although the Mach number, angle of attack, and dynamic pressure of the stack were still within the predicted range. At L +13.02 seconds, the rudder's electrome-chanical actuator (EMA) stopped responding to guidance system commands. The differential elevon and roll rates increased dramatically. The sideslip of the stack had remained within the expected range until L +12.5 seconds, after which the loss of yaw control provided by the rudder caused the sideslip angle to diverge rapidly, to more than eight degrees. At L +13.5 seconds, the right elevon was overstressed and suffered structural failure. This was followed by the loss of the left elevon, the rudder, and finally the wing. Telemetry from the Hyper-X launch vehicle was lost at L +20.78 seconds. With the vehicle breaking up and tumbling out of control toward the Pacific, the Navy range control transmitted a destruct command at 48.57 seconds.

After the destruct command was sent, the X-43A detached from the rest of the stack at L +49.31 seconds. No separation command was sent, and the loss of the X-43A was caused by the gyrations of the stack during the descent. The aft S-band antenna began to transmit data at L +49.63 seconds. Two cameras had been added to the adapter to provide high-speed video of the separation. One of the cameras successfully transmitted images.

Remarkably, given the gyrations of both vehicles, clear images of both the X-43 and the adapter were transmitted to the ground stations. The X-43A was nose down, with the vehicle's top surface and tail to the camera. The left wing had rotated backwards, as the control horn had broken. A section of sheet metal on the drop jaw was also seen to have been lost. The X-43A continued sending data to receiving stations until L +77.51 seconds, when the transmit-ter fell silent, and the mission was over.[15]

With the fault-tree and failure scenarios established, the understanding of the data, conditions, and the timeline of events complete, the mishap investi-gation board had several more steps to take. Investigators now had to refine and analyze the data. From this, the board would add new fault trees, close the inapplicable fault trees, and establish any anomalies that had occurred.

The failure-to-reach-desired-separation-point fault tree had six subtiers—loss of control (4.1), structural (4.2), flight termination system initiation (4.3), fire/explosion (4.4), collision with air vehicle (4.5), and loss of X-43 data (4.6). The data pinpointed the critical subtier as loss of control (4.1). The other subtiers all were closed out as not having contributed to the loss. There had not been a structural problem until after the loss of control; the flight-termination-system (FTS) command was sent after the failure occurred, not before; no fire or explosion was detected; the stack had not collided with another vehicle, and the X-43A's telemetry system had continued to transmit data during the long fall.

The loss-of-control subtier had five branches: external disturbance (4.1.1), structures (4.1.2), aerodynamic/control (4.1.3), motor (4.1.4), and avionics (4.1.5). Of these, the flight data and postflight analysis eliminated all of the branches except aerodynamics/control (4.1.3) as having contributed to the accident. The mishap investigation board was now at the last level of the fault tree.

Aerodynamic/control (4.1.3) had no less than eight fault boxes. Of these, autopilot design (4.1.3.1), autopilot implementation (4.1.3.2), and structural dynamics modeling (4.1.3.3) were found not to have been involved in the accident. Of the remaining four, mass properties modeling (4.1.3.4), aerodynamic modeling (4.1.3.5), vehicle configuration (4.1.3.6), and fin actuation system (4.1.3.7) all directly contributed to the loss of the vehicle. Finally, the aeroelastic effects (4.1.3.8) fault box was judged by the MIB to have been a potential factor in the loss, but this could not be confirmed.[16]

The mishap investigation board submitted their report on March 8, 2002. It concluded:

> Root Cause: The X-43A HXLV failed because the vehicle control system design was deficient for the trajectory flown due to inaccurate analytical models (Pegasus heritage and HXLV specific), which over estimated the system margins.
>
> • The key phenomenon which triggered the mishap was the divergent roll oscillation motion at a 2.5 Hz frequency.
> – The divergence was primary caused by excessive control system gain.
> • A second phenomenon was that a consequence of the divergent roll oscillation was a stall of the rudder actuator that accelerated the loss of control.
> • Neither phenomenon was predicted by preflight analyses.
> • The analytical modeling deficiencies resulted from a combination of factors.
>
> The mishap occurred because the control system could not maintain the vehicle stability during transonic flight. The vehicle instability was observed as a divergent roll oscillation. An effect of the divergent roll oscillation was the stalling of the rudder actuator. The stall accelerated the loss of control. The loss of control resulted in the loss of the X-43A stack. The rudder actuator stalled due to the increased deflections that caused higher aerodynamic loading than preflight predictions. The deficient control system and under prediction of rudder actuator loads occurred due to modeling inaccuracies.

Determining the cause of the X-43A mishap was a complex effort requiring a significant commitment of time and resources. This effort consisted of in-depth evaluations of the Pegasus and HXLV system and subsystem models and tools as well as extensive system level and subsystem level analyses. To support the analysis, extensive mechanical testing (fin actuation system) and wind tunnel testing (6 percent model) were required.

The major contributions to the mishap were modeling inaccuracies in the fin actuation system, modeling inaccuracies in the aerodynamics, and insufficient variations of modeling parameters (parametric uncertainty analysis, Pegasus heritage and HXLV specific models were found to be inaccurate.

1) Fin actuation system inaccuracies resulted from:

- Discrepancies in modeling the electronic and mechanical fin actuator system components
- Under prediction of the fin actuation system compliance used in the models.

2) Aerodynamic modeling inaccuracies resulted from:

- Errors in incorporation of wind tunnel data into the math model
- Misinterpretation of wind tunnel results due to insufficient data
- Unmodeled outer mold line changes associated with the thermal protection system (TPS).

3) Insufficient variations of modeling parameters (parametric uncertainty analysis) were found in:

- Aerodynamics
- Fin Actuation System
- Control System

Less significant contributors were errors detected in modeling mass properties. Potential contributing factors were found in the areas of dynamic aerodynamics and aeroservelasticity.

Linear stability predictions were recalculated using corrected nominal models. Stability gain margins were computed for all axes. Aileron gain margin (roll axis) was examined in particular and showed a sizeable reduction from the 8 dB preflight prediction. Model corrections led to a revised prediction of less than 2 dB at nominal conditions. This was well below the requirement of a 6 dB gain margin. Although this prediction was very significant and close to instability boundaries, the revised prediction was still stable. This meant that the nominal model corrections alone were insufficient to predict the vehicle loss of control and that parameter uncertainty had to be included. Accounting for parameter uncertainties in the analyses replicated the mishap. This was confirmed by nonlinear time history projections using 6-degree of freedom (6-DOF) flight dynamics simulation of the X-43A stack.

No single contributing factor or potential contributing factor caused this mishap. The flight mishap could only be reproduced when all of the modeling inaccuracies with uncertainty variations were incorporated in the system level linear analysis model and nonlinear simulation model.[17]

The events that led to the failure began long before June 2, 2001 and had their origins with the selection of the lower-altitude launch profile. There were significant differences between the Hyper-X launch-vehicle launch of the X-43A and the launch of a standard Pegasus. This was because of the requirement of a Mach 7 separation speed. Had the X-43A been launched at the standard Pegasus launch altitude of about 40,000 feet, the separation speed would have been Mach 10. To reduce burnout speed, the lower drop altitude was used. The excess energy would be used climbing to the higher altitude. However, this had major effects on the conditions the stack would experience. On a standard Pegasus launch, the dynamic pressure on the vehicle at nearly Mach 1 would have be around 300 pounds per square foot (psf). The dynamic pressure being experienced at 13.5 seconds after launch by the Hyper-X launch vehicle was 650 psf, more than double that normally experienced on a Pegasus launch.

Although the goal was to use the Pegasus "as is" to the extent possible, the Mach 7 requirement meant a major departure from the booster's proven and well-tested launch profile. The higher dynamic pressure on the HXLV at transonic speed was a factor in the mishap.[18]

Within seconds of ignition, the Pegasus began its pitch-up maneuver and experienced a 2.5-Hz roll oscillation. Paul Reukauf noted, "We had seen in the past the booster started into an oscillation like the oscillation we had [on the X-43A launch], but it only got one or two cycles before it [the Pegasus] went supersonic, the center of pressure moved to aft on the fins and consequently the loads go way down on the fins and it stabilizes immediately."

With the X-43A booster, launched at 20,000 feet, the oscillation did not damp out, and in fact became divergent. This, in turn, led to the rudder actuator stall, which led to the loss of control. Neither of these events had been predicted by the preflight wind-tunnel testing and simulations. The question became why this had not been detected in the tests before the flight.[19]

The WIRE Pegasus launch on March 4, 1999, which carried a satellite payload, was of particular significance to the mishap investigation board. At between approximately 6 and 12 seconds after that launch, while the Pegasus was flying at transonic speed, the booster experienced a roll excursion, which quickly became coupled in yaw and then in pitch. The booster experienced large sideslip and bank excursions, but recovered as it reached supersonic speeds. Despite the control problems, the booster was able to place the WIRE satellite into the correct orbit. Following the anomaly, autopilot changes as well as improvements to the aerodynamic and fin actuation system modeling were made. The WIRE launch had been made at 40,000 feet; with the lower dynamic pressure and higher launch speed, the booster had been able to pass through the transonic speed regime before control was lost.[20]

X-43A project engineers knew beforehand that stability of the stack at transonic speeds was, as Corpening later observed, "going to be dicey." The Hyper-X launch vehicle was flying at transonic speeds and an angle of attack of about 10 degrees. There was the contributing factor of the X-43A's oddly shaped body, which had never before been flown on the nose of the booster. The sharp edges of the chines and wings also could generate vortices, which might interact with HXLV control surfaces in unpredictable ways. The thermal protection material, added to protect against the higher heat loading during ascent also had the potential to alter the HXLV aerodynamics. Accordingly, a number of wind-tunnel tests had been run to determine the aerodynamic forces and moments on the stack under these conditions. Corpening also noted:

> Now we also had a certain amount of direction at the beginning of the project that we would treat the launch vehicle as a quasi-off-the-shelf system. It was proven hardware. It was a proven launch system. We were just modifying it slightly—or not so slightly. And what we wanted to do was focus on those changes in the launch vehicle, not the things that were similar between [the HXLV] and Pegasus. We inherited a number of things. One of them was the launch vehicle wind-tunnel model. And we'd modified now, of course, the research vehicle on the front end. Now this model was set up where the control surfaces that rolled the vehicle– the two downward dihedral fins would go in opposite directions to roll the vehicle—the increment that it was set up to roll was in five-degree increments.
>
> So we went into the wind tunnels, and we didn't want to design a new wind-tunnel model; we didn't see a reason to. So we went in there, and we would test at 8 degrees angle of attack with the fins neutral, [then] with the fins at plus or minus 5 degrees, plus or minus 10 degrees. And we would do that at various angles of attack and sideslip angles to develop the database. And what you do is take the 0-to-5-degree deflec-tions, and connect those directly in a linear fashion. So if you were at 2-1/2 degrees, you'd simply take the force that you get at 0 degrees and at 5 degrees, and divide it by 2. So it's a linear average. What we were looking at was our roll authority. In other words, how quickly and with what authority the launch vehicle would roll the stack. We had that data at 0, 5, and 10 degrees. Then we just extrapolated linearly in between those conditions.
>
> Within hours, if not a day or two, of the mishap, the Orbital engineers knew that this vehicle rolled a lot faster than we had predicated, and had gone unstable because of that. So we knew right away that something was up—why this thing was rolling and not recovering quickly. We

focused on that, but it took us about six months to really dig down. And we finally ended up going in for a new wind-tunnel test, and this time we put in a new wind-tunnel model where we could move the fins in two-and-one-half-degree increments. So now instead of 0, 5, 10, we're 0, 2-1/2, 5, 7-1/2, [and] 10 [degrees].

And lo and behold, right at the fin positions that we were flying at the time the vehicle departed, there was a nonlinearity [in the amount of rolling moment]. The 2½ [degree position] actually shows more rolling moment than we had predicted. I think part of it might have been this vortex interaction. So we were in a nonlinear area. So we were getting more roll authority out of the fins than we had predicted.[21]

Corpening also noted that there were problems with the fin actuation system and the control system.

The other thing that we had inherited from the Pegasus program was a couple of the models: how the systems worked together and how the structure of the vehicle worked. The first one was called a compliance model. ... [the] fin actuation system measures the position of the fin at a certain point in the shaft or the gear of the actuator. It's not all the way out into the control surface. Now it's recognized ... that because the aerodynamic force on the fin is forward of the hinge position, it actually flexes the fin back more than you would expect. Just like your fingers bend up when you stick them out the window. It's called compliance. So you take into account where you think your fin position is, based on your measurement point, and then you add a little bit extra because of all the linkages and the structure flexing outboard of that position.

Well, it turned out that the fin was more flexible, that whole system was more flexible, than we had predicted. So we were in greater compliance. So now, for [a hypothetical] example, we would think we were at 1 degree; we would put in a compliance number. For the control law design we would assume we were at 1.1-degree angle of attack, when in actuality we were at 1.2. And as you go up in angle of attack, you get more force and more rolling moment. So not only had we under predicted the rolling moment itself, but we were also grabbing more angle of attack.

Then the last one was the onboard computer that runs all of the systems and has the inertial navigation system and everything, that's up forward in the forward part of the rocket—it has to talk the computer in the aft end of the vehicle that's controlling the fins, and then that fin computer talks, has a talk-back thing, as we saw. So in other words, the forward computer sends a command to the actuator and says, "[move] your fins to this position, based on what I'm seeing going on up here on my inertial navigation system." And then the onboard computer goes, "Okay, I've done that." Sends a command back, "I'm reading for the next command." So you have this move back and forth as these two computers talk to each other. And there's a certain delay in all these electronics commands going back and forth. And we had predicted that delay based on what Pegasus used. It turned out that delay was longer in reality than what we had predicted.

Okay, so now you have higher aerodynamic forces because of the nonlinearity of wind tunnels [testing], and the compliance, and the communication between the computers is slower than you had predicted. Not only is the vehicle rolling with more authority, but it's rolling further than you would like because the computers can't talk to each other quick enough. And this just set up a very nasty situation where the vehicle's rolling, rolling, rolling, rolling. The computer onboard is saying, "Turn back! Turn back!" The actuator's saying, "Not yet. I'm not done yet." And then finally it gets the command, and now the flight computer's says, "Turn back a lot." And it goes back the other way even more, and back and forth, and back and forth until the computer was telling the actuators to go to full throttle, and [the higher-than-expected dynamic pressure] exceeded the structural limits of the fins, and they ripped off, one, two, and three. And it was over.[22]

The final steps in the mishap investigation were to develop the fault-and-anomaly-closure action plan; perform analyses, testing, and evaluations; refine failure scenarios; and determine technical causes. Based on this, the project engineers then developed corrective actions. The final steps were to develop the lessons learned from the mishap and to publish the final report.

For those connected with the X-43 project, this period had been emotionally trying. Reukauf recalled later,

I would say that psychologically, it's a very difficult time because number one, you're in a situation where you no longer get to direct what's happening. And, number two, you're doing lots of work going down avenues which you know are not direct contributors to the accident. But you have to do it. So it seems like you're doing a lot of extra work.[23]

DECISION AS AN ART, NOT A SCIENCE

The loss of the first X-43A points out the often difficult and subtle nature of decision making for aerospace projects. Early in the Hyper-X project, managers faced two options for the Mach 7 launches—off load fuel or use a lower-altitude launch. Both involved changes to the Pegasus, but off-loading was seen as too risky. In contrast, the lower-altitude launch profile seemed attainable. To make sure, the engineers used Pegasus wind-tunnel data and the design models to determine whether the HXLV would be stable under the different launch conditions. When the analysis was completed, the data showed a lower-altitude HXLV launch would be successful. The models were accurate for a standard Pegasus; they had been proven in a decade of launches, and so their results were considered to be valid. The matter seemed settled.

What the engineers did not realize prior to the first X-43A launch was that the conditions being tested were outside the design test case. The original Pegasus models were designed with the 40,000-foot launch altitude as an assumption. The use of a different altitude was not factored into the models, the result being that the models were not valid design tools for the lower-altitude launch situation being considered.

The end result was a paradox. The decision to launch at the lower altitude seemed correct, based as it was on the best-available data. That decision underwent a complete review, and project personnel were comfortable with the decision. There was nothing to indicate that the decision was flawed. The focus instead was on issues such as separation, which were seen as the significant unknowns. The only flaw in the process was that no one asked if the assumptions in the models and data were correct for the new launch profile.

DEALING WITH FAILURE

Beyond flaws in the models and the interaction of several different factors, there was a human dimension to the loss of the X-43A #1. Project personnel had transformed an idea into a complete vehicle. They had cared for it, dealt with its problems, worked nights and weekends to prepare it, and now, after four years, the X-43A was about to make its first foray into the unknown. They watched the B-52B's long flight out, experienced the suspense of the countdown, and felt the thrill of the launch. The stack fell free from the B-52B, and there was the long, long wait for ignition. There was a tiny doubt—will it fire? Then the yellow-white flame erupted from the nozzle, and the stack began to accelerate. All of the years of work were about to be realized, but then they were gone in the blink of an eye. The Hyper-X launch vehicle tumbled out of control and fell toward the Pacific Ocean. It was over.

Looking back on the experience, Yohan Lin observed that to cope with failure, each member of the team had to adopt a positive attitude. He recalled that Vince Rausch had said during the debrief that more is often learned from failure than from success. This was because success only confirms what is already known. Failure reveals what *was not* known. As part of the positive attitude, Lin observed that the team did not blame others and did not point fingers. The failure was of the team as a whole. So will its success.[24]

Corpening gave an example of this attitude at the meeting that immediately followed the crash:

> We met as a large team, in the large conference room [in building] 4800.
> I believe it was Kevin Peterson, the Dryden center director—he got up
> and said, "You know, we knew it was high-risk. We obviously ran into

some problems here. We've got to sort them out and push through. We've got two other vehicles to fly."

And that support from upper management never wavered, which was really amazing to me. But immediately after the large meeting, we broke up into a smaller group with a couple of Orbital folks, Phil Joyce, the project manager; Mike Pudoka, the chief [Orbital] engineer, I believe, and a couple of their key engineers; Joel [Sitz] and I and Brad [Neal] and a couple of others; Vince Rausch and a couple of other folks from the government side. And it was a tough meeting. Orbital took it very, very personally. Phil Joyce immediately—*immediately*—accepted responsibility. He said, "Hey, we let you guys down. Our job was to get you to separation, and we didn't get there. It's our responsibility to do that, we take that responsibility." It was, to me, an indication of the character of Phil and his team and the character of the team. At no point was there any finger-pointing and saying, "Well, it's your fault. It wasn't mine. I did everything I could do. It's on your watch." There wasn't any of that.[25]

Lin also made a final point. The reason that the Hyper-X team persisted after the failure is the same reason that they were part of the project in the first place. And that was because the Hyper-X was so important an effort. More than four decades had passed since the scramjet concept had been originated. But the potential of the concept had yet to be realized despite all of the efforts and resources that had been expended. The Hyper-X project was on the verge of realizing that potential. This was to be one of the great milestones in aerospace history; this was to be the opening chapter of the second century of flight. The team had known failure. They would now fix what had gone wrong. And they would now succeed.[26]

NOTES

[1]Peebles, Curtis, personal observations of the events of June 2, 2001.

[2]Soden, Linda, history interview, Aug. 25, 2005, NASA Dryden Flight Research Center History Office, p. 14.

[3]Peebles, Curtis, personal observations of the X-43A #1 launch and aftermath.

[4]Fullerton, Gordon, history interview, Aug. 3, 2005, NASA Dryden Flight Research Center History Office, p. 16.

[5]Losey, Lori, interview, Nov. 16, 2006.

[6]Ross, Jim, history interview, Aug. 24, 2005, NASA Dryden Flight Research Center History Office, p. 5.

[7]Grindle, Laurie, history interview, tape no. 1, Jan. 19, 2005, NASA Dryden Flight Research Center History Office, pp. 4, 15.

[8]Corpening, Griff, history interview, Dec. 20, 2004, NASA Dryden Flight Research Center History Office, pp. 40–43.

[9]Soden history interview, pp. 17–19.

[10]Soden history interview, pp. 17, 18.

[11]"Report of Findings: X-43A Mishap by the Mishap Investigation Board Volume 1," May 5, 2003, pp. 1, 2, 21, 24. (This is the publicly released version, with ITAR-sensitive material removed.)

[12]Corpening, Griff, history interview, tape no. 2, Dec. 20, 2004, NASA Dryden Flight Research Center History Office, p. 44.

[13]"Report of Findings: X-43A Mishap by the Mishap Investigation Board Volume 1," p. 20.

[14]"Report of Findings: X-43A Mishap by the Mishap Investigation Board Volume 1," p. 22, and Corpening history interview, tape no. 2, p. 44.

[15]Ibid, pp. 15–19.

[16]Ibid, pp. 22–24.

[17]Ibid, pp. 5–7.

[18]Ibid, p. 11.

[19]Reukauf, Paul, history interview, p. 47.

[20]"Report of Findings: X-43A Mishap by the Mishap Investigation Board Volume 1," p. 24.

[21]Corpening history interview, tape no. 2, pp. 45–47.

[22]Ibid, pp. 47–49.

[23]Reukauf history interview, pp. 43, 45, 46.

[24]Lin, Yohan, interview, Nov. 15, 2006.

[25]Corpening history interview, tape no. 2, pp. 42, 43.

[26]Lin interview.

Chapter 6

RETURN TO FLIGHT

Experience is a hard teacher. First comes the test, then the lesson.
Anonymous

The mishap-investigation-board report was issued in March 2002 and served as the basis for planning the X-43A return-to-flight effort. The report recommended technical reviews as well as changes in management procedures to correct the problems and shortcomings that had been revealed during the first flight. The technical aspect of the investigative process involved an extensive review of the hardware, software, and system designs; new wind-tunnel tests and computational-fluid-dynamics analysis; and refinement of the mathematical models used in creating the initial flight plan. All were areas in which the MIB identified deficiencies. To avoid similar inaccuracies, the board's postflight analysis and simulations were done using several different methods in order to cross-check critical areas and to reduce the possibility of an error slipping through. Small groups known as "tiger teams" were organized to examine specific fixes for problems that had been identified by the MIB.

REVISITING THE SIMULATIONS AND PROCEDURAL CHANGES

Before the first X-43A flight, the big issue in the minds of engineers was the separation. The actual launch had been subjected to a significantly smaller amount of analysis and simulation. This reflected a perception that the Hyper-X launch vehicle, as off-the-shelf hardware, was a well-enough-known quantity.

The loss of the first Hyper-X launch vehicle (HXLV), however, made clear that the heritage data from the previous Pegasus launches were not adequate to show that the low-altitude/lower-speed launch profile used on the first flight could be flown successfully. The mishap investigation board found that inaccurate modeling of the vehicle characteristics was the cause of the failure. To prevent similar errors, during the return-to-flight work new high-fidelity models of the vehicle aerodynamics, fin actuation system, vehicle structure, and autopilot system were developed.

Reducing the risk involved writing high-fidelity models of the separation and using additional wind-tunnel and new computational-fluid-dynamics analyses. The separation mechanism on the adapter was further tested. The new data were used for additional modeling of the pyrotechnic pistons that fired to separate the X-43A from the adapter. Beyond work on the separation itself, the X-43A control laws for the time period of the separation also were refined, to improve the research vehicle's ability to survive unpredicted events.

To confirm the earlier predictions made for the boost, separation, and research flight, a series of independent computer programs was used. The primary program used to model the boost was Orbital's NRT Sim. This was a full-stack simulation up to point of separation, which was based on Pegasus heritage data. It included HXLV analysis, autopilot design, and trajectory analysis. The primary separation program was Langley's SepSim. This was a 6 + 6 degree-of-freedom simulation of both the HXLV and the X-43A. SepSim included separation analysis, sensitivity studies, and collision detection. The simulation for the X-43A's free flight was Dryden's RVSim. This software covered the X-43A's flight from separation to ocean impact. It used the Dryden simulation environment and included X-43A analysis, autopilot design, and sensitivity studies.

The backup boost simulation program was Dryden's LVSim-D. This was an independent check and analysis of the HXLV booster, run in the Dryden simulation environment. The backup separation simulation was done with Post 2 Sep from Langley, another 6 + 6 degree-of-freedom simulation of both the HXLV and X-43A, but made independently of that with Langley's SepSim program. Different code was used to write the two programs—MCS/ADAM code for SepSim and POST2 code for Post 2 Sep.

Further safeguards included running simulations as full end-to-end missions at both Dryden and Langley, using different linking, integration, and interfaces. The Dryden "drop-to-splash" simulation used NRTSim, SepSim, and RVSim. This required the manual linking of the simulations and provided validation of the individual phases and the integrated flight. The Langley end-to-end sim used the same three programs, but with a single user interface, with automatic linking and interface. The test served as an independent check on both the separate programs and the complete flight profile.

Another change was the use of new uncertainty models for parameters in the Monte Carlo analysis. These verified that the vehicle could survive if the trajectories diverged from the planned profiles. Even with conservative uncertainty margins, the 1200 Monte Carlo analyses results showed a 97% probability of successful separation. Less than 1% of the runs resulted in a collision with the adapter. This outcome was similar to those of the Flight 1 results, even with the new margins.

The other set of changes made was to management and review procedures. Part of this involved a strengthening of the existing integrated-product-team (IPT) structure through improved communications and teamwork. The IPT for each discipline developed a return-to-flight plan that contained all of the necessary action items. Responsibility for each of these was then assigned to a specific individual. His or her work was then tracked until the item was closed. The IPT also determined what activities required additional checks and how these were to be done within the group. All IPT decisions and actions were reviewed by the engineering review board before being implemented.

As an external check on these activities, a hierarchy of independent review panels also was involved. These ranged from peer assessors, who were experts in a particular field but were not directly associated with the Hyper-X project, to the flight readiness review, the integrated mission assurance review, and finally the airworthiness and flight safety review board. At each step, the independence of the group increased, while the depth of their review decreased. This provided that independent sets of eyes looked at every aspect of the project at different but overlapping levels. A group that has been working on a specific area for many months or years can become so familiar with an issue that they can miss its significance. New individuals, lacking such familiarity, were potentially more likely to spot a danger it might pose.

As with configuration control issues, all decisions and actions made by the project staff were documented at each level. This was to prevent an issue from slipping through without resolution.[1]

OPTIONS FOR REDUCING TRANSONIC DYNAMIC PRESSURE

Although the lower launch altitude had been seen by Hyper-X project engineers as the best option for achieving a Mach 7 burnout speed, this decision had, in fact, set in motion the events that doomed the first flight. A new approach would be required. As a result, a range of options was examined following completion of the mishap-investigation-board report. These were intended to both reduce dynamic pressure on the Hyper-X launch vehicle at transonic speeds and increase booster reliability. The obvious solution was launching the booster at 40,000 feet to more closely duplicate standard Pegasus conditions. But this again raised the issue that had led to the decision in the first place—the huge amount of excess energy that would have to be eliminated in order for separation to occur at the planned speed, altitude, and dynamic pressure. Griff Corpening recalled later that the engineers "looked at some crazy ideas." The options as of early March 2002 were as follows: 1) add new trajectories to reduce transonic dynamic pressure; 2) off-load propellant from the Mach 7 booster; 3) modify the Pegasus nozzle; 4) use Orbital's modified L1011 airliner as the launch aircraft, rather than the NASA B-52B; 5) upgrade the fin actuation system; 6) add an in-flight liquid ballast transfer system; and 7) construct a new B-52B pylon, which could carry a heavier stack.[2]

These were soon narrowed down. New trajectories were eliminated, as were use of the L1011 launch aircraft and a new nozzle design. The obvious solution was adding several thousand pounds of ballast to the launch vehicle. A liquid ballast system would address this possibility, though this solution too created new problems. Corpening noted,

> Well, two things happened. One was kind of a no-brainer. The vehicle's now heavier. So, yes, you have less dynamic pressure at 40,000 feet, but you're yanking and banking a heavier vehicle. So in the end the forces on your fins, which are what we're trying to reduce, didn't reduce because it's a heavier vehicle. Less pressure, but you're moving it around. So that didn't make any sense.
>
> The second thing we started finding out as we started diving into the actual design and structural characteristics of the Pegasus adapter and the X-15 adapter [was that] we shouldn't be heavier. Maybe we actually need a lighter vehicle because of what we were finding out with the adapter.[3]

The only remaining option for increasing the launch altitude was off-loading the solid rocket propellant from the Hyper-X launch vehicle in order to reduce the stack's speed at burnout. This was still seen as involving a significant unknown, as it would require removing about a ton and a half of propellant from the vehicle. The earlier doubts about the idea's feasibility remained. Corpening recalled that the prospect of offloading "just scared the heck out of everybody."

Although solid rockets had been machined to remove propellant before, and the idea of a reduced propellant load had been considered earlier in the project for the Mach 5 and 7 flights, no Pegasus ever had undergone the procedure. There were many who believed it simply was not doable. Langley's Mel Lucy headed a tiger team devoted to studying the problem. Doubts remained, however. Corpening recalled, "every time we'd briefed this stuff to upper management, they would say, 'no, not on my watch.' Jerry Creedon at Langley was famous for saying that: 'No way in hell are you doing this on my watch.'"[3]

There were sound reasons for the doubts expressed. Some 3345 pounds of solid fuel, amounting to 12% of the total propellant load, would have to be machined from the fin slot region, located in front of the Hyper-X launch vehicle nozzle. The result was a much larger cavity at the nozzle, which raised concerns about a successful rocket ignition. A large solid rocket has a hole running through the propellant from the nozzle to the forward end. The solid propellant burns outward from this hole simultaneously along the entire length of the rocket. To ignite the fuel and keep it burning, backpressure must build inside the rocket. There was concern that this large, nonburning area in front of the nozzle would prevent the necessary amount of backpressure from building.

Other issues also were raised. One of these was acoustic resonance. The flame front created a large amount of acoustic energy as the propellant burned, energy that could be amplified by the large empty area at the nozzle. (The effect was akin to that of a large speaker horn.) The final issue was the effect of the "big dead spot," as Reukauf called it, on the thrust profile.[4]

By the end of May 2002, these issues had been analyzed, and the basic return-to-flight strategy had been finalized. It contained three elements. The first was off-loading the Hyper-X launch vehicle to reduce its weight and the dynamic pressure on the vehicle at transonic speeds. The fin actuation system (FAS) also would be modified to double the hinge torque capability. Although the 40,000-foot launch altitude would reduce dynamic pressure, some of the Monte Carlo analyses seemed to indicate that the existing FAS torque limit could be exceeded in certain situations. Finally, studies continued to determine whether or not the existing B-52B pylon could carry the lighter stack. If not, a new pylon would have to be fabricated to replace the existing X-15 pylon.

Return-to-flight briefings were prepared for the NASA research associate administrator and the Langley and Dryden Center directors in June of 2002. A study by ATK also was underway to confirm that propellant removal could be safely completed. The fin-actuation-system modifications and B-52B pylon tests also were to be addressed in the briefings.[5] The briefings were presented on July 18, and the options were approved. A second review was scheduled for mid-October 2002, with the Langley and Dryden Center directors requesting regular updates. The ATK review of the propellant off-loading process determined that the operation could be accomplished, but that risk mitigation was necessary.[6]

With management approval, and the technical feasibility of the plan confirmed, NASA directed Orbital Sciences to have its subcontractor, ATK, begin initial planning for the propellant off-loading. The process would be reviewed before work could proceed so that off-load procedures could be assessed and the accuracy of performance predictions for the modified booster could be verified.[7]

The final question looming over the off-loading plan was whether a static test firing of the modified "Hyper-X Lite" booster was needed before clearance could be given for an X-43A launch. The issue was not a trivial one. Only two Hyper-X launch-vehicle boosters were available for use in the program. A test firing would mean the sacrifice of the Mach 10 mission, as there was no money to replace the booster that would be used in the test. If engineers opted to forego a static test, then the off-loaded booster for the Mach 7 flight could be delivered in the April 2003 time frame. If a static test were judged to be necessary, however, the Mach 7 flight would be delayed still further, putting the Hyper-X project at risk of cancellation.

The tiger team assigned to this issue went about resolving the question very methodically. After considerable effort, the team was convinced they could predict the rocket's performance with the reduced propellant load. They then convinced ATK, the contractor that produced the Hyper-X launch-vehicle booster, and NASA managers of the same. NASA and the contractor's engine predictions were cross-checked. Project managers at NASA Headquarters finally agreed to forgo a static test of the off-loaded booster.[8]

Originally, the third HXLV booster scheduled for use in the Mach 10 flight was to undergo the machining process. This rocket lacked the fins and other equipment with which the second HXLV already had been fitted, which meant there would be no delay before machining began while these were removed. Technicians at ATK began working on the tooling configuration, while at Orbital Sciences data were collected for an independent government review panel that was to make an assessment.[9]

By early October of 2002, however, the plan had been changed to off-loading of the second booster. This would save several weeks of stack reintegration time. Off-load data produced by Orbital Sciences and ATK were delivered to the review panel, which was to examine it and make an interim status report by late October.[10]

As the panel deliberated, project staff continued working toward the return to flight. At Dryden, Orbital Sciences personnel removed the aft skirt and fins from the second booster, in preparation for shipping the stage to ATK. At the same time, the issue of the B-52B pylon was cleared up; hook tests were completed, clearing the way for the pylon's use at the off-loaded HXLV launch weight. Additional wind-tunnel tests were run with a B-52B/stack model. These data were compared with the analytical aerodynamic data to ensure that the B-52B pylon's load limits would not be exceeded if the Pegasus fin position should be abnormal. The data showed there would not be a problem, and plans to build a new pylon were subsequently abandoned.[11]

During the final week of October 2002, the government panel and ATK engineers met to discuss the off-loading issues. It was not until the end of the year, however, that the work was completed. The last major issue was the motor's internal acoustic stability analysis, and the government and ATK were working toward a December 18 meeting in which the problem would be addressed. The Orbital/NASA off-load contract changes were completed on December 12, 2002. NASA's legal office expedited the contract approval process. By this time, the second booster was nearly ready for shipping to ATK's Promontory, Utah, facility. The wing, ballast module, and motor skirt all had been removed from the rocket, and early January 2003 was the scheduled time frame for its shipment.[12]

After a year of work, study, and debate, the initial off-loading of the Hyper-X launch-vehicle booster propellant began on February 12, 2003. The off-loading effort went smoothly, and just over a week later it had passed the halfway point.

By the end of the first week in March, the 3345 pounds of propellant had been successfully removed, and the rocket was undergoing X-ray inspection. No major issues were discovered, and the operation had gone extremely well. A postmachining review was planned for March 17 at ATK's Bacchus, Utah, facility.[13]

The review found the booster to be flight worthy. The booster was shipped back to Dryden, arriving on April Fools' Day.[14] The off-loading of the solid propellant had been seen as a major risk, but had actually gone very well. The result was a major change in the flight conditions the Hyper-X Lite would experience.

From launch to a speed of about Mach 1.5, the dynamic pressure on the Hyper-X Lite booster varied little from that experienced by a standard Pegasus booster. Above this speed, the differences in dynamic pressure measurements between the two boosters increased rapidly. The peak dynamic pressure for a Pegasus first stage was about 1300 pounds per square foot (psf) at a speed of Mach 3. Dynamic pressure on the booster then decreased rapidly, as it ascended steeply into thinner air. The Hyper-X Lite's maximum dynamic pressure, or max q, was about 1700 psf at just above Mach 3. (In contrast, max q for the first HXLV would have been just under 2000 psf, at about Mach 2.5). The dynamic pressure profiles for both the first HXLV booster and Hyper-X Lite were similar beyond Mach 4, with the Hyper-X Lite actually flying at a slightly higher dynamic pressure—1400 psf compared to about 1300 psf that of the first HXLV launch profile.

The thrust profile of the two rockets also was different because of the propellant off-loading. The original HXLV baseline thrust profile was a little under 90,000 pounds at ignition, building to over 120,000 pounds of thrust at about 18 seconds after ignition. (Because of the different altitudes, this is the vacuum thrust.) The amount of thrust then begins a slow decline until about 73 seconds after launch, when the thrust drops from 95,000 pounds to 10,000 in just 2 to 3 seconds. Over the next 7 seconds, the HXLV's thrust trails off to zero as the booster burns out.

With the Hyper-X Lite, the ignition thrust was only 80,000 pounds, building to 110,000 pounds after 15 seconds. Over the next 5 seconds, the thrust dropped to 70,000 pounds, then gradually increased between 20 and 77 seconds after launch to 100,000 pounds (vs 95,000 for the original HXLV thrust profile). As the altitude was the same for both boosters but the thrust was higher for the off-loaded Hyper-X Lite, the dynamic pressure was also higher for the modified rocket. The rest of the thrust profile was similar to that of the original configuration, although longer in duration—a drop in thrust to 10,000 pounds in a few seconds and then a tapering off to burnout at 85 seconds after launch.

The Hyper-X Lite thus had a lower peak thrust (110,000 pounds vs more than 120,000 pounds for the original HXLV), an inverted thrust profile (an increase, a sharp drop, then a gradual buildup before burnout vs the first HXLV's longer and higher thrust buildup, followed by a gradual decline until burnout), and a longer burn time.[15] Off-loading the solid rocket propellant eliminated the high transonic dynamic pressure of the lower launch profile.

The other return-to-flight issue was the modification of the fin actuation system, which would increase the torque margin should the dynamic pressure estimates again be in error. The FAS modifications, in contrast to the propellant off-loading, were viewed as a straightforward engineering problem. Events would prove otherwise.

FIN ACTUATION SYSTEM

Among the events that had led to the failure of the first X-43A launch was the stalling of the fin actuation system. The root cause was the inability of the FAS to produce sufficient torque to move the rudder against the higher-than-expected dynamic pressure. Although the new launch profile, with the drop altitude raised to 40,000 feet, would result in a lower dynamic pressure, the simulations indicated the possibility that a fin stall could still occur with the original Pegasus FAS design.[16]

The Hyper-X launch-vehicle guidance system used on the first X-43A launch was based on the closed-loop feedback design of the existing Pegasus hardware. The guidance system used a "single-string" design, meaning that there was no backup system for its elements. This was because of size, cost, and the difficulty of integrating two control systems. It also meant that a system failure would result in the loss of the HXLV and payload.

The HXLV's inertial measurement unit (IMU) was a Litton LN-100LG global-positioning-system-aided inertial navigation system. The IMU measured the accelerations, rates, velocities, and positions of the HXLV from activation and alignment before launch from the B-52B through X-43A separation. The IMU output was sent to the 68030-based flight computer and a pair of 68302-based communications boards. The flight computer took the IMU's pure inertial measurements and translated the output into path-steering commands for the fin actuation system, which moved the three control surfaces at the HXLV's aft end.[17]

The original FAS design consisted of an electronic control unit (ECU), which included the signal conversion and power output boards that received steering commands from the flight computer. The ECU then converted the computer's commands into analog signals, which then were sent to the three electromechanical actuators (EMA). These consisted of a permanent magnet motor, reduction gear train, position potentiometer, and metal housing. Each of the three control surfaces had an individual EMA. A thermal battery supplied electrical power, which was activated shortly before launch, during the HXLV's ascent. (Once activated, the launch had to be made on schedule or be aborted, as the battery had sufficient power for only a single attempt.) The three EMA units were mounted in the aft skirt assembly, a two-part aluminum cylinder attached to the aft end of the ATK Orion 50S rocket motor.

As an EMA moved a fin, its potentiometer measured the change in its position and reported this back to the ECU, which filtered the sensed actuator position measurements. This "fin actuator position talkback" was sent by the ECU to the flight computer. Simultaneously, the IMU measured changes in the flight path caused by the fins' movements and generated new outputs for the flight computer.[18]

This back-and-forth transfer of data and commands introduced electronic delays into the control system. The IMU took a small amount of time to measure the vehicle's movements and then compare these to the planned flight path, determine the differences, and generate the output for the flight computer. The flight computer also took time converting the IMU output into fin actuator commands and sending them to the ECU. Additional time was required for the ECU to convert these into analog signals for the actuator. Similar delays occurred on the feedback half of the loop.

Beyond these electronic delays, there also were mechanical factors, called "compliance." It took time for the actuators to move the fins to the commanded position. The fins also operated in a highly dynamic environment; during the X-43A boost phase, the HXLV fins were subjected to dynamic pressures of 1700 psf or more. These aerodynamic forces would cause the fins to bend and the linkages to flex. The effects of such compliance had to be correctly modeled if the HXLV were to be stable in flight. Operating conditions for the HXLV were more demanding than those for more stable vehicles. In these vehicles compliance errors had the potential to "eat up" margins.[19]

The mishap-investigation-board report had found that errors in the modeling of these elements contributed to the loss of the first vehicle. Much of the return-to-flight work focused on refining these models to allow accurate predictions for the HXLV-specific operating conditions.

Project engineers believed that increasing the torque capability on the actuator system would provide a quick fix for increasing the margin. The contractor indicated that this could be accomplished by removing a brake on each electromechanical actuator and replacing it with a second actuator motor in a torque-summing configuration. These modifications would increase the hinge torque from 1850 foot-pounds to over 3000 foot-pounds. Even in a three-sigma situation, this provided about a 25 to 30% torque margin. The project engineers wanted a 50% margin, but the lower torque margin did cover the worst-case scenario.

Although project engineers knew this fin-actuation-system modification work would be difficult, what loomed larger in their minds was the even more problematic option of off-loading Hyper-X launch-vehicle propellant. The FAS modification seemed, by contrast, to be a simple fix. Reukauf said later "it turned out that [the FAS modification] was the fix that almost killed the program."[20]

Adding a second actuator set in motion a series of significant modifications to the original Pegasus electronic-control-unit configuration. These consisted of a signal conversion board, control board, predriver board, three power-boards (one for each fin), and motherboard. To handle the doubled current produced by two actuators on each fin, the powerboard and predriver board had to be redesigned. The new powerboards replaced the analog design of the original Pegasus ECU with a digital system. The new ECU powerboards used complex programmable logic devices (CPLDs) to control the direction of the fins' movement. The CPLDs activated opposing pairs of field effect transistors (FET) mounted in an "H-Bridge" configuration. The opening of an FET pair would cause the motor to rotate in the desired direction, while the amount of current determined the extent of the fin's movement. To reverse the fin movement, the initial pair of FETs would be closed, and then the other pair activated.

The ECU motherboard, signal conversion board, and control board were all Pegasus heritage, but the powerboard and predriver board for each ECU now were Hyper-X specific. The new design posed several challenges. The CPLDs were low-voltage logic devices that controlled high electrical currents. All of the hardware was collocated on a powerboard. In addition, the high-current switching could create electrical effects that might cause CPLD failure.[21] To cope with the higher torque, the material from which the housing was constructed was changed from aluminum to stainless steel, to make it stiffer and to prevent flexing as a result of higher loads. For the same reason, the gear material also was made stronger.[22]

By the first week in May 2002, the FAS modification work had begun, and the specifications were distributed for review.[23] The preliminary design review was scheduled for June 18 by the FAS contractor.[24] The modification work on the FAS continued through the summer, and by mid-August the contractor had released all of the mechanical and electrical drawings. The controller test boards were being manufactured, with a completion date of early September to allow for development testing.[25] The FAS critical design review also was planned for September. The schedule at this point called for the modified FAS to be delivered to Orbital Sciences in early March of 2003, with the second X-43A flight set for June.[26]

By early October, the elements of the new FAS were beginning to take shape. The powerboard testing was underway, and the subcontractor was cutting the new Vascomax gears. The modifications were on schedule for integrated test unit checks to be conducted in mid-October.[27] As 2002 ended, the FAS modifications seemed to be going well. The manufacturing of the actuator gears was progressing on schedule in December, while the qualification actuator completed its burn in time during the second week in February 2003. With this completed, the actuator could be shipped to Orbital Sciences to begin temperature and vibration testing.[28]

The initial vibration and thermal tests of the control unit and actuator were completed in late February 2003 without incident. The actuator was then shipped to Orbital Sciences' Chandler, Arizona, facility on March 7 to begin qualification testing.[29] Over the next month, the modified actuator was successfully loaded to the design goal of 50% over the three-sigma expected loads. At the same time, the flight actuators and controller were assembled and then underwent burn-in testing during mid-April.[30] These ran into instrumentation problems, halting the tests. Because of the setback, engineers from both the FAS contractor and Orbital, along with Dryden quality assurance representatives, worked during early May to reconfigure and check the contractor's laboratory. The actuator also had to be reassembled as a result of the gear train being replaced.

Despite these efforts, the contractor continued to have test equipment problems during tests with the actuator. To maintain the schedule, a switch in the test sequence was made. While troubleshooting of the test procedures continued at the contractor's facility, the actuator was shipped to the Chandler facility. Making the switch prevented the problems with the actuator tests from impeding the schedule, but weekly progress updates were made, and final assessments of the difficulties would be saved for later.[31]

FIN-ACTUATION-SYSTEM LATCH-UP

The first sign of a serious design problem with the FAS modifications came in early October 2003. An electronic control unit failed during a cold-soak test simulating temperatures at high altitudes. The failures occurred when the actuators were commanded to slew at a high rate. Instead, the complex programmable logic devices ceased processing, which is known as a "latch-up" condition. Should this occur in flight, the fins would stop moving, control would be lost, and the mission would fail.

The unit was returned to the vendor for analysis. The contractor attempted to reproduce the failures with the ECU instrumented for diagnostic data. Although several cold-temperature cycles were made, each time the channel controlling the fin operated normally.[32] Griff Corpening, the Dryden chief engineer for the two X-43A Mach 7 flights, recalled that "as soon as you hooked up your diagnostic equipment, it wouldn't [latch up] anymore. So the problem was so subtle that as soon as you interfered in any way with the circuitry, it wouldn't [latch up]."[33]

Not until January of 2004 was the problem resolved. The latch-up was triggered by excessive electronic noise in the ECU powerboards during current-limit states. These occurred when the maximum electrical current value was being sent to the field effect transistors. Once the noise reached a certain level, it would cause the CPLDs to latch up.

The failures could be reproduced in ground tests, even though the exact process through which the electronic noise caused the latch-up was not entirely clear. Engineers concluded that this failure mode could occur at only two points during the planned flight profile. The first was soon after ignition, when the booster pitched up into the ascent path, putting the maximum stress on the fin actuation system during the flight. The second was after the solid rocket burned out and X-43A separation had occurred. When the Hyper-X launch vehicle was at hypersonic speeds prior to separation, the fin movements were small and did not reach the current-limit state.

Two changes were made to solve the problem. The complex programmable logic devices firmware was changed to eliminate programming that could not function properly across the required temperature range. Resistors also were added to the CPLD outputs that minimized (but did not eliminate) the electronic noise in the output signals. Although the investigation was time consuming and extremely thorough, the actual fixes were minor.

The FAS to be used on the second flight underwent preflight testing. This consisted of 200 command step inputs at 5-degree increments—during which the current-limit state was attained each time—at cold, ambient, and hot temperatures, for a total of 600 cycles. These tests created much greater stress on the FAS than would the planned flight profile. The FAS latch-ups occurred only under these stress-test conditions and never during a standard flight profile.[34]

Reukauf summed up the FAS problem as "a very, very complex failure," adding,

> [T]here was a lot of testing [that] went on and there were some fixes made. And, ultimately, those fixes worked and we were able to get all the way through our initial testing and acceptance testing and all of the other testing that they do with the fin-actuator combinations. We decided to fly the second flight, thinking we had solved that problem. But it held up the second flight by almost six months.[35]

FINAL FIXES

Most of the return-to-flight effort was focused on correcting errors that had resulted in the loss of the first X-43A and ensuring that nothing had been overlooked in the wind-tunnel tests, simulations, and computational-fluid-dynamics analysis.[36] To remove any potential threat of another failure, there also were issues that had no direct bearing on the mishap but had to be addressed nonetheless.

The mishap information board had to deal with data-latency issues in its investigation of the first flight. Board members examined computational delays within the computer as it called up subroutines, or control laws, and converted steering commands into voltages to move the actuators, or similar activities. Data-latency issues also arose from transport delays as electrons flowed through the wiring. This was not the same as compliance, which related to the physical movement of mechanical systems. Data-latency issues resulted from delays in the transfer of data within the X-43A's electronic systems. Aircraft-in-the-loop timing tests were done to document and eliminate these effects.[37]

Considerable efforts also were made as part of the return-to-flight effort to improve engine operation. Two sets of wind-tunnel tests were done with the HyPulse scramjet model (HSM). This was a full-scale-length, partial-width replica of the scramjet flowpath. To fit in the HyPulse wind tunnel, the ramp and nozzle had to be truncated. Unlike the previous tests in 2000, the HSM was fitted with the new Mach 10-Keel Line 8 (M10-KL8) flowpath.

The initial series of HyPulse wind-tunnel tests was done between July and November of 2001, at flight Mach numbers of 9 and 10. The Mach 9 tests consisted of three calibration runs, one unfueled tare run, and then two hydrogen–silane runs and four hydrogen-only tests. The Mach 10 tests involved four calibration tests, three tare runs, and nine tests each with hydrogen–silane and with hydrogen alone.

Nearly a year passed before the eighth and final series of Hyper-X engine wind-tunnel tests was made. These were conducted between October 2002 and March of 2003. As before, tests were made at two different speeds— Mach 10 and 10.3—and with the M10-KL8 flowpath. The Mach 10 effort was more extensive, with a single calibration run and five tare tests, followed by 11 hydrogen–silane and 7 hydrogen-only tests. The Mach 10.3 efforts were, in contrast, minimal. There was a single calibration run, no tare runs, three hydrogen–silane tests, and two with hydrogen alone.[38]

These wind-tunnel tests led to the discovery that a small increase in the angle of attack resulted in greater thrust from the engine and a reduced chance of a flameout. This increased angle of attack was added to the flight software. A related matter was the unstart control logic for the engine control system; this was developed and proven during the wind-tunnel tests, and then it, too, was added to the flight software.

The time was also used to fix structural and mechanical problems in the adapter and X-43A. Two of these were discovered in adapter camera system images taken as the X-43A was torn from the adapter. One set of images showed a piece of sheet metal being ripped off of the adapter during the gyrations. This would not have occurred during a normal ascent, but the adapter was reinforced nonetheless to prevent a reoccurrence.[39]

Another potential threat also appeared in the images. The X-43A's left tail was seen to have rotated 180 degrees and was turning freely on its shaft.

The control horn connecting the tail's shaft to the actuator had been broken by the Hyper-X-launch-vehicle gyrations. As with the sheet metal, this would not have occurred under normal flight stresses. The incident did indicate a possible lack of margin. Corpening said in a later interview:

> I believe that it was an adequate design. And had we been in a nominal situation, it would have been adequate. But what we found as we investigated this aluminum control horn is that it had a little bit more slop to it than we'd like, and the strength was marginal. It probably would have been okay. But we had time. And at that point we were under direct orders to reduce risk wherever we could. So we went back in and redesigned it out of steel. And [we] also designed it so it would have essentially zero slippage in its attachment mechanism. That was a whole challenge in and of itself.
>
> [It] turned out the design was very difficult to fabricate and very difficult to install. There was a whole bunch of problems there, and that took a lot of time and energy. I remember the summer of '03—I went on vacation, and I had every intention of coming back from vacation and the control horn would have been fabricated and installed. I got back from vacation, and it wasn't. It took another two months to get it designed and installed. So that was a challenge there.[40]

The final mechanical issue to appear during the first X-43A's brief flight was the failure of the adapter's nitrogen system. The failure occurred before control of the HXLV was lost and was unrelated to it. The nitrogen gas supplied the pressure to spray a water–glycol mixture on the scramjet's leading edge, to cool it during ascent. When a pyrotechnic valve fired, releasing the gas, debris caused a regulator to fail. The nitrogen gas began to vent overboard. The postmishap analysis indicated that even with the regulator failure there would have been sufficient nitrogen for a successful engine test. To prevent a reoccurrence, a filter was added to catch any debris.[41]

It was now the spring of 2004. Almost three years had passed since the 13.5 seconds that had sealed the fate of the first flight. After the end of the program, Corpening recalled his feelings as the second X-43A mission neared:

> For Flight 2—there was very much a depth of confidence, a maturity of confidence, a maturity, if you will, having been tempered by fire, so to speak. And I think through that tempering there was also a humility. It's hard for me to describe. There was a strong sense that we had done what we should do, that we had done everything we could think of.
>
> But there was also a deep appreciation for Mother Nature and the physics and what we were trying to do. We still recognized we had to depress the Pegasus trajectory and fly through the negative-angle-of-attack regime. We still had to separate, which was viewed still as a very high-risk event. And nobody had ever flown a Mach 7 research vehicle

shaped like this under free-flight conditions. So I think there was very much a healthy respect for what was still ahead of us, but with a depth of confidence and calm.

Myself, personally—I remember right before Flight 1, I was as stressed as I have ever been. Going into Flight 2, I was less stressed, but yet very much more aware, I think, of all the challenges that were still out there.[42]

NOTES

[1]Reubush, David E., Luat T. Nguyen, and Vincent L. Rausch, "Review of X-43A Return to Flight Activities and Current Status," pp. 4–7.

An example of an error overlooked because of familiarity was the use of a 15-psi pure-oxygen atmosphere in U.S. manned spacecraft during ground tests. This procedure was simpler than using a mixed oxygen/nitrogen atmosphere and had caused no problems during all of the Mercury and Gemini flights. Personnel at all levels—management, pad operations, and the astronauts themselves—had no concerns over the flammability of the high-pressure pure-oxygen atmosphere during pad tests. No flammability testing had been done on materials inside the spacecraft under these conditions. On Apollo 1, faulty wiring caused a spark, which ignited the pure-oxygen atmosphere, killing the three crewmen during a prelaunch checkout.

[2]*Aerospace Projects*, March 8, 2002, pp. 1, 2.

[3]Corpening, Griff, history interview, tape no. 2, Dec. 20, 2004, NASA Dryden Flight Research Center History Office pp. 53, 54, and *Aerospace Projects*, March 15, 2002.

[4]Reukauf, Paul, history interview, Feb. 17, 2005, NASA Dryden Flight Research Center History Office, pp. 50, 51, and Reubush et al., "Review of X-43A Return to Flight Activities and Current Status," p. 5.

[5]*Aerospace Projects*, May 31, 2002, NASA Dryden Flight Research Center History Office, p. 1, and June 6, 2002, p. 1.

[6]*Aerospace Projects*, July 19, 2002, p. 1.

[7]*Aerospace Projects*, July 26, 2002, p. 2, and Aug. 2, 2002.

[8]Corpening interview, tape no. 2, p. 54, and *Aerospace Projects*, Aug. 2, 2002.

[9]*Aerospace Projects*, Aug. 16, 2002.

[10]*Aerospace Projects*, Oct. 4, 2002.

[11]*Aerospace Projects*, Oct. 11, 2002, and Oct. 28, 2002.

[12]*Aerospace Projects*, Oct. 28, 2002, and Dec. 13, 2002, p. 2.

[13]*Aerospace Projects*, Feb. 14 and 21, 2003, p. 4, and March 7, 2003, p. 5.

[14]*Aerospace Projects*, March 21, 2003, p. 5, and April 4, 2003, p. 5.

[15]Reubush et al., "Review of X-43A Return to Flight Activities and Current Status," p. 5.

The terms "HXLV" for the Flight 1 booster and "Hyper-X Lite" for the off-loaded booster on Flight 2 were used in these paragraphs to differentiate between the two versions. While "Hyper-X Lite" was used in documentation, both boosters officially were designated the "HXLV."

[16]Reukauf history interview, p. 73.

[17]Joyce, Phillip J., John B. Pomroy, and Laurie Grindle, "The Hyper-X Launch Vehicle: Challenges and Design Considerations for Hypersonic Flight," AIAA Paper 2005-3333, p. 4.

[18]X-43A Mishap Investigation Board, "Report of Findings: X-43A Mishap Volume I," p. 12.

[19]Ibid, p. 11, and Corpening history interview, tape no. 1, Dec. 20, 2004, NASA Dryden Flight Research Center History Office, pp. 44–46.

[20]Reukauf history interview, pp. 45, 46, 71, 72, and e-mail from Yohan Lin to Curtis Peebles, July 5, 2006.

[21]Reubush et al., "Review of X-43A Return to Flight Activities and Current Status," p. 5, Yohan Lin history interview, NASA Dryden Flight Research Center History Office, p. 62, and additional information from Lin.

[22]Reubush et al., "Review of X-43A Return to Flight Activities and Current Status," p. 5, and Corpening history interview, tape no. 1, pp. 51, 60.

[23]*Aerospace Projects*, May 3, 2002, p. 1.

[24] *Aerospace Projects*, May 31, 2002, p. 1.

[25]*Aerospace Projects*, Aug. 16, 2002.

[26]*Aerospace Projects*, Aug. 2, 2002, p. 2.

[27]*Aerospace Projects*, Oct. 4, 2002.

[28]*Aerospace Projects*, Dec. 13, 2002, p. 2, and Feb. 14, 2003, p. 4.

[29]*Aerospace Projects*, Feb. 21, 2003, p. 4, and March 7, 2003, p. 5.

[30]*Aerospace Projects*, April 4, 2003, p. 5.

[31]*Aerospace Projects*, May 3, 2003 p. 3, and May 9, 2003, p. 4.

[32]*Aerospace Projects*, Oct. 3, 2003, p. 3, and Oct. 31, 2003, pp. 2, 3.

[33]Corpening history interview, tape no. 1, p. 48.

[34]*Aerospace Projects*, Jan. 9, 2004, p. 3, additional information from Dryden X-43A project manager Joel Sitz, Lin, and Reukauf, and e-mail from Lin to Curtis Peebles, June 27, 2006.

[35]Reukauf history interview, p. 51.

[36]Reubush et al., "Review of X-43A Return to Flight Activities and Current Status," p. 6.

[37]Ibid, p. 6, and Yohan Lin interview, Nov. 22, 2006.

[38]Rogers R. C., A. T. Shih, and N. E. Hass, "Scramjet Development Tests Supporting the Mach 10 Flight of the X-43," AIAA Paper 2005-3351.

[39]Reubush et al., "Review of X-43A Return to Flight Activities and Current Status," p. 6.

[40]Corpening history interview, tape no. 1, pp. 53, 54.

[41]Reubush et al., "Review of X-43A Return to Flight Activities and Current Status," p. 8.

[42]Corpening history interview, tape no. 1, p. 59.

Chapter 7

$C_t > C_d$

It was only a flight of 12 seconds, and it was uncertain, wavy, creeping sort
of flight at best; but it was a real flight at last and not a glide.

Orville Wright

The checkout of the second X-43A vehicle went smoothly, despite the long
delay and numerous modifications. Yohan Lin recalled that whereas the first
vehicle "went through the growing pains," the second vehicle "went very
smoothly, no problems. By that time we pretty much understood the systems
fairly well and, in terms of operations, there were no significant problems."[1]

Looking back on the experience, Griff Corpening observed:

> We had taken all the lessons learned on the launch vehicle to the separation
> event and to the research vehicle. And we had processes and additional
> players in place. And we had done, again, in my mind everything reason-
> able and prudent. And it was once again very much time to go fly. Now,
> what was different between Flight 1 and Flight 2 is that I think we all had
> a very healthy respect and understanding [of failure].[2]

As the second flight approached, the stakes were high for the Hyper-X
project. The first flight had shown what had been wrong with the Hyper-X
launch vehicle, but had failed before even reaching supersonic speed.
The unknowns facing the X-43A still were unknown. Among these were the
HXLV's ability to fly the ascent profile and then pitch down to a negative
angle of attack. Separation and stabilization of the X-43A still were unex-
plored. Finally, the scramjet engine had yet to prove its performance, or even
that it could work.

The vehicle had been prepared as thoroughly as possible. Controllers could
monitor the stack telemetry before launch to determine whether any problems
were cropping up. But once the stack was launched from the B-52B, controllers could do nothing more. Like a baby bird being pushed out of the nest, the
X-43A would be on its own. If the X-43A succeeded, it would be the fastest
airbreathing aircraft in the world, and the scramjet would be proven as a
workable engine design.

But if an unknown had been missed, Flight 2 might fail. And if Flight 2 failed, the consensus among project personnel was that there probably would not be a third flight. The Hyper-X would become just another failed project, and the scramjet would still remain an unproved and possibly unworkable technology.

FLIGHT 2

The captive-carry flight of the second X-43A was made on January 26, 2004. Like the captive flight in 2001, this one would test the various B-52B, X-43A, and HXLV systems under actual flight conditions, with the test process encompassing all operations except the actual launch. All flight objectives were met, and only minor issues were found.[3]

The launch was scheduled for Saturday, March 27, 2004. As before, a weekend flight was scheduled so that the full capacity of the Point Mugu range could be utilized. One factor that made scheduling difficult was squeezing the flight into springtime weather patterns in southern California. Launch day fell between cutoff lows, which were weather fronts that typically appeared during this time of year on the California coast. The crew of the B-52B was Dana Purifoy (pilot), Gordon Fullerton (copilot), Dave McAllister (X-43A panel operator), and John Pomroy of Orbital Sciences (HXLV panel operator).

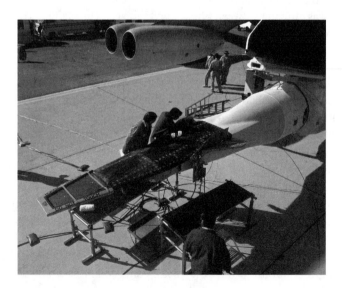

X-43A #2 undergoing final preparations after being slung under the wing of NASA's B-52B at Edwards Air Force Base. The protective covers are placed over the carbon–carbon leading edges on the nose. (NASA photo EC04-0091-49.)

The B-52B launch aircraft flying over the Pacific Ocean during the January 26, 2004, captive-carry flight. This mission was used to verify the different systems in preparation for the second launch later in the spring. (NASA photo EC04-0029-44.)

The B-52B crew for the second X-43A launch. From left to right: John Pomroy (Orbital/ HXLV panel operator), Gordon Fullerton (NASA/copilot), Dana Purifoy (NASA/pilot), and Dave McAllister (NASA/X-43A panel operator). The insignia on the aircraft fuselage was originally added when it launched the X-15, the only other hypersonic aircraft flown. (NASA photo EC04-0091-118.)

McAllister had started work at Dryden Flight Research Center as a co-op student in the fall of 1992, joining NASA full time in January 1996. He transferred into the Hyper-X project in November 2003, following the mishap-investigation-board investigation. His primary responsibility was to develop and deliver the flight cards, the checklists, and emergency procedures used by ground controllers. In his role as X-43A panel operator for the second launch, he was introduced to the peculiarities of flying in the B-52B.

B-52B, serial number 52-0008, was first flown in June of 1955, making it not quite half as old as heavier-than-air flight itself. Ironically, it was not only the oldest B-52 still flying but also had the lowest number of flight hours of any B-52 aircraft still flying—just 2443.8 hours when it was retired at the end of the X-43A program. McAllister's position in the plane was in the lower area, below and behind the cockpit where the pilot, copilot, and HXLV panel operator were seated. His work area was about the size of a large closet. McAllister commented that, "there were no windows and your only connection to the outside world is your radio and [the X-43A panel] video monitor."

The launch aircraft's environmental control system was a very old and quirky one. On the January 2004 captive-carry flight, McAllister recalled, it was initially too cold in his position. Then, during takeoff, "I was engulfed by a significant amount of water vapor that lasted for probably about 5 minutes. It didn't make it [so] I couldn't see the monitor or anything like that, but certainly filled my lap and the floor around me with water vapor." He called Purifoy and Fullerton to warn them that condensation had formed on the equipment. ("Back seaters" learned not to complain about the temperature to the pilots.) The pilots replied that they were a little cold, and they turned the heat up a little. By the time the B-52B had crossed the coastline, McAllister could see smoke was now coming from the vent and had to pull his feet back as the air was too hot.[4]

A pair of two-seat F-18s served as chase planes for the second X-43A launch. NASA research pilot Frank Batteas and Dryden still photographer Jim Ross were in F-18 NASA 852, while pilot James Smolka and Dryden videographer Lori Losey were in F-18 NASA 846. Jim Ross recalled the mood on the eve of Flight 2:

> I was with Frank Batteas on the second one. I think there was a lot of tension for the whole program in general just because we weren't sure exactly what was going to happen. So we were hoping that everything was fixed and they felt comfortable that everything was fixed. But I think there was still a little bit of the problem with the first one hanging over everyone, just waiting to see when that first drop and ignition happened whether it was going to go off without a hitch or not.[5]

Chase-plane pilots and backseaters on the January 2004 captive-carry flight. Because several of the captive-carry and launch flights occurred in the winter and fall, F-18 crew members had to wear these Mustang suits to protect them against the cold Pacific water. From left to right: Craig Bomben (NASA/pilot), Carla Thomas (Arcata/photographer), Frank Batteas (NASA/pilot), and Lori Losey (Arcata/videographer). (NASA photo ED04-0019-22.)

The B-52B took off from the Edwards main runway at 12:40 p.m. PST. Soon after the launch plane climbed into the air, it was joined by the two chase planes. The formation then turned west and headed out toward the Pacific. The Flight 2 stack consisted of the off-loaded HXLV booster with a steel aft skirt replacing the aluminum skirt to shift the stack center of gravity aft, a steel adapter, and the X-43A research vehicle. Total weight of the Flight 2 stack was about 37,537 pounds.[6]

Douglas Clark Taylor was a member of the Hyper-X project. Following his death in 2003, this memorial was placed on the side of the second HXLV. (NASA photo EC04-0087-23.)

The weight of the stack and its position under the right wing, between the fuselage and the inboard engine pylon, created balance problems during the flight to the launch point. The fact that the B-52B lacked a main tank in the inboard right wing created further difficulties. This tank had been removed for installation of the structure that held the X-15 pylon. The result was that the aircraft had two main tanks in the left wing but only one in the right wing.

To keep the heavily loaded and lopsided aircraft in proper balance, a center-of-gravity plan was made. Normally, a pilot dealt only with the fore and aft center of gravity of his aircraft, to ensure that it did not move outside allowable limits. With the B-52B, the lateral center of gravity also had to be considered when carrying an experiment as heavy as the Hyper-X stack. To keep track of the two shifting centers of gravity, the crew carried a laptop computer running an Excel spreadsheet program. The crew entered the fuel quantities for each of the tanks, and the program automatically calculated both the fore and aft and lateral centers of gravity.[7]

When the B-52B took off from Edwards, most of the fuel was in the two left main tanks, to balance the weight of the stack for taxi and takeoff. This fuel had to be transferred to the right wing tank for launch, however. If the lateral center of gravity remained in this configuration, when the stack was released from under the right wing the B-52B would suddenly be 37,537 pounds heavy on its left wing. To partially balance the change in the lateral center of gravity, some fuel had to be pumped into the right wing. This added fuel would result in the left wing being only about half-a-rocket heavy when the stack was launched. Balancing the aircraft in this manner also caused the B-52B to gently roll to the left (toward the heavy wing). This resulted in a separation maneuver that opened the lateral distance between the airplane and the HXLV at ignition.

Fullerton transferred the fuel to the right outboard tank during the climbout to rebalance the B-52B for launch. At this point, however, he realized there was a problem. Fullerton recalled later:

> I was trying to get fuel transferred over there to make that right wing heavier and it just wasn't getting there. The fuel system is controlled by the co-pilot, and I had a transfer going [but] it wasn't going at the rate I thought it ought to be and in fact we [were] losing quantity rather than gaining quantity on the right outboard tank. Part of that, I think, was because of the slow speed and the high engine setting for a long period of time.
>
> We had a flakey valve out there, so I'm pretty sure that one of the valves that allowed fuel transfer wasn't open ...there's no direct feedback whether it's open or closed. We found, due to the engine wiring or the engine switches, it would sometimes open and sometimes it wouldn't. It was probably closed when it should have been opened. And so there are low-level lights in the main tanks, yellow lights that come on when you're

down to 4000 pounds, and by golly we had a low-level light on that right main tank. That's not good. That means turn around and get on the ground before things get worse. And I'd call the problem out on the radio. [Gary] Beard, [a B-52 avionics technician] mentioned another route for fuel that was passed along by ground control, which I was doing about the same time they suggested it, and that got it going. It went a different path and we got fuel in there and we got the yellow lights out and we decided to keep going.[8]

This was not the only in-flight problem. Batteas and Ross, in F-18 NASA 852, experienced a difficulty that threatened the still photography. Ross recalled later:

About 45 minutes prior to launch I had icing happen on the [canopy] side I needed to shoot out of, and I was [hoping] that it would fix itself. Frank tried to turn the heat up as high as he could and it didn't seem to be helping so I ended up having to try and chip ice away [for] the rest of the flight. And it never did go away, so I just kept trying to clear a spot I could shoot out of. I did that up to about fifteen seconds before the drop and then just kind of had to go with it from there and get a focus and then just wait.[9]

Flight controllers at their stations in the Gold Room. Visible in the photo, taken two days before the second X-43A's captive carry flight in January 2004, are front to back: Tony Kawano (range safety officer), Brad Neal (mission controller), and Griffin Corpening (test conductor). (NASA photo ED04-0019-10.)

A group of NASA and contractor personnel watch Flight 2 from a control room. Front row, left to right: Randy Voland (NASA Langley, Propulsion); Craig Christy (Boeing); Dave Reubush, (NASA Hyper-X deputy program manager); and Vince Rausch, (NASA Hyper-X program manager). Back row, left to right: Bill Talley (DCI); Pat Stoliker [NASA Dryden director (acting) of research engineering]; John Martin (NASA Langley Guidance and Control); and Dave Bose (AMA). (NASA photo EC04-0095-21.)

At the 9-minute mark, the countdown entered its final phase. Controllers in Dryden's Gold Room ran through final checks. The B-52B was heading toward the launch box, at an altitude of 40,000 feet and a speed of Mach 0.8. The Point Mugu range crew was ready, and the pair of P-3 tracking aircraft was in position. As with the first attempt, a large number of reporters and VIPs were on hand at Dryden. CNN was covering the mission live. The press watched the live video feed in the cafeteria. In offices at Dryden, personnel watched the events unfold on CNN.

Spectators in the Dryden cafeteria watch the onboard video as Flight 2 nears the launch point. (NASA photo ED04-0090-7.)

"Launch, launch, launch." The HXLV falls away from the B-52B on Flight 2. (NASA photo EC04-0092-28.)

At 1:55 p.m. PST, the B-52B's onboard cameras showed the X-43A's wings and rudders being tested. The fin actuation system's batteries were activated soon after; because of their limited lifetime, the launch would now either be made on time or cancelled. The fin sweeps of the HXLV were performed at 1:58:30 p.m. PST. The stack could be seen to shake on the pylon as the fins moved. The seconds were ticking away. The video F-18 chase plane was about 2000 feet from the B-52B—twice that of the first launch. James Smolka had flown the still photo F-18 on the first launch, when the out-of-control HXLV flew toward his aircraft. The increased distance made videographer Losey's task of keeping the image centered more difficult. Her camera weighed 8 pounds—the limit that flight safety would allow. Losey said later that she was ready for anything this time.[10]

McAllister recalled: "we were so well rehearsed that when I got down to 1 minute prior to launch, time kind of slowed down for me instead of compressing or speeding up."[11] The clock ran down to zero, and in the Gold Room mission controller Brad Neal called out, "launch, launch, launch."

FASTEST AIRPLANE IN THE WORLD

With a sharp blow that the crew could feel reverberating through the B-52B's structure, the pylon hooks released at 1:59:58 p.m. PST, and the stack fell free. McAllister recalled, "when the hook is released, you're releasing a lot of energy so there is a loud bang. You get this vibration through

Ignition of the HXLV about 5 seconds after launch. Within a few seconds it was supersonic, and under a minute and a half later the stack reached nearly Mach 7. (NASA photo EC04-0092-32.)

the airplane. It's like a single-hit vibration. You can feel that vibration for maybe a half a second."[12]

The B-52B banked to the left, opening the distance between it and the booster. The stack began to roll as it fell, reaching a higher-than-expected angle of about 30 degrees. At 1 second after release, the booster control system was enabled, and the vehicle immediately stabilized. The Hyper-X launch vehicle ignited 5 seconds after release and began to accelerate. This was followed by the call of "supersonic." The only sign of the HXLV exceeding Mach 1 was a wing rocking, which had been seen in previous Pegasus launches. The autopilot corrected for this, and the rocking was quickly damped out.[13]

The HXLV pitched up into its climb, pulling about 1.9 *g*s, and the B-52B crew saw the booster, though they could not see or hear the ignition. Fullerton commented: "your first clue that its working is when it comes flying out in front of you. The big surprise on Pegasus was seeing how steeply it was going out. It looked like it was vertical."[14]

At the same time, the video F-18 chase plane made its slow, 20-degree turn away from the booster's flight path. The HXLV and its long smoke trail were centered in the viewfinder, without the canopy frame interfering with the shot. The booster dwindled in size as it accelerated away from the chase planes. Optical tracking was now taken over by a modified Grumman G-III business jet called the "HALO-II." This U.S. Army aircraft had been fitted with a package of visible light and infrared cameras mounted in a faring on the top of the fuselage.[15]

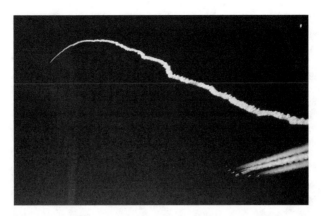

The B-52B and the smoke trail from the HXLV against a pure blue sky. The HXLV flight path was initially a steep climb, followed by a pitch down into level flight at a nearly 100,000-foot altitude. (NASA photo EC04-0092-39.)

The stack's maximum dynamic pressure (max q) occurred about L +40 seconds. This was about 1600 pounds per square foot at a speed of about Mach 3.5. The adapter fluid systems started 48 seconds after the launch, spraying a water–glycol mix on the scramjet's inlet for cooling. The regulator failure on the first flight did not reoccur. At about L +52 seconds, the HXLV began a pushover maneuver to a negative angle of attack, putting maximum loading on the HXLV wing during ascent.

As the rocket motor neared burnout, about 90 seconds after launch, the HXLV systems calculated the optimum separation time, to minimize errors in Mach number, dynamic pressure, and flight-path angle, and then sent the "ready to separate" signal to the X-43A flight management unit (FMU).[16]

At L +93.44 seconds the HXLV had reached the predetermined separation conditions. The stack was traveling at a velocity of Mach 6.95 and an altitude of 94,069 feet. Dynamic pressure was 1024 psf, slightly less than the target value, with the flight-path elevation, angle of attack, and sideslip within desired limits.[17] The X-43A's FMU issued the separation command at L +93.46 seconds; the HXLV received it, and the explosive bolts fired. The ejector pistons fired simultaneously, generating very little lateral-directional error. As the X-43A was pushed away from the HXLV, it experienced transience effects that were within predicted values.

The two adapter cameras transmitted video of the separation. Run at normal speed, the video seemed to be only static and snow, like a black-and-white 1950s television screen. When slowed, however, the images showed the X-43A separating smoothly from the adapter and then rapidly becoming smaller as it moved away from the HXLV. There had been no recontact, and the research vehicle flew rock steady.

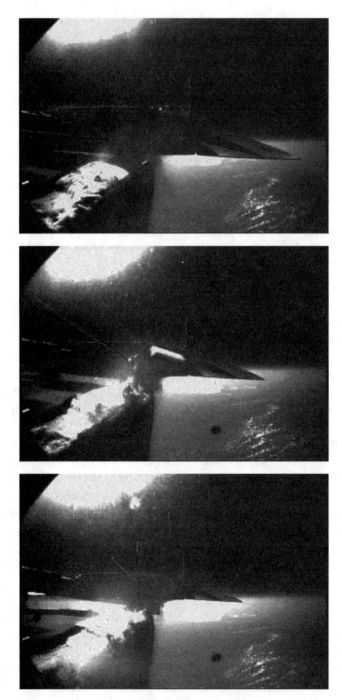

Images from the onboard camera showing the separation of the second X-43A from the adaptor. The separation was considered to be among the most difficult elements in the mission profile and was subject to extensive computer analysis and ground tests. In the end, the separation went smoothly. (NASA photos.)

The next step was for the X-43A to stabilize on the correct angle of attack for the scramjet test. This had to take place within a 2.5-second interval, and Monte Carlo analysis had indicated it would take just over 0.5 seconds. But now a problem arose. The X-43A took longer than expected to stabilize. The vehicle's angle of attack continued to decrease after separation for nearly a half-second before beginning to slowly increase. At 0.75 seconds after separation, the angle of attack was outside the worst-case Monte Carlo predictions. It was not until about two seconds after separation that the angle of attack was within acceptable parameters. The vehicle arrived at the nominal angle of attack just within the 2.5-second interval, creating proper conditions for the scramjet test to begin.[18]

The scramjet cowl door opened as programmed, allowing air to flow through the engine. Preflight Monte Carlo analysis had predicted that this would cause a nose-down transient. What actually occurred, however, was a nose-up motion that was outside the predictions. The control system corrected the transient within one and one-half seconds.[19]

Drag had slowed the X-43A, but it maintained a velocity of about 7000 feet per second—or about 1.3 miles/second. The vehicle bow shock and the oblique shock waves sent up by the lower fuselage inlet ramp slowed the airflow, reducing it to about 3000 feet per second through the 30-inch-long scramjet. Measurements were made within the engine to determine the efficiency of the pressure recovery of the ramp and engine inlet. This fuel-off tare pressure data would be compared to those of the preflight wind-tunnel tests and calculated predictions.

After about 5 seconds, the engine fueling sequence began. Gaseous hydrogen fuel was injected into the combustion chamber along with silane. When the silane came in contact with oxygen, the silane/hydrogen/air mixture in the scramjet ignited immediately. Once the combustion was self-sustaining, the silane shut off, and the hydrogen flow increased.

The hydrogen and oxygen burned, producing water in the form of steam. Combustion had to be sustained and the position of the engine's internal shock waves maintained. The flame-front's position in the engine had to be maintained in a 3000-feet-per-second airflow (in a space only 30 inches long). If the shock wave's position moved forward, an "unstart" followed; if combustion became unstable, then the engine would no longer develop thrust.

The complete process—airflow into the engine, final compression of the air, injection of the hydrogen gas and silane, the ignition and stable combustion, and finally the expanding of hot exhaust gases out the nozzle to produce thrust—all had to occur within about 0.001 of a second.[20]

Down below, the HALO II aircraft's infrared camera recorded the burnout, separation, and scramjet ignition. The HXLV appeared as a glowing ball with a long tail. At the separation, a small dot appeared ahead of the booster. Then a long, thin tail was visible as the scramjet engine burn began. The HXLV, its booster burned out and guidance control lost, safely fell below and behind the X-43A vehicle. The issue of separation, which was a major concern for so long had passed without incident.[21]

Telemetry data showed the vehicle's speed had rapidly increased once combustion began. This continued for most of the 10-second burn, before acceleration began to trail off. It was not until the final moments of the engine burn that the acceleration became less than the vehicle's drag, and its speed began to slow.

For the first time ever, the engine test had successfully demonstrated that a scramjet could not only work in flight, but actually produce positive acceleration.[22]

The peak speed during the scramjet-powered phase was calculated to be Mach 6.83, making the X-43A the fastest airbreathing aircraft ever to fly. During the 10-second burn, the X-43A traveled 15 miles.[23] The previous airbreathing record holder was an SR-71 that reached Mach 3.32 during a 1976 flight. The X-43A flight represented a speed increase of Mach 3.51, more than doubling the previous record.

Following the engine burn, the cowl door remained open to perform the four-second postexperiment tare. As with the preburn tare, pressure data were gathered to compare with ground-test results. The data gathering was followed by a cowl-open parameter identification maneuver (PID) lasting 17 seconds. These were simultaneous control surface sweeps. The vehicle's angle of attack was increased and decreased several times by differing amounts. The data from the PID maneuvers would later be analyzed to determine the X-43A's hypersonic stability and control characteristics. With the PID maneuvers complete, the cowl closed, and the Hyper-X program's primary research objectives were complete.

The vehicle now began the flight's secondary research phase. This involved gathering hypersonic flight data during the glide to impact in the Pacific Ocean. The X-43A's angle of attack increased to begin the tests. This recovery maneuver halted the increased temperatures and dynamic pressure the vehicle had been experiencing. As before, a surprise resulted. The X-43A's angle of attack showed small-amplitude oscillations at a 0.65-Hz frequency during the maneuver. No preflight predictions had indicated such oscillations would occur.[24]

After the recovery maneuver was completed, the X-43A began a steep descent. As the vehicle rapidly slowed, test maneuvers were made at Mach 5, 4, 3, and 2. In addition to PIDs, the vehicle made frequency sweeps—small but rapid control surface sweeps that changed the angle of attack—and pushover, pull-up (POPU) maneuvers, which involved slowly raising and then lowering the angle of attack before it returned to the original value. The amplitude of a POPU was larger than that of a parameter identification maneuver, but took longer and involved only a single cycle.[25]

This long descent path took the X-43A beyond the horizon of the Point Mugu and Vandenberg ground tracking stations. When ground contact with the X-43A was lost, airborne P-3 aircraft acted as receiving stations. Data were received by the P-3 and recorded onboard. The Vandenberg data were sent first to Point Mugu and then to Dryden, in near-real time. The P-3s provided the only means of retrieving data during aerodynamic tests after the scramjet burn. The parameter identification maneuvers were successfully completed, and the data collected.

At about 492 seconds after separation, with the maneuvers completed, the X-43A began its approach mode. The rate and angle of descent were reduced, and the vehicle headed toward the preplanned impact area. The P-3 was able to receive data continuously. The last data showed the vehicle at an altitude of 41.86 feet and flying at a speed of Mach 0.92. It then plunged into the Pacific Ocean about 442 nautical miles from the launch point, within the planned impact area. Total time from separation to impact was 508 seconds.[26] Flight 2 was now over.

The problems that had beset Batteas and Ross before the launch continued afterward. But they had been able to successfully photograph the launch from their F-18. Ross recalled that the ice on the canopy "seemed to come back pretty quickly but most of the images came out all right." He continued:

Frank was going to try and get a shot where the smoke trail and the bomber [were] in the same shot. So when it dropped, I was kind of trying to give him direction because we were not quite as low and the rocket fell below us and I couldn't quite see it, and then he wasn't responding back to me.

It turned out that his mike on his mask was busted. I said, "You can't talk to anyone, right?" and he goes, "No." And I said, "Do you need me to talk?" and he gave me a big head nod. Well, we're [the photographers and videographers] not really that up to snuff on radios and things. So I got information from him on how to work the radio. I called Jim Smolka and told him that we were having a problem. And he told me that I'd probably have to make the radio calls and I said that I probably needed some direction with that because I've never done that before.

So I called Dana [Purifoy] in the bomber and told him that we had a situation and Dana said he heard the conversation between Jim and I and that he was just going to have us fly on their wing and they would give calls for us all the way back. So we just did that all the way back, and then I had to make the call for the tower for landing and clear the taxiway. It all worked out.[27]

After the Flight

Griff Corpening was in the Gold Room and recalled the emotional experience of the launch:

> We just went through the flight cards, one after another, and launched. This time, though, once we saw motor ignition, everybody just kept watching, ticking the events off as we went. And I was just hearing them going along, motor ignition .... We passed transonic. Because we were at a higher altitude when we launched, we went through transonic very quickly. It seemed like within seconds I heard Mike Pudoka say, "We're supersonic," which was past the problem area. And then we were at Mach 3, and the cooling water came on. Everything was looking good. We started into the negative angle of attack. Everything still looking good. Mike [Pudoka] was making regular announcements that all systems on the launch vehicle were nominal. The trajectory [was] on track.
>
> And then we were through the boost, motor burnout. "Ready to sep[arate]. Sep." And that's when I was holding my breath. First of all I heard that the fuel was on. So I thought, well, okay, at least those systems are working. And then I heard Cathy Bahm, the lead GNC [guidance, navigation, and control] engineer, say, "The RV is stable." And I thought, "My gosh! We might do this," because the fuel was on, and the research vehicle was flying pointy-end forward. And I heard, "Fuel off." And, "Cowl open PID," which was our parameter identification maneuver. "Cowl closed." And we're still flying, and it was absolutely astounding.
>
> During the descent is when I think it finally hit me that we'd actually pulled this off. I remember going between elation and almost being overwhelmed to the point of tears that this team had pulled this off after all these years. It was just a tremendous moment.

The engineers monitoring the engine data soon reported that not only did the systems all work, but it looked like the performance of the vehicle was what had been expected.[28]

Joel Sitz, the Dryden X-43A project manager, added in a postflight statement: "Today was a grand-slam in the bottom of the twelfth. It was fun all the way to Mach 7. We separated the research vehicle from the launch vehicle, as well as separating the real from the imagined."[29]

It had been a long road—nearly three years since the loss of the first X-43A, and some four decades since the scramjet was first proposed. Linda Soden recalled later:

> Emotionally, here we are on another roller coaster. Again, it's elation; it's anxieties, it's everything all at once right now. And it was a lot of hoping, too. When the launch was made and the Pegasus came off of the B-52B, you could almost see everybody watching their watch and saying, "Okay, we've made it past 7 seconds. Everything is level; everything is straight,

looking good." When the announcement came that they had hit hypersonic speed there was a shout of joy in the control room. So separation
went smoothly, and now we're at the hypersonic speeds and the engine
has ignited. It was pure joy. Pure elation.

When ship two went off without a hitch I don't think there was a dry
eye in the control room again. That was just amazing... Because we
won.... I think the biggest emotion was relief. We've done it. We've been
through the trial of fire and we came out ahead and now we're standing
in the cool waters.[30]

When the flight data were analyzed, they showed that the mission met all
of its goals. The X-43A had successfully demonstrated an airframe-integrated
scramjet engine in actual flight at Mach 6.8. The engine performance was
within 3% of preflight predictions. The resulting thrust was sufficient to
overcome the airframe drag and provide positive acceleration, as predicted.
The scramjet test conditions also were well within preflight uncertainty
levels. During the engine burn, the vehicle flew at the correct angle of
attack. The postscramjet maneuvers, and their unexpected results, allowed
a better understanding of the vehicle's aerodynamics to be developed. The
flight data served to validate the ground design and test procedures, including
the SRGULL analytical design method for the scramjet. The use of engine
module test techniques and the secondary effects of test gas also were
proven.[31]

The major concern during development had been with the separation
maneuver. The difficulties in predicting the actual separation conditions

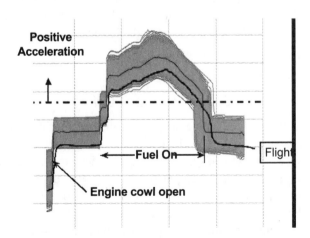

The scramjet engine burn data from the second X-43A flight. The black line is the thrust
level, while the shaded area is the range of predicted thrust. The scramjet successfully
generated more thrust than the vehicle's drag at Mach 7, thus producing a positive
acceleration. (NASA diagram.)

were caused by uncertainties in the total impulse of the solid rocket, atmo-spheric variations, winds, and the limited flight data available for the HXLV airframe. The seeming ease of the actual maneuver came as a result of exten-sive preflight analysis. This included development of high-fidelity models of the inertial navigation system and of the structural, thermal, and rocket motor ballistics during initial development efforts, and additional work undertaken after the failure of the first launch, which included the fin-actuation-system nonlinear model and revised aerodynamic models.

Other efforts included extensive post-Flight 1 wind-tunnel testing to flesh out a sparse data matrix. Navier–Stokes computational-fluid-dynamics studies of vehicle aerodynamics also were made. Roll disturbance models were developed to test the ability of the autopilot to operate under extreme flight conditions. Rotary derivatives, which were very difficult to obtain from wind-tunnel data, were parametrically varied to determine the results of different derivations from the flight data.

In addition, thermal models were successfully developed by taking the Monte Carlo results, identifying the worst-case design reference mission and then incorporating safety factors into the analysis. This was critical in development of a thermal-protection-system (TPS) design for the HXLV. The composite Pegasus structure was unable to withstand significant local heating or local failure of the TPS. The gap heating of the fins was dealt with through additional modeling and verification efforts. The result was that the actual flight conditions proved quite benign compared to the worse-case analysis and testing.[32]

Beyond showing that the Pegasus-derived HXLV was a workable booster, Flight 2's success also proved nonsymmetrical vehicle designs to be practical. These included Hyper-X-derived test vehicles, on up to scramjet-powered first-stage vehicles either carrying expendable rocket upper stages or reusable lifting vehicle second-stage designs.

SIGNIFICANCE OF FLIGHT 2

Beyond the "high fives" and elation that followed Flight 2's success, it was more than the story of how a dedicated team overcame terrible setbacks. Flight 2's success also meant more than just a new speed record. Its impor-tance was not strictly the length of the flight or the distance covered. The engine's burn time was measured in seconds, and the distance the X-43A traveled under power could be covered by a car in a few minutes.

What was important about Flight 2 was much more—and far simpler. It had been four decades since the idea of the scramjet engine first appeared. Despite all of the efforts made during that time, despite all of the high hopes and great potential, all of the arm waving and salesmanship, all of the skepti-cism, all of the proposals made and rejected over the years and all that had been learned, despite all of the calculations and ground tests and simulations, one single important fact set Flight 2 apart. Without it, all of the work of the past four decades did not matter. With it, however, all things scramjet now became possible. The importance of Flight 2 was that it ultimately added the last important component of the hypersonic picture.

On Flight 2, a scramjet engine actually *worked*.

NOTES

[1] Lin, Yohan, interview, Aug. 12, 2005, NASA Dryden Flight Research Center History Office, pp. 27, 28.

[2] Corpening, Griff, history interview, Dec. 20, 2004, NASA Dryden Flight Research Center History Office, p. 57.

[3] *Aerospace Projects*, Feb. 6, 2004, NASA Dryden Flight Research Center History Office, pp. 2, 3.

[4] McAllister, Dave, interview, March 2, 2005, NASA Dryden Flight Research Center History Office, pp. 6–11.

[5] Ross, Jim, interview, Aug. 24, 2005, NASA Dryden Flight Research Center History Office, p. 11.

[6] Joyce, Phillip J., John B. Pomroy, and Laurie Grindle, "The Hyper-X Launch Vehicle: Challenges and Design Considerations for Hypersonic Flight Testing," AIAA Paper 2005-3333, pp. 10, 11.

[7] Fullerton, Gordon, interview, Aug. 3, 2005, NASA Dryden Flight Research Center History Office, pp. 12, 13.

[8] Ibid, pp. 18, 19.

[9] Ross interview, pp. 12, 13.

[10] Losey, Lori, interview, Nov. 16, 2006.

[11] McAllister interview, p. 14.

[12] Ibid, p. 14.

[13] Joyce et al., "The Hyper-X Launch Vehicle: Challenges and Design Considerations for Hypersonic Flight Testing," pp. 11, 12.

[14] Fullerton interview, pp. 20, 22.

[15] NASA Dryden Flight Research Center Web site, http://www.dfrc.nasa.gov/Gallery/Movie/Hyper-X/HTML/EM-0015-09.html (launch video) and http://www.dfrc.nasa.gov/Gallery/Movie/Hyper-X/HTML/EM-0015-10.html (HALO II video).

[16] Joyce et al., "The Hyper-X Launch Vehicle: Challenges and Design Considerations for Hypersonic Flight Testing," pp. 11, 12, and Laurie A. Marshall, Griffin P. Corpening, and Robert Sherrill, "A Chief Engineer's View of the NASA X-43A Scramjet Flight Test," AIAA Paper 2005-3332, pp. 12, 14. Times are approximate.

[17] Bahm, Catherine, Ethan Baumann, John Martin, David Bose, Roger E. Beck, and Brian Strovers, "The X-43 Hyper-X Mach 7 Flight 2 Guidance, Navigation, and Control Overview and Flight Test Results," AIAA Paper 2005-3275, pp. 9, 10.

[18] Marshall et al., "A Chief Engineer's View of the NASA X-43A Scramjet Flight Test," pp. 12, 14.

[19] Bahm et al., "The X-43 Hyper-X Mach 7 Flight 2 Guidance, Navigation, and Control Overview and Flight Test Results," pp. 11, 12.

[20] Ibid, p. 14, and 2004 Collier Award Handout, slide 20. The airflow speeds are approximate. The combustion process of a scramjet engine is often likened to "keeping a candle lit in a hurricane." This is an imprecise analogy. The maximum winds of a hurricane are about 150 miles per hour. The airflow inside a scramjet is at supersonic speed.

[21] NASA Dryden Flight Research Center Web site, http://www.dfrc.nasa.gov/Gallery/Movie/Hyper-X/HTML/EM-0015-10.html.

[22] Marshall et al., "A Chief Engineer's View of the NASA X-43A Scramjet Flight Test," p. 15, Fig. 15, axial acceleration profile during engine test.

[23] "Air Force Rocket Laboratory X-43A Data Briefing," Dec. 9, 2005, unclassified draft version, p. 39.

[24] Marshall et al., "A Chief Engineer's View of the NASA X-43A Scramjet Flight Test," p. 15, and 2004 Collier Award Handout, slide 47.

[25] Bahm et al., "The X-43 Hyper-X Mach 7 Flight 2 Guidance, Navigation, and Control Overview and Flight Test Results," p. 15.

[26] Ibid, pp.15, 18, and Marshall et al., "A Chief Engineer's View of the NASA X-43A Scramjet Flight Test," pp. 16–19.

[27] Ross interview, pp. 13–15.

[28] Corpening history interview, pp. 58, 59.

[29] "NASA's X-43A Proves Hypersonic Scramjet Flight," March 27, 2004, Release: 04-16.

[30] Soden, Linda, history interview, Aug. 25, 2005, NASA Dryden Flight Research Center History Office, pp. 30, 31.

[31] Ferlemann, Shelly, Charles McClinton, Kenneth Rock, and Randall Voland, "Hyper-X Mach 7 Scramjet Design, Ground Test and Flight Results," AIAA/CIRA 13th International Space Planes and Hypersonic Systems and Technology Conference, Capua, Italy, May 2005, pp. 15, 21.

[32] Joyce et al., "The Hyper-X Launch Vehicle," p. 16.

Chapter 8

To the Edge of the Envelope

A ship in port is safe, but that is not what ships are for.
Sail out to sea and do new things.

Rear Admiral Grace Murray Brewster Hopper, Pioneer computer scientist, 1906–1992

By early 2004, beyond difficulties facing Hyper-X personnel after the loss of the first flight, the modifications and delays resulting from the failure, and issues such as the fin-actuation-system problem, the operating environment for the project also had changed. On February 1, 2003, the Space Shuttle *Columbia* was lost during reentry. This led to a reexamination of U.S. space activities. From this came a commitment for a long-term program to return humans to the moon and then undertake manned landings on Mars. The focus shifted away from aeronautical projects like the Hyper-X. Additionally, the project had continued longer than originally envisioned, increasing the costs. And so project managers came under pressure to complete the third flight by the end of the year.

When Flight 2's projected flight date was pushed back into 2004, project personnel realized a more aggressive checkout schedule would be needed if Flight 3 were to be made by year's end. A plan was developed for streamlining preflight testing of the Mach 10 X-43A vehicle, and certain tests were eliminated. Done away with were aircraft-in-the-loop and X-43A compliance tests, which had been successful in earlier stages of the project and had produced predictable results.

As it turned out, however, elimination of these tests proved unnecessary. The second and third X-43A vehicles had undergone simultaneous checkout and modification. Some Flight 2 tests actually had been done using Flight 3 hardware, leaving the third vehicle in an advanced stage of readiness in the spring of 2004. The ground crew also had recent experience with the checkout procedures, allowing Flight 3 checks to be completed more quickly than those for the second vehicle. These were completed so quickly that the cancelled testing could be rescheduled into the test flow. The team's experience level was so high that rescheduling the tests did not create any delays or require anything in the test procedures to be sacrificed.

Processing and analysis of Flight 2 data continued through April of 2004. The team shifted its attention at the beginning of May to the third X-43A flight. As it was imperative that the flight be completed by the end of 2004, project managers decided against incorporating the Flight 2 data analysis into the Flight 3 models programmed into the vehicle systems. This, together with planned changes to preflight testing, would save time and allow the flight software to be ready to meet the flight schedule.

Project engineers recognized that this was not an ideal approach, but there was no longer room in the schedule for incorporating the analysis into the software. The scramjet-engine test region was to be the research focus of the third flight, and so was given the highest priority. The initial schedule called for the third flight to be made in mid- to late September 2004. As a compromise, the Flight 2 data *were* used to determine modifications needed for Flight 3 and for the Monte Carlo stress cases. The immediate goal was correcting problems that had appeared during the second flight.[1]

The first of these was the inordinate amount of time the vehicle had taken to reach the correct angle of attack. This was addressed by increasing the gain on the angle-of-attack integrator. A more complicated problem was the oscillation that had occurred during the recovery maneuver; among possible causes were actuator friction and aerodynamic uncertainties. The solution was to lower the angle of attack throughout the trajectory to avoid flying the third X-43A under the same conditions as the second.[2]

The Mach 10 flight featured a different Hyper-X launch-vehicle configuration than that of the second flight. The stack did not carry additional ballast or the heavier steel aft skirt and adapter structure used on Flight 2, but it did have a full load of propellant. This resulted in a vehicle of approximately the same weight, but with its center of gravity shifted aft, causing reduced static stability and autopilot margins.

Limiting the stack's maximum angle of attack increased these margins but reduced the maximum burnout speed caused by higher drag. This, along with the added weight of the modified fin actuation system and earlier weight increases in the X-43A and adapter, meant a Mach 10 burnout speed was risky. Rather than incur this additional risk, program managers decided to accept a Mach 9.6 nominal separation speed.[3]

As the scramjet featured a single-point design, analysis was necessary to make sure it could still operate in the lower speed range. Grindle noted,

> We were looking at a separation condition of 9.6, plus or minus 0.6. And the deceleration between separation and the actual engine test in that 2½ seconds is really minimal. So basically that separation Mach is pretty much what we were thinking of for an engine Mach. So there was the potential, then, [that] it could be as low as nine and we hadn't accounted for that. So it required more work with the propulsion model. But that work was done and it worked out.[4]

Early in May 2004, a Flight 3 planning meeting was held at Orbital Science's Chandler, Arizona, facility. The final modifications and acceptance testing of fin-actuation-system hardware was on the critical path for a mid-September launch. Final control laws for both the HXLV and the X-43A were near the critical path. The schedule for the X-43A control laws was particularly tight. The control-law design had to be fully developed by the end of that week. The directional/lateral control laws were ready to be implemented into the simulations. The cowl-open propulsion increments were being added to the aero database the same week the meeting was held, whereas the cowl-closed pitch control was expected to be ready the week after.

A problem with the hardware had also appeared. During a leak and function check of the X-43A fluid system, a motorized valve failed.[5] The cause of the valve failure was traced to copper debris from corrosion in the hydrogen heat exchanger. This required a replacement unit to be fabricated by ATK General Applied Sciences Laboratory (GASL). By late May, work on a modified heat exchanger was about 70% complete. Fuel-valve bench checks were underway at Dryden Flight Research Center. Fifty pounds of tungsten ballast also was being added to the X-43A#3 at ATK GASL to shift the vehicle's center of gravity.

Software development was on schedule at this point. The X-43A Mach 10 guidance algorithm design was underway, and Dryden engineers had initiated the Monte Carlo analysis of the preliminary flight control design. Final modifications to the propulsion-system-control law model had been completed at Langley. The Mach 10 trajectory was not yet completely bounded for all transonic angle-of-attack conditions. A study for the best approach was still being conducted.[6]

As the month of June began, preparations for Flight 3 continued on schedule. ATK personnel were at Dryden to finish installing the thermal-protection-system material on the adapter and to complete the final ballast fit check. The project, meanwhile, hosted tours of the Hyper-X facility on May 27, 2004, for local community leaders and a group of Italian students.[7]

The significant issue facing the project at this point was a review by the X-43A flight control team of the preliminary software design. Late changes to the model were putting the development of the flight control laws at risk. The design was scheduled for completion by June 22. If the deadline were missed, the software schedule could not be maintained.

Another serious issue was the potential need for additional wind-tunnel testing of the HXLV 6% stack model. The wind-tunnel tests were to validate several transonic points in the model being used to develop the Mach 10 trajectory. These points had been obtained through extrapolation, rather than direct measurements. The existing wind-tunnel database originally had been obtained using a 15-degree angle of attack at Mach 0.8. Hyper-X launch-vehicle stability concerns led to a change in the Mach 10 trajectory's angle of attack to about 11 degrees. The design approach was to use larger uncertainties in the areas of extrapolation, and the wind-tunnel tests were to validate this approach.

There were positive events as well during this period. The replacement heat exchanger was delivered and installed in the X-43A. Before the fluid system could be reintegrated, however, an additional hydrogen regulator had to be delivered. It was due on Monday, June 7, at which time the system would be reintegrated for leak testing.

The Dryden *Aerospace Highlights* weekly project report for June 4, 2004 also noted, "The Hyper-X Launch Vehicle (HXLV) actuator and electronic control unit passed pre-environmental acceptance testing. The hardware will begin environmental acceptance testing today (6/4)."[8]

This was to be the last good news about the fin actuation system for a long time.

FIN ACTUATION SYSTEM, AGAIN

X-43A personnel believed they could move quickly to the third flight because preliminary work already had been accomplished during the return-to-flight effort. In particular, "one of the real confidence builders," as Paul Reukauf put it, "was that we thought we had fixed the fin actuator problem on the Mach 7 flight."[9] The powerboards for the FAS electronic control units (ECUs) were integrated, and burn-in testing began. The actuator integration was scheduled to start soon after. This preenvironmental acceptance testing had been successfully completed by the end of May. Environmental testing of the components, at high and low temperatures, began during the first week of June.[10]

The situation radically changed when two powerboards failed during the low-temperature environmental tests. The failures occurred at significantly colder temperatures than experienced during previous flights. The recovery plan called for replacing the two failed powerboards with spare units, which would be ready by mid-June. A second step involved the addition of a heater plate to the electronic control unit, so that a warmer ambient temperature would be maintained during the flight. Completion of the heater was scheduled for mid-July. Despite all of these issues, at this point a September 2004 launch still was seen as possible.[11]

The replacement fin-actuation-system hardware was delivered, but failed its initial testing on June 30. Two of the channels passed, but the third latched up. And unlike in earlier such incidents, this failure occurred at room temperature, not during the cold test cycle.[12] "Our fix," Reukauf recalled, "which we had come up with on the Mach 7 flight, obviously had not worked for the Mach 10 system."[13]

As troubleshooting continued in early July, it became clear that the Flight 3 boards had more electronic "noise" than those in the Flight 2 fin actuation system.[14] Grindle later noted that the FAS design was the same for both flights but that,

> some of the components on the board were from a different lot than the other and this lot seemed to be noisier. And so the fixes we had in place that worked fine for Flight 2 wouldn't stand up to the noise they were getting from Flight 3. So we had to basically go right back to the drawing board with another design cycle.[15]

The problem was similar to that on the second flight—the complex programmable logic devices (CPLDs) were adversely affected by electronic noise from the powerboards. This resulted in the CPLDs ceasing to process, which caused them to latch up. Even the minor differences among the individual parts were sufficient to negate the earlier fix.

As with the Flight 2 boards, the solution was to use "more of the same" of the earlier fix to reduce the electronic noise. By the third week of July, a fix had been determined, and the powerboards had successfully passed low-temperature test cycles. With the FAS problem apparently resolved, the fix was accepted by government and contractor representatives. By the end of July, the flight boards had been modified by the manufacturer and were scheduled to begin qualification testing the first week of August. However, the FAS problems meant a September flight was no longer possible. October 5 was now the earliest realistic flight date.[16]

But the new schedule was short-lived. On August 16, the electronic control unit undergoing acceptance testing suffered an anomaly. High current flow through the field effect transistors (FET) caused the powerboard to burn up, leaving it severely damaged. The cause appeared to be an ECU component failure.

The NASA/contractor team that had investigated the Flight 2 FAS problem was reassembled to examine the new anomaly. A fault tree was developed to help the team determine the root cause.

The hardware was inspected and then sent for testing. Analysis indicated that the cause was a high-current switching component failure on the rudder powerboard. Rereviews of the previous design changes, test procedures, and the component/board heritage were conducted, as were additional engineering checks of the powerboards. These showed no indications of design or testing problems. Simultaneously with the investigation, a rebuilt ECU was assembled to replace the damaged components, and additional powerboards were manufactured.

Despite an intensive analytical effort, simulations of the failure, and development testing, a root cause for the failure could not be conclusively determined. The best that the team could provide were several likely causes, and these became the basis for modifications.

Analysis indicated that the electronic noise also disrupted the complex programmable logic devices' timing of the opening and closing of the field-effect-transistor pairs. This, in turn, controlled the movement of the fin. The switching of the two pairs of FETs had overlapped. Both went on, and the high current flow shorted them out, literally melting them.

To reduce the potential for this timing error, the CPLD firmware was modified to increase deadband time between switching, providing additional margin. The gate resistance also was increased to reduce the time it took for the FETs to turn on. In addition, researchers decided to add a ground jumper wire to connect the electronic-control-unit heat sink and the powerboard, to minimize ground noise. Changes to the test procedures were made to avoid damaging the systems while providing the necessary level of stress testing.[17]

The repeated failures during the testing of the third fin actuation system indicated serious problems. Originally, engineers believed the failure mode would occur only in the event of a 2-degree change on the fin angle. This occurred only twice during the flight, one of these after separation. But engineers now realized there was the potential for a failure anytime after the FAS was activated, which happened in the last two minutes prior to drop.[18] This unknown vulnerability was present in the FAS of the second flight, but no failure occurred. About the consequence of this realization, Reukauf said, "then the question became, 'Well, since we didn't really fix the system for Mach 7, did we just get lucky at Mach 7, and can we take the risk for Mach 10 or can't we?'"[19]

The FAS problems highlight the difficulties in assessing risk in research aircraft programs. The Hyper-X program made use of existing systems, including the Pegasus booster and its associated flight models. To meet the demands of the X-43A mission profile, however, these existing systems had to be modified. And modifications inevitably mean some loss of certainty, if not increased risk.

Lin summed up the prospects: "Whenever you tweak a system that's already working you're always asking for problems, because the system is balanced and you upset that balance, you introduce elements in there that were never there or intended, unknowns will come out, or new problems will arrive."[20]

When the heritage of the existing systems is lost, program engineers, managers, and contractors can no longer rely on the reliability data of the production systems, as the products have become one-of-a-kind units. As a result, the revised systems may have to undergo extensive development work, analysis, and checkout procedures. And the work must be allowed for in both the program's schedule and budget.

Yet even after all of the analysis was complete, no one was 100% certain they knew what was causing the problems. The assurances that X-43A personnel could provide to the different review panels were not conclusive. The latch-up was caused by the different sensitivities of lot variations among components. By careful selection of components, engineers were confident that the fin actuation system would work in flight for the approximately 90 seconds required. Dryden X-43A project manager Joel Sitz later admitted that though this had worked, it was not an elegant way to deal with the issue.

The confidence that X-43A engineers had in prospects for Flight 3's success was based on a relative certainty that they could reproduce the failure conditions, on their ability to show that the FAS would not experience these conditions during ascent, that no failure had occurred during normal flight conditions, and that there was an adequate margin for uncertainty. The modified fin sweep procedures before launch would give a measure of assurance that the FAS was operating properly. They also knew that the FAS for the second and third flights had been tested nearly 1000 times each under high-stress conditions. The large number of tests indicated that predictions for Flight 3's success were valid. But at the same time, the X-43A team had doubts about the FAS' reliability.[21]

Hard-pressed to find a better explanation for the FAS problems, Corpening dryly noted: "At one point I think we were having things go wrong so much that the only thing we could attribute it to was that at that time Mars was as close to the Earth as it had been in thousands of years. We figured it was the influence of Mars."[22]

Acceptance testing of the rebuilt electronic control unit began in mid-September. The delay caused by the failure was estimated at the time to be three weeks, with a late-October launch still a possibility and an early November date as a backup.[23] One-hundred-hour burn-in tests of the rebuilt ECU were completed on September 22, with all three channels passing successfully. Another month was required to complete FAS acceptance testing, and all of the flight hardware was then delivered to Dryden.[24] Although the FAS had, at last, successfully passed its tests, the launch had been delayed almost two months.

Some team members felt it might have been better to develop a new FAS design, but there was neither the time nor the money available for such an effort. Even if doing so had been possible, moreover, there were no guarantees a new system would be more reliable.

And the FAS was not the team's only concern during preparations for the third flight. On June 30, representatives from Boeing and MER (manufacturer of the carbon–carbon material that coated the leading edges) were at Dryden for a fit check of the leading edges. Although able to withstand both the heating and the 1000-pounds-per-square-foot (psf) dynamic pressure experienced during the ascent and scramjet test, the material was relatively fragile.

During the fit check, technicians discovered the left-side leading-edge chine had a delamination. The carbon–carbon chine was not flyable in this condition and could not be repaired. The incident could have eliminated any possibility of meeting the flight schedule. The manufacturing process for the carbon–carbon components involved extensive machining and heat-treating, and there was not enough time to produce a replacement from scratch.

Side view of the X-43A #3 scramjet. Although only 30 inches long, the engine was able to produce enough thrust to maintain the velocity of the 3000-pound X-43A against a dynamic pressure of some 1000 pounds per square foot. (NASA photo EC04-0285-55.)

There was, however, a spare billet that already had been through some of the heat-treatment cycles. This allowed fabrication of a replacement chine to be completed without interfering with the schedule. By mid-August, the work had been finished, and fit checks of the carbon-carbon leading edges had been successfully completed.[25]

A problem that took longer to analyze and correct was the X-43A left-rudder/wing contact incident, which had occurred during a wing trim operation in mid-June. The test had been scheduled for the day following the incident, but personnel conducting the test were asked to do it early. As part of the test, the vehicle's left rudder was moved, striking the left wing in the process. This incident had the potential of damaging the rudder shaft and causing in-flight control problems.[26]

A multipronged effort was launched to clear the rudder for flight. Test procedures to electrically and mechanically check the rudder were reviewed. Calculations of the loads the rudder experienced during the incident were made using computational and finite element models, and the structural integrated product team (IPT) performed analysis to determine the material strains on the rudder. By the middle of July, a risk analysis was being developed.[27]

Based on that analysis, project engineers concluded that the rudder had not been damaged to the point that the flight would be in danger of failing. The actions needed to recover from the rudder/wing contact incident were presented to a joint Dryden and Langley Flight Readiness Review Board on August 10 and to the joint Airworthiness and Flight Safety Review Board the following day. The boards accepted the recommendation that the left rudder was acceptable for flight, and the issue was closed.[28]

Beyond mishaps such as these, Flight 3 also faced the uncertainties of Mach 10 scramjet operations. Additionally, higher temperatures on both the Hyper-X launch vehicle and the X-43A during launch and flight meant that the margins for the thermal protection system were smaller than those for the Mach 7 flight.

The B-52B had become another worry. This became apparent on the September 7, 2004 captive-carry flight. The X-43A preflight crew had worked through the Labor Day weekend to get both the B-52B and the stack ready for the test, which would take place on Tuesday after the holiday. The attempt ended in a ground abort because of a leak in the #2 hydraulic pack. This device used high-pressure bleed air to spin a turbine to generate pressure in the aircraft's hydraulic system. There were 10 hydraulic packs on the B-52B used to operate the aircraft's hydraulic systems. Each was about 3 feet long and 18 inches in diameter.

A second attempt was made the following day, and initially everything seemed to be going well. But when the B-52B reached its takeoff position, the #4 hydraulic pack was discovered to be leaking fluid at a higher-than-acceptable rate. This forced a second ground abort in as many days. The captive-carry flight was postponed, and work began on repairing the hydraulic packs. By mid-September the #4 pack had been successfully bench checked and reinstalled on the aircraft. The #2 pack was awaiting the bench-check results. Once positive results were confirmed, it was rein-stalled. After both packs were in the aircraft, the hydraulic system could be rechecked.[29]

The captive-carry flight was rescheduled for Monday, September 27. To ready the flight, B-52B and X-43A ground crews had to work 12-hour shifts over the preceding weekend to get both vehicles ready. During the preparations, yet another leak was discovered, and the #1 hydraulic pack had to be replaced before the flight.

After all of the problems, the September 27 captive-carry flight went off smoothly. The only major issue to arise from the flight was that the HXLV global positioning system did not realign after the power transfer on the B-52B. A team was organized to examine options for addressing the bad alignment. These included procedural changes and addition of a battery backup to the GPS antenna system. Adding the backup would ensure that the antenna inputs were never unpowered. While the installation was underway, the primary work done to the B-52B was directed toward completing the postflight checks and performing general aircraft maintenance.[30]

Finally, there was X-43A #3's "personality." Lin noted that "vehicle three was by far the most difficult vehicle to test. It behaved as if saying, 'I don't want to go, you're not going to make me go.'"[31]

TECH BRIEF

The X-43A technical briefing, scheduled for October 28, 2004, was the remaining major milestone on the road to Flight 3. After that, all of the remaining discrepancy reports, system test reports, and configuration change requests would have to be completed, closed, approved, or rejected, the emergency procedures training had to be completed, and other preparations finished.

The meeting began at 8:30 a.m. with Marta Bohn-Meyer, Dryden's chief engineer, presiding. This was a formal examination of the project's status. Bohn-Meyer asked questions of each of the engineers making the presentations on each aspect of Flight 3 and each of the issues. Her questions were detailed and probing. Each engineer had to be prepared, know the problems, and show that the problems had been corrected. Lin said later,

> She's trying to bring the best out of us. The reason why she's doing that is she's trying to bring our engineering reasoning and our assumptions to the floor so we understand what we're saying and believe ourselves, that this is the correct solution to the problem. And so in a way, that's her way of making sure that we are confident in the solution that we've arrived at.[32]

Over the next three hours each of the issues was tackled. With Flight 3, the engineers hoped that the vehicle would accelerate under the thrust of the scramjet, even though it would be near its maximum design speed. They also hoped to get data all of the way to splashdown in the Pacific. It might not be possible for the P-3 to receive data down to the splash, the engineers warned, as its position had been moved closer to the coast to provide backup separation and engine burn data. This meant that the X-43A could go beyond the P-3's radio horizon before splashdown occurred.

The tech brief then began addressing captive-carry flight issues. During the flight, an oxygen sensor reading had shown erroneous data indicating a 1.5% oxygen concentration in the vehicle. It was replaced after the flight. Another problem was a display lockup in the control room during the first in-flight bit check. A work around and new procedures were developed, to the satisfaction of the project.

An issue stemming from the captive-carry flight was that the air-conditioning system cooling the avionics had been turned off when pilots arrived at the aircraft. Because of the length of time before takeoff, during which the cooling system was off, the temperature in one avionics box had redlined. It had cooled off by the time the B-52B reached the launch point, but engineers discussed whether the air-conditioning disconnect should be made at the direction of the ground controller. There was also an issue with the HXLV's inertial-measurement-unit gyro bias exceeding permitted limits during the flight out. There were also the various safety requirements for the Navy range.

Overshadowing all of these was the issue on all of the participants' minds: the fin actuation system. The actuators had been run to their specific torque. They then were delivered, aligned, and checked out with no problems arising. Mission simulations and step functions were checked and found to be correct. The FAS heater also worked properly. But that still left uneasiness among the project members.

Bohn-Meyer presided over the tech brief, but she was not the only person who would question the speakers; other engineers attending the session raised questions as well. One asked whether, if a mission constraint were waived and a failure should occur, could the thought process that went into making that decision be reconstructed afterwards, during the investigation? Another noted that the launch card listed a launch speed of 240 knots indicated air speed but the trajectory simulation called for 255 knots. He asked whether a check of the flight cards, simulations, and other materials had been made to ensure that all values were consistent.

The issue of inconsistency in documentation was brought up. Two issues closed with discrepancy reports, whereas a different procedure was used to close another issue. The B-52B hydrogen and silane pressure measurements were unreliable, one engineer noted, but these measurements were being displayed on control-room monitors. Separate measurements of the pressures were available. He questioned why the bad data were being displayed, and the possible result that in an emergency, a controller might mistakenly look at the bad rather than good data.

Unlike the first and second flights, Flight 3 would take place on a weekday. This meant tighter Federal Aviation Administration limitations on flying through controlled airspace. On the other hand, because the Air Force's flight testing of the F-22 was winding down, the difficulties over range availability, frequency allocations, and other issues that the first and second flights had experienced were eased. Regarding the captive-carry open items status, all of the open discrepancy reports had to be closed in time for the crew brief. The meeting concluded with discussion of the issues brought up during the tech brief. These include the backup controllers being brought in at the last minute.[33]

After the official tech brief ended, an informal meeting took place around the table to discuss the outstanding concerns related to the fin-actuation-system issue. A wide range of opinions were presented. The worst-case estimate gave a probability of 80 to 90% that Flight 3 would be successful. One engineer noted that the problem he was having was the difference between the calculated/estimates of success vs a gut feeling.

Another engineer noted that the Flight 1 failure had reinforced for him the reality that unknowns existed, though enumerating them was virtually impossible. The problem, he felt, was giving a qualitative probability that actually meant something. Even if the probability of success were just 50/50, he went on to say, he still would vote in favor of a launch. But what he felt most worrisome was that they were unable to give project managers an accurate risk-level assessment. A NASA engineer felt that the amount of testing conducted had been inadequate. A contractor engineer responded to that concern by saying that he felt everything possible had been done.[34]

2004 had been an intense year. The X-43A team had been working almost constantly including weekends and holidays. Managers, in fact, were worried that the team had been working too hard. Grindle recalled: "These people, when presented with the option of working a three-day weekend vs never see anything come of it all—they'll work that weekend every time." Another factor was that the project faced a threat of cancellation if the third flight were not completed by the end of the year.[35]

As October became November, there was a change in the mood of the team. The FAS still represented a threat, but the number of unresolved items was growing smaller. There was a sense that the team was nearing the end of its struggles. In terms of paperwork, the engineering review board and configuration control board meetings held during the final weeks before launch still had many discrepancy reports, system trouble reports, and configuration change requests (CCRS) to approve. Most were quickly closed or approved. Others only required signatures, although a few required additional analysis or testing. The work was done in short order. In one meeting, 22 items were dealt with in just over a half-hour.

There was even time for humor. Item CCR-824, which dealt with timeline documents, was approved at the November 2 configuration control board meeting. A comment was made, however, that the word "research" in the document was missing an "h."[36]

At the time of the tech brief, the third X-43A launch was scheduled for November 9. This was delayed to allow a Pegasus satellite launch from Vandenberg using Orbital Science's L1011 aircraft to leapfrog ahead of the X-43A mission. Ironically, that the L1011 launch was then itself postponed because of satellite and booster issues.[34]

The Mach 10 flight had much less margin for error, in terms of heating, system operation, and scramjet performance. It would as the saying goes, "push the envelope." This cliché is often used without realizing its real meaning. Admiral Rick Hunter, a U.S. Navy pilot, once observed that the lower-left corner of a letter envelope represents zero altitude/zero airspeed, with the top right corner of the envelope representing the vehicle's maximum altitude/maximum airspeed. Hunter noted that this is the corner a pilot pushes when he pushes the envelope. "What everybody tries not to dwell on," Hunter added, "is that that's where the postage gets canceled, too."[38]

Flight 3 was finally scheduled for Monday, November 15, 2004.

A LONG DAY

The night was pitch black on the drive to Edwards Air Force Base. Jupiter was high in the eastern sky. Lower down was Venus, the brightest object in the night sky. The pilots, ground crew, control-room personnel, and other participants assembled in Dryden's large mezzanine conference room in Building 4800 at 6:00 a.m. for the crew brief.

The first agenda item was open technical issues. Among these was the removal of the protective blankets on the Hyper-X launch vehicle. Only one P-3 was available that morning. A KC-135 aircraft was added to provide downrange coverage of the flight path. The KC-135 was positioned to the south of the X-43A flight path to accommodate the angle of the sun. The timeline called for the control room to be manned at 8:30 a.m., taxi to begin at 12:30 p.m., and takeoff at 1:00 p.m.

The B-52B status was "go." This would be the last research flight it would make after 49 years of service. The X-43A was serviced and ready to fly. The faulty oxygen sensor that had malfunctioned during the captive-carry flight had been replaced. There had been changes with the ground battery and control room. On the HXLV, the inertial-measurement-unit gyro bias was now within its original limits. The erroneous readings it had given on the captive carry had been cleared up. The error was not an issue because of the short flight time of the HXLV booster. All flight-critical instrumentation was working.

Range status was "go," as well. There were no mission conflicts. Controllers were warned that in the event of an incident, all notes and materials would be impounded. The weather forecast was good. The clouds in the range area were disappearing, but these were below launch altitude. The mission rule list was then reviewed, and a question was raised that if the stack had to be jettisoned, were mission controllers to check with senior management before making that decision? Stress was also put on the importance that the B-52B and chase planes were not to enter the range area early, before the launch window opened.

The next items on the briefing agenda were takeoff information and divert fields. The B-52B required a 9000-foot takeoff roll on runway 04. In the event of an emergency, the B-52B divert fields would be Vandenberg and Palmdale. The two F-18s would land at Point Mugu, Vandenberg, or Palmdale.

Controllers were reminded that the flight cards they were to use were Revision T, and someone commented that they had "killed a small forest" with all of the versions that had been produced over the years. The final item to be addressed was that of the emergency calls that would be made; in the event of a stack jettison, the timing would depend on what was under the B-52B at the time (i.e., a built-up area, open desert, or the restricted ocean test range). The briefing ended at 7:00 a.m.; outside the windowless building, the sun was up. What the long day would bring was uncertain.[39]

The controllers entered the Gold Room, which was a secure facility. Because of the classified nature of the engine data, only authorized personnel could enter, and the curtains were drawn in the viewing gallery overlooking it. NASA and contractor personnel were in the Blue Room, which had rows of tables and several large monitors on the forward wall.

The preflight preparations went smoothly for an hour and a half. Controllers actually were ahead of schedule on the flight cards. The first indication of a problem came at about 10:27 a.m., when controllers noticed that the electronically scanned pressure #4 (ESP #4) reading was high. This device was connected to several onboard sensors. A hold was called, and controllers estimated a 40-minute delay. Project engineers began discussing in the visitor's gallery whether the flight could proceed. The question was whether the necessary data could still be acquired even though not all of the sensors would be operating. As the engineers' discussion continued, controllers tried different procedures to correct the problem, but none were successful.

Langley and Dryden personnel decided the flight could be made even though some data would be lost. Other than the ESP #4 problem, the B-52B and stack both were ready for flight. The ground crew began the X-43A closeout at 12:25 p.m. but the delay had lasted two hours. According to the original timeline, the B-52B should have been about to taxi. The window for the flight plan was closing.[40]

Then a new problem appeared: the X-43A's aft S-band transmitter temperature spiked and went into the red zone. Apparently it had turned on by itself. Lin noted: "there was some sense of puzzlement as to why those things happened, because certain things could physically not have happened—such as the S-band transmitter turning on by itself." Apparently, X-43A #3 was still unwilling to go.[41]

The controllers decided to power down the X-43A, wait five minutes, and then power the vehicle up again. Once the problem was cleared up, the B-52B was nearly ready to taxi to the runway. As controllers waited, the possibility was raised that the transmitter had turned on because of the premature separation of a lanyard. This was a serious matter, for, if it were true, when the stack dropped it would automatically self-destruct. A check of the connection's integrity started. Discussions began about the possibility that the transmitter was the cause of the ESP#4 problem. After the 5-minute wait was up, the X-43A was powered up again. The primary transmitter was on, but the aft S-band transmitter was off. The test confirmed that the lanyard had not separated. The transmitter also was determined not to have been the cause of the ESP #4 problem.

The various delays had taken a further toll on the mission plan. The P-3 had to leave the range at about 3:15 p.m., while the B-52B and chase planes would not return to Edwards until after sunset. Another complication involved the B-52B fuel supply. The B-52B used JP-4 jet fuel, rather than the JP-8 that was the standard fuel used by the military, because JP-8 fuel caused leaks in the launch plane's rubber fuel bladder-wing tanks. In contrast, the JP-4 fuel had no harmful effects on the rubber material. Unfortunately, JP-4 was no longer being mass produced by refineries, and a specific, large amount had to be custom ordered. If the B-52B taxied out to the runway and the launch were aborted, there would not be enough JP-4 on hand at Edwards to fully refuel the aircraft, and no more was locally available. A limited amount of JP-8 would have to be added to the tanks. The B-52B's crew chief gave his approval for the use of JP-8, should it be required.

Controllers were polled as to whether the B-52B's engines should be started, and approval was given. The radio calls indicated that the B-52B's radar beacon was being received, global-positioning-system data were good, and the Gold Room's displays were operating properly. The next step was the X-43A system checks. A call was made that the aft S-band transmitter had turned on again. This sparked a quiet groan in the Blue Room. Then there was a call that the signal was *not* from the aft S-band transmitter, but from the primary transmitter, which *should* be operating. There was, however, now a problem communicating with the KC-135 aircraft. Controllers were trying to contact it through the Los Angeles traffic control center.

Because of all of the delays and problems in the preparations, a bare 20-minute margin in takeoff time now remained. The B-52B's engines had been running, and it was ready to begin taxing. The launch aircraft's four-man crew was Gordon Fullerton (pilot), Frank Batteas (co-pilot), Brad Neal (X-43A panel operator), and Brian Minnick of Orbital Sciences (HXLV panel operator). A request by controllers to the Federal Aviation Administration for an extension was made, but the FAA's response was that the HXLV and X-43A had to be in the water by 4:00 p.m. Insufficient time now remained for the B-52B to taxi out, take off, fly the route, and make the launch before the window closed. There was no option but to end the attempt. The B-52's engines were shut down, and the controllers went through their abort check-lists. The ground equipment to service the stack's onboard systems was reattached, and work began on analyzing the ESP#4 and S-band transmitter anomalies. The team faced the emotional rollercoaster of an abort. They would try again the next day.[42]

To the Edge of the Envelope

The second attempt to fly the third X-43A mission came on November 16, 2004. The team tried to relieve preflight tension by joking around while waiting for the briefing to begin. The briefing information was much the same as for the first try. If the X-43A were to hit the water before 4:00 p.m., then 3:45 p.m. was the latest possible launch time. All of the B-52B tanks were filled with JP-4, for there was enough left in the tanker truck to replace the fuel used in the engine startup the day before.

The instrumentation seemed to be working when it had been shut down following the first day's abort. The solution for the problem with the aft S-band transmitter was to connect it to the battery at a later point in the countdown. In the previous day's attempt, the battery had been connected much earlier than it had been in earlier ground tests. If the ESP #4 problem did reoccur, the takeoff still would proceed. Engineers put the chances that the ESP #4 would work at 50/50.

The sequence on the second day's attempt would follow that of the previous tests. Dealing with the problem the day before had involved a fair amount of improvising; as a result, it was hard to correlate the sequence of events. The range facilities and personnel were ready for the flight to proceed. The KC-135 no longer was available, as it had a scheduled commitment elsewhere, but the two P-3s were ready. Mission rules required that at least one telemetry aircraft be available. The weather forecast was good. The cirrus had dispersed overnight and was at 25,000–30,000-foot altitude, again putting it below launch altitude. Headwinds were within the Hyper-X launch-vehicle capability. There were no changes in the earlier mission rules or ground track. Only two minor changes were made in the day-of-flight cards. The crew brief was completed in about 40 minutes. Personnel then dispersed to their assigned positions.

The preparations went smoothly, but the problems of the previous day were on everyone's minds. The range was ready, the telemetry was up, and there was a good signal lock. The inertial-navigation-system alignment was then completed, and the internal power checks began. The ground crew recharged the nitrogen gas supply in the B-52B.

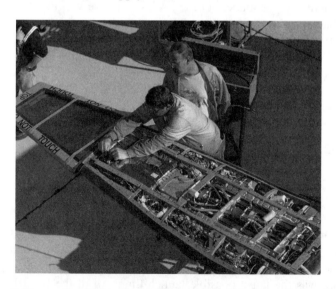

Preflight activities on the X-43A #3 by NASA avionics technicians Randy Wagner and Terry Bishop. The upper surface has not yet been attached, showing how tightly the systems are packed within the fuselage. (NASA photo EC04-0323-53.)

The ground crew's preparations of the stack continue into the night. The task of getting all of the systems ready was complicated by darkness and a cold desert wind. (NASA photo EC04-0323-118.)

When the point in the flight cards was reached at which the ESP #4 malfunctioned, a call was made that the pressure checks still looked good. The new procedures developed to deal with the ESP #4 were successful, and the aft S-band transmitter stayed off. The X-43A #3, which had been for so long reluctant to fly had apparently decided to behave.

The Orbital ground crew removes the yellow protective blankets from the third HXLV on launch morning. The blankets helped control the temperature in the booster to ensure that the propellant grain did not crack. As with the preflight testing, the final preparations before takeoff were extensive and detailed. (NASA photo EC04-0327-16.)

Brad Neal in the X-43A panel operator's position onboard the B-52B for Flight 3. The lower flight deck is cramped, subject to fog, and can be too cold or too hot because of the old bomber's quirky environmental system. (NASA photo ED04-0320-13.)

The B-52B crew arrived at the aircraft at 11:12 a.m., and final preparations of the X-43A were completed by 11:52 a.m. The crew was now ready to start the B-52B engines. The final X-43A closeout was completed, and at 12:34 p.m., when the B-52B was cleared to taxi, a cheer from the spectators went up in the Blue Room. A minute later, the aircraft began to roll down the taxiway. The B-52B crew was the same as on the previous day. Chase-plane crews were Dana Purifoy and Carla Thomas in F-18 NASA 852, with Richard Ewers and Jim Ross in F-18 NASA 846. This time, Thomas would take still photos, and Ross would shoot video footage.[43]

The F-18s were first to take off, at 1:03 p.m., and were followed by the B-52B at 1:08 p.m., and the chase planes joined up with the B-52B for the flight out to the launch point. Unlike with the fuel-transfer drama of the second launch, the flight out to the launch point was uneventful. Fullerton recalled later:

> Yeah, it went real smooth. I was in the left seat for the final launch. We were going up to where we were used to going—40,000 feet or so, where Pegasus liked to be and the airplane performed well. I can't remember any maintenance glitches. With navigation—we found our way out with the GPS map system we have to the right place with very little squawk-ing from the Navy range people. And so it went nicely and [was] a great day for all concerned.[44]

In Dryden's Blue Room, where NASA and contractor personnel watched the flight, the chase-plane video was displayed on a large monitor. Ross found his role as a videographer very demanding. He later recalled that,

NASA's B-52B launch aircraft takes off on November 16, 2004, for the third and final X-43A flight. This was also the last mission the 49-year old aircraft would fly. (NASA photo ED04-0320-16.)

The video is a lot harder to do because you're downlinking the whole time, so you've got to shoot for about two hours straight, continuous. I knew that this one was kind of a big deal because the last one had gone so well that there were a lot of people watching this one, and they were downlinking live to CNN and all the different news agencies.

So we just have to try and keep it as stable as we can because there's no way to know when [Dryden video] is sending it up to the world and then—you're moving it all over the place and that's what they're seeing on CNN to the world. So you always have to keep it as steady and clean as you can. It's a lot more taxing on your body, especially because the drop time is two hours into it. So you've been holding the camera for two hours during the most crucial part and that's when it starts to get really uncomfortable to hold.[45]

The results of Ross' efforts were spectacular. The B-52B against the blue sky, with a crescent moon visible was among images he captured.

The B-52B and its chase planes now were off the California coastline. Controllers went through the flight card items. The only problem was that the B-52B's autopilot was not working. This was traced to a switch in the wrong position, after which the autopilot was turned on. The ESP #4 was working properly. The tracking stations were checked as the formation continued on to the launch area. At 10 minutes before launch (L-10 minutes), the P-3 crew reported that they were ready to receive the signals from the X-43A.

At L-9 the Gold Room door was locked. As controllers had done so many times in emergency-procedure training sessions, they ran through checklist

An in-flight view of the B-52B carrying the Flight 3 stack as it headed toward the launch point. The Mach 10 flight represented the true unknown of the Hyper-X project, in part because of the uncertainties of scramjet operation at speed that wind tunnels could not fully simulate. (NASA photo EC04-0325-23.)

items. At L-2, the batteries powering the HXLV flight controls were activated. The launch would now either be made on time or be aborted, as the batteries' lifetime was too short to permit a second try. A fin-actuation-system failure also could now occur at any time. The fin pins were retracted, and the HXLV's three control surfaces moved through their full sweep. The movement could

Senior NASA and contractor officials in the Blue Room at the NASA Dryden Flight Research Center awaiting the launch of X-43A #3. The onboard video from both the B-52B and the F-18 chase plane was displayed on several large televisions at the front of the room. (NASA photo ED04-0320-21.)

be seen on the Blue Room television screen, and the audience cheered. The telemetry showed no indication of an impending FAS failure.

At L-1, the "arm" light was on, and the HXLV guidance system switched into inertial navigation mode. Fullerton and Batteas followed the final minutes before launch with the only digital instrument in the cockpit—a square, white plastic egg timer attached with Velcro® to the top of the instrument panel. At L-30 seconds, the go was given for the launch. A few of the spectators in the Blue Room asked each other "Are we having fun yet?" and "Are you excited?"

The final seconds ticked off. At 2:34 p.m. operations engineer Dave McAllister in the Gold Room called, "launch, launch, launch," and the B-52B's pylon hooks released.[46]

As the stack fell free, airflow around the B-52B caused the stack to roll to the right. A large roll angle had been seen on the second flight, and this posed a risk of FAS failure. To prevent this, engineers reprogrammed the booster control system so that it would activate immediately, rather than after a one-second delay as originally programmed. The HXLV stabilized the vehicle's rates and attitudes.[47] After falling for 5 seconds, the solid rocket ignited, and then pulled up into a steep 2.5-g climb. As it reached transonic speeds, a "bump" similar to one on the second flight and those seen on the Pegasus launches was observed in the telemetry data.

The stack was being subjected to higher heat loads during the faster climb. The coolant flow to the leading edges and cowl door of the scramjet began 43 seconds into the boost, with the HXLV just past Mach 4. Then, at 64 seconds after launch, at a speed of Mach 7.4 and an altitude of around 92,000 feet, there was an "abrupt disturbance" in the HXLV vehicle dynamics. Wing fillet strain and temperature data indicated that an "anomalous shock event" had caused a shift in the vehicle's structure. This resulted in a change in rudder trim, but the ascent was not affected.

In the Blue Room, a computer-driven display of the HXLV speed, altitude, and heading was displayed on the big screen. Spectators were awestruck at the Mach numbers they were seeing. The HXLV quickly passed Mach 3, 4, 5, and 6. When the booster exceeded Mach 6.7, it broke the record held for nearly four decades by the X-15A-2. The speed continued to increase, through Mach 7, 8, 9, and approaching Mach 10. But as they cheered each milestone, the fin-actuation-system issue was in all of the spectators' minds: everything could still be lost in the blink of an eye.

The peak speed of the HXLV was reached at about 75 seconds after launch, at just over Mach 10. The solid rocket burned out, and the stack began to coast. The onboard systems began the separation sequence at L +88.16 seconds, or about 1.6 seconds earlier than the target time. At that point the vehicle's speed was Mach 9.74, at an altitude of 109,440 feet and a dynamic pressure of 959 pounds psf. When the X-43A successfully separated

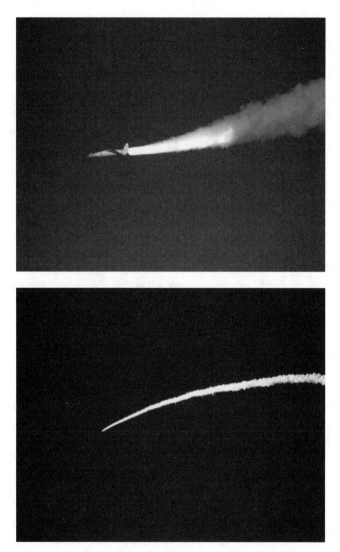

The launch and ascent of the third HXLV. The heavier propellant load of the solid rocket theoretically could achieve Mach 10, but because of potential stability problems at high angles of attack, the final trajectory reduced the separation speed to just under this mark. (NASA photos EC04-0325-37 and -54.)

from the HXLV, a loud cheer went up in the Blue Room—the FAS worries were finally over.[48]

The X-43A then began to orient itself for cowl opening, taking nearly one second—longer than expected—to reach the proper angle of attack. A similar problem had occurred on the second flight; the gain of the angle-of-attack integrator had been increased to prevent a reoccurrence. Although this solution

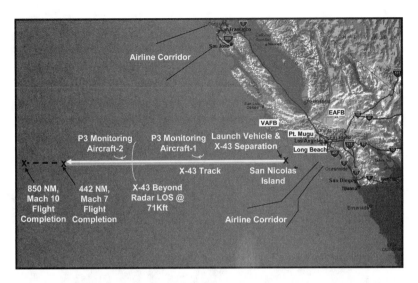

Ground-track diagram for the X-43A Mach 7 and 10 launches. The X-43A flights were a complicated effort involving ground stations, data-reception aircraft, and the Los Angeles airport. (NASA diagram.)

was not entirely successful, the time needed for the vehicle to reach proper conditions was reduced relative to Flight 2.

The cowl door opened as planned 2.5 seconds after separation. The power-off tare lasted 3 seconds, and then hydrogen fuel was injected into the scramjet and ignited with the silane. The burn lasted about 11 seconds, during which time the X-43A covered about 20 miles. The test goal was to show that the scramjet could produce as much thrust as the drag on the vehicle and thus maintain a cruise condition. The top speed reached during the scramjet-powered flight was Mach 9.68; this was Mach 2.85 *faster* than the peak speed achieved by the second X-43A less than eight months earlier. Once the burn was complete, a 6-second power-off tare was performed. The cowl door then closed, ending the engine test and the primary phase of the flight. As the door closed, the pressure inside the scramjet dropped. In the Blue Room and the visitor's gallery, the cheering and handshakes began.[49]

Postflight data showed the cruise requirement had been met and scramjet measurements were in "excellent agreement" with those predicted. The scramjet data collected during the flight represented—by orders of magnitude—not only the largest volume of Mach 10 measurements, but also, in terms of quality and type, an amount far surpassing that previously acquired during more than four decades of wind-tunnel measurements.[50]

The X-43A then began the secondary mission of collecting hypersonic flight data. The recovery maneuver was initiated, and the angle of attack increased to 6 degrees. The angle-of-attack oscillations during the second flight's recovery maneuver did not reoccur on the third flight. Instead,

Home at last, the B-52B crew and their families are reunited after the landing. (NASA photos EC04-0326-26 and -30.)

the third vehicle responded with a roll oscillation. At the same time as the roll oscillation occurred, the internal engine pressure readings increased, indicating that air was flowing through the engine. This caused a vehicle nose-down attitude that the wings had to correct. Then, about 90 seconds after separation, the wings' position changed sharply in response to a disturbance. Because the venting of the silane gas began at approximately the same time, program engineers attributed the disturbance to ignition of the silane. When the venting was complete, internal pressure decreased, and the roll oscillation stopped. This came to be referred to as "the Mach 8 unpleasantness."

How air could have flowed through the engine to ignite the venting silane was not clear. The cowl door actuator data showed that it had closed following the engine experiment, and that it remained closed through the descent. If, as some engineers thought, part of the scramjet casing burned through, or the cowl door was distorted, the airflow would have been reflected in the data as increased pressure. Yet, had this occurred, the airflow/pressure increase would have continued rather than stopped. In the end, one report on the Mach 10 flight noted: "there is no known cause for either the initiation or cessation of this phenomenon."[51]

Despite the anomalous event, the X-43A successfully completed all seven of the parameter identification maneuvers (PID) during the descent. By the time the seventh and final PID was made at Mach 2, the vehicle was slowing rapidly. Some of the inputs were actually made in the transonic speed regime. The X-43A then entered the approach mode, which reduced its descent angle and speed. When radio contact was lost with the P-3 aircraft, the vehicle was at an altitude of 918 feet and a speed of Mach 0.72. The X-43A had flown a total distance of about 850 nautical miles from the drop point.[52]

The B-52B and the two chase planes headed back to Dryden. Personnel climbed the stairs to the roof of Building 4800 in anticipation of their arrival while others from inside the center's main building gathered outside to wait. When the aircraft reached Edwards, they descended and flew over the main building, leaving a thunderous roar in their wake, the B-52B with an F-18 on each wing tip. The bomber circled twice and then landed on the Edwards main runway, and then taxied back to Dryden. When the B-52B first took to the air in June of 1955, a hypersonic aircraft was a distant dream. As the plane touched down for the final time at the dawn of the 21st century, one era had ended, and another was about to begin. It was a moment both exhilarating and bittersweet.

And in a wonderful turn of fate, the same B-52B that had launched more than half of all of the X-15 flights—the world's first hypersonic aircraft—performed the launch of the first hypersonic scramjet and did so from the same wing adapter the X-15 had used all those decades earlier.

N<small>OTES</small>

[1] Marshall, Laurie, Catherine Bahm, Griffin Corpening, and Robert Sherrill, "Overview, Results, and Lessons Learned of the X-43A Mach 10 Flights," AIAA/CIRA 13th International Space Planes and Hypersonic Systems and Technological Conference, Capua, Italy, May 2005, p. 22.

[2] Baumann, Ethan, "X-43A Flight Controls," March 6, 2006, pp. 37, 38.

[3] Joyce, Philip J., John B. Pomroy, and Laurie Grindle, "The Hyper-X Launch Vehicle: Challenges and Design Considerations for Hypersonic Flight," AIAA Paper 2005-3333, p. 12.

[4] Grindle, Laurie, history interview, tape no. 2, Jan. 20, 2005, NASA Dryden Flight Research Center History Office, pp. 2, 3.

[5] *Aerospace Highlights*, May 7, 2004, NASA Dryden Flight Research Center History Office, p. 4.

[6] Ibid, May 21, 2004, pp. 4, 5.

[7] Ibid, May 28, 2004, p. 3.

[8] Ibid, June 4, 2004, pp. 5, 6.

[9] Reukauf, Paul, history interview, Feb. 17, 2005, NASA Dryden Flight Research Center History Office, pp. 57, 58.

[10] *Aerospace Highlights*, May 21, 2004, p. 4 and June 4, 2004, p. 5.

[11] Ibid, June 10, 2004, pp. 3, 4.

[12] Ibid, June 25, 2004, p. 3, and July 2, 2004, p. 3.

[13] Reukauf history interview, p. 58.

[14] *Aerospace Highlights*, July 9, 2004, p. 3.

[15] Grindle, Laurie, history interview, tape no. 3, Jan. 20, 2005, NASA Dryden Flight Research Center History Office, and Yohan Lin, private communication.

[16] Lin, Yohan, private communication, and *Aerospace Highlights*, July 23, 2004, p. 3, and July 30, 2004, p. 4.

[17] Ibid, Aug. 20, 2004, p. 3, and Aug. 27, 2004, p. 3. Additional information provided by Yohan Lin.

[18] Grindle history interview, tape no. 3, pp. 15, 16.

[19] Reukauf history interview, pp. 58, 59.

[20] Lin interview, p. 60.

[21] Sitz, Joel, interview, June 2, 2006.

[22] Corpening, Griff, history interview, Dec. 20, 2004, NASA Dryden Flight Research Center History Office, p. 49.

[23] *Aerospace Highlights*, Aug. 20, 2004, p. 3 and Aug. 27, 2004, p. 3.

[24] Ibid, Sept. 24, 2004, p. 5, and Oct. 22, 2004, p. 4.

[25] Marshall et al., "Overview, Results, and Lessons Learned of the X-43A Mach 10 Flights," p. 22, and *Aerospace Highlights*, July 2, 2004, p. 3, and Aug. 13, 2004, p. 4.

[26] Lin, Yohan, interview, Dec. 12, 2006.

[27] *Aerospace Highlights*, June 18, 2004, p. 4, June 25, 2004, p. 3, and July 16, 2004, p. 3.

[28] *Aerospace Highlights*, Aug. 13, 2004, p. 4.

[29] Fullerton, Gordon, history interview, Aug. 3, 2005, NASA Dryden Flight Research Center History Office, pp. 22–24, *2004 Daily Flight Log*, NASA Dryden Flight Research Center Pilot's Office, and *Aerospace Highlights*, Sept. 10, 2004, p. 3, and Sept. 17, 2004, p. 4.

[30] *2004 Daily Flight Log*, and *Aerospace Highlights*, Oct. 1, 2004, p. 3, and Oct. 8, 2004, p. 4.

[31] Lin interview, pp. 28, 29.

[32] Ibid, pp. 58, 59.

[33] Peebles, Curtis, X-43A notes, NASA Dryden Flight Research Center History Office, pp. 15–17.

[34] Peebles X-43A notes, p. 17.

[35] Grindle history interview, tape no. 2, pp. 17, 18.

[36] Peebles X-43A notes, p. 18.

[37] *Aerospace Highlights*, Nov. 12, 2004, p. 5.

[38] *Great Aviation Quotes*, http://www.skygod.com/quotes/index.html.

[39] Peebles X-43A notes, pp. 28, 29.

[40] Ibid, pp. 29, 30.

[41] Lin interview, p. 55.

[42] Peebles X-43A notes, pp. 30, 31, and Fullerton interview, pp. 24–26.

[43] Peebles X-43A notes, p. 32.

[44] Fullerton history interview, p. 27.

[45] Ross, Jim, history interview, Aug. 24, 2005, NASA Dryden Flight Research Center History Office, pp. 19, 20.

[46] Peebles X-43A notes, pp. 33, 34.

[47] Reukauf history interview, pp. 61, 62.

[48] Vachon, M., T. Grindle, C. St. John, and D. Dowdell, "X-43A Fluid and Environmental Systems: Ground and Flight Operations and Lessons Learned," AIAA/CIRA 13th International Space Planes and Hypersonic Systems and Technology Conference, Capua, Italy, May 2005, pp. 12, 14, and Joyce et al., "The Hyper-X Launch Vehicle: Challenges and Design Considerations for Hypersonic Flight," pp. 14, 15, and Peebles X-43A notes, p. 34.

[49] Marshall et al., "Overview, Results, and Lessons Learned of the X-43A Mach 10 Flights," pp. 6, 17, 18, and "X-43 Flight Data Briefing Air Force Rocket Laboratory, Dec. 9, 2005, p. 39, and Peebles X-43A notes, pp. 33, 34.

[50] Marshall et al., "Overview, Results, and Lessons Learned of the X-43A Mach 10 Flight," pp. 13, 17.

[51] Ibid, pp. 19, 20.

[52] Ibid, p. 16, and Baumann, "X-43A Flight Controls," p. 41.

Chapter 9

To the Far Horizon

> Earth is the cradle of mankind, but man cannot live in the cradle forever.
> *Konstantin E. Tsiokovsky, Russian rocket theorist, 1857–1935*
>
> We are on a journey to keep an appointment with whatever we are.
> *Gene Roddenberry, television producer, 1921–1991*
>
> All civilizations become either spacefaring or extinct.
> *Carl Sagan, astronomer, 1934–1996*

Laurie Grindle commented that the mood after the third flight was very mixed.

> The one thing about it [is] that everyone is very happy about the flight itself and the success that we had, but it's also very sad, because for a lot of us we've been working with the same group of people since 1996 and now, all of sudden, we aren't working with them anymore. And that's government and contractors alike, and it's just kind of weird. But also, it's just kind of sad to see everybody go off, go their separate ways and do their own thing. I mean, it's a positive conclusion, but it's also tempered with some sadness. And I think that the Flight 3 flight party had some of that as well.
>
> The Flight 3 party was also about saying goodbye to people. And so I think that made it even have a stronger impact than the Flight 2 party, just because it was a celebration of success but also kind of a celebration of the team too, but it's also kind of a, "well, it's been nice working with you!"

The Hyper-X team had been a "band of brothers" who had gone through a wonderful, heartbreaking, and ultimately triumphant experience. Now that effort had suddenly ended, leaving a feeling of emptiness. Grindle continued:

> Yeah, I had told Joel [Sitz] he needed to go out and find another project and keep us all together, because it would be so hard for all of us to ramp up again. Right now we just sit across the table from each other and we know what we're all thinking, what's going through everybody's mind. You don't even need to go down a certain path, because you already know where that's going to lead you.

Adding to the feeling of emptiness was the abruptness of the project's end. The project personnel were happy after the third flight and were looking forward to taking long-deferred vacations. Grindle commented:

> The unfortunate thing was that we had no money and literally ran out in December. And so, for that first week of December, it was a happy thing at the beginning and by the end of the week it was a disaster. We had one week left and then we were done. And there was no money to write reports and there was no money to do any of this stuff. We ultimately managed to get to write the reports, but the first two weeks of December were just horrible. It was a conclusion when you didn't even expect one.
>
> We thought we were funded all the way through March. So we knew it was ending, but we thought we had until March to see that end. And now it ended in two days. We came in on the second [of December], and everything was cool, and then by the fourth [of December], it was a disaster.
>
> I think the way I felt in December was like we had failed. And the reason why I felt that way was because they weren't going to allow us to analyze the data or any of that kind of stuff. And I was thinking, "Wow, we're being punished, and they don't punish you for succeeding, they punish you for failing so we must have failed in some way." Those first two weeks of December were just a really, really, hard time. And yeah, I basically looked back at our success as a failure [in those two weeks], because that's how I felt we were being treated.[1]

Money for data analysis was ultimately found. Over the following two years, a substantial number of AIAA papers and other reports were written on the accomplishments of the Hyper-X program. Many of the Hyper-X engineers were assigned to NASA's Orion launch abort test program, whereas others joined unmanned aerial vehicle efforts underway at Dryden Flight Research Center. Some of the contractors who worked on the project were laid off.

In terms of technology, the X-43A/Hyper-X represented a singular milestone. After nearly a half-century of high hopes, studies, wind-tunnel tests, proposals, and cancelled projects, a scramjet-powered vehicle had *flown*. The performance of the engine validated the scramjet design tools and scaling laws. In turn, the theoretical calculations and ground testing could be used to design more advanced engine concepts. Just as important, both the scramjet and vehicle systems had successfully operated in the variable temperatures and densities of the atmosphere.

The X-43A systems were able to maintain the flight conditions necessary for the scramjet to operate properly. Control deflections to correct the engine-induced moments were very close to preflight predictions. And when the unexpected occurred, such as when the vehicle pitched up during the cowl opening on the second flight, the control system was sufficiently well designed to correct the situation.

The airframe and wing structure, the thermal protection material, and the internal conditions of the X-43A performed largely as predicted. The Hyper-X launch-vehicle thermal anomaly during the ascent on Flight 3 and "the Mach 8 unpleasantness" during the descent indicated there were still unknowns. Despite this, neither of the anomalies resulted in the loss of the booster or research vehicle.

The X-43A's airframe drag and lift both were slightly higher than predicted, but still within preflight uncertainty predictions. The stability and control were as predicted, as was the boundary-layer transition. The biggest aerodynamic worry before the flight was the separation of the HXLV and the X-43A. After all was said and done, this went as predicted, proving that nonsymmetrical/high-dynamic pressure stage separations could be performed. This in turn meant that two-stage-to-orbit vehicles employing this technology were feasible.[2]

HYPERSONIC LESSONS LEARNED

In assessing the lessons learned during the Hyper-X project, it must first be observed that the particular nature of the effort, such as its mission profile, system design, limited number of flights, and use of a rocket booster and air launch, meant that some of the standard practices long used for conventional aeronautical and astronautics projects did not directly apply. In other areas, the Hyper-X reaffirmed the experiences of generations of engineers.

The first lesson learned from the Hyper-X illustrated the basic difference between academic research activities and flight research. An example of the first would be an astronomer making observations of a star. He first determines what data are needed for his research project and chooses the types of observations through which he will collect this data. With the plan complete, the astronomer is allotted time on an observatory's telescope. He makes the observations using the telescope's existing imaging and/or spectrographic instruments. With this completed, the astronomer then returns to his university and processes the data, using a preexisting computer and software program. His final step is to use the processed data to write up the results of his research efforts as a scientific paper.

The important point is that all of the astronomer's efforts were directed at conducting the experiment. He did not have to design and build the telescope, instrumentation, or computer, nor did he have to write and debug the software before beginning his research; the equipment and software necessary for his research already existed.[3]

With flight research, the picture is very different. To perform a research experiment, project personnel must first design, fabricate, and assemble the research vehicle from scratch, then conduct ground tests of the vehicle and its individual components, validate the control laws and software, and finally fly the vehicle. Only then, when the project has been underway for years, are the research data finally collected. The project staff might end up conducting research in areas, such as control system design, far removed from the official research goals of the project. This is an aspect that must be accepted as an inevitable result of having to develop the means of conducting the experiment before it can be made.

The differences between academic and flight research can be seen in the level of personnel involved in the two. Academic research activities are conducted by an individual or, at most, a relatively small group. In contrast, flight research requires a large team effort involving multiple companies, subcontractors, vendors, and government organizations, hundreds if not thousands of personnel, large sums of money, and considerable amounts of time.

The first question an aerospace research and development project faces is both simple and critical. What do you want to do? One example of this to be found in the Hyper-X project work was the question of whether to recover the X-43A after the Mach 5 flight.

Although the issue was a minor one, it did contain a potentially serious pitfall. There is a tendency to add extraneous goals to a project once it has begun. The tendency for planetary probes to be fitted with every possible experiment, causing them to grow in size, complexity, and expense, is one example. This resulted in fewer and more expensive missions, until their cost was too high to be politically feasible.

With the National Aerospace Plane, the X-30 was designed to demonstrate a single-stage-to-orbit profile. It was to be a research aircraft that would, project personnel hoped, lead to what was called a "NASP Derived Vehicle" (NDV). This would be the operational version of the X-30, which could fill all of the many and contradictory roles envisioned by the project's supporters. There was pressure on managers to have the experimental X-30 demonstrate some operational capabilities, or at least have some of the features of a NASP derived vehicle. These included something simple such as adding a cargo door to the research vehicle. Other ideas were far more demanding. Among them was the ability to go into space, reenter the atmosphere, and then "pop up" into space again. Another proposal called for the vehicle to have sustained low-speed flight capability. The National Aerospace Plane project office also considered a "go-around" capability, in which the aircraft could abort an initial landing approach if necessary then make a second attempt.

Any of these ideas, even if technically feasible, would have added billions to program costs and increased the vehicle's weight by from 50,000 to 100,000 pounds. And it was by no means clear if any of them were technically feasible. Additionally, incorporating them would transform the X-30 into a far different vehicle than that planned, radically altering the National Aerospace Plane effort from the one originally proposed.[4]

The Hyper-X project, however, was structured as a tightly focused research effort. The decision to avoid adding "nice-to-have" features such as an X-43A recovery capability prevented a blurring of this focus. In such a structured program, priority research efforts must be kept central. Any additional research activity cannot be allowed to interfere with the primary goals. An example of this was with the aerodynamic maneuvers the vehicle would make after the scramjet test. If the X-43A survived long enough for the engine test to be completed, the primary goal of the mission had been met. The aerodynamic maneuvers added to the productivity of the flight without modifying or interfering with this primary goal.

If a project involves an ongoing series of flights, then additional goals can be added to the later flights once primary goals have been met. The X-15 program offered one such example. Once the speed and altitude expansion flights had been completed, NASA and the Air Force flew scientific and technological experiments on the vehicle. Plans also were made for Hypersonic Research Engine tests and for potential modification of an X-15 with delta wings. If, on the other hand, the program's cost and schedule were being compromised, then deleting a marginal goal in the interest of remaining focused on principle research objectives might be necessary.

The Hyper-X project underwent just such a restructuring in late 1997. Project managers realized that unexpected problems during the design and manufacturing phases had increased costs. There was insufficient funding to carry out the original plans calling for four flights. Additionally, the Mach 5 flight continued to be problematic in the eyes of project personnel. It required an off-loaded booster, about which engineers felt far from confident. Moreover, Reukauf recalled that earlier wind-tunnel testing had provided significant information about dual-mode scramjet operations at Mach 5.

Typically, development of a research vehicle requires that a great deal of work be undertaken early in the project. This was because of the complexities inherent in starting up the project, bringing different contractors into the effort, refining initial design concepts, and dealing with early technical issues and problems, all of which translate inevitably into high initial cost. Ideally, this inevitability should be allowed for in the project budget. In reality, it rarely is.

In the case of the Hyper-X, there was such an early cost rise. This, in turn, drove a reassessment of the research program. The Mach 5 flight was dropped, and the lone Mach 7 flight and two Mach 10 flights were switched to a pair of Mach 7 missions and a single Mach 10 launch. The danger of the rapid cost increase at the beginning of the work was that it could put the project's future in doubt.

One area in which the Hyper-X differed from earlier research vehicles was in its operational profile. This would have a major effect on how the vehicle was prepared for flight. Conventional research vehicles (both manned and unmanned) will typically use a step-by-step envelope expansion plan. The initial X-15 tests were glide flights, for example, which tested the rocket plane's basic aerodynamics and control systems. These were followed by the initial low-speed/low-altitude powered flights (up to Mach 3 and 100,000 feet) using a pair of XLR11 rocket engines. These tests identified a number of control and structural issues, which were then corrected. When the XLR-99 engine was finally ready, speed and altitude envelope expansion with the X-15 began. This process took some three years, reaching Mach 6 and 354,200 feet. The final elements were flights of various engineering and scientific experiments, the HRE, the advanced X-15A-2 vehicle, and the proposed delta wing X-15.

This step-by-step procedure avoided the undertaking of too many firsts on a single flight. It also meant flights with the X-15 could begin before all of the systems (and software) had been developed and tested. Had the interim XLR11 engines not been used, the X-15's first powered flight would have been delayed for a year and a half, increasing costs without producing data.

With the Hyper-X, the situation was very different. There were only going to be three flights. Every flight was an all-up, full-performance mission—no glide flights, no envelope expansion, no preliminary test flights could be made in attempts to discover problems. All of the testing had to be done before the flights. Without the ability to undertake the step-by-step envelope expansion, such as the X-15 had done, the ground testing had far greater importance than normal. This testing was critical to the Hyper-X's mission success, as it was the only chance engineers had to discover design flaws, assembly errors, damaged components, or software problems with the vehicle.

Griff Corpening made several observations about the X-43A testing process around 1999. He wrote:

> My thoughts on the development of flight test equipment include the "common sense" application and the correct balance of analyses, design, and testing to produce reliable flight test equipment, including both hardware and software subsystems. We can now systematically tie these disciplines together by the use of systems engineering and integration processes of which probably the most important aspect is requirements definition, maintenance, flow down, and tracking. The technical requirements, including performance and reliability, will drive all aspects of the hardware development. One must keep in mind that from a technical viewpoint the available tools are analyses, design, and testing, so the proper balance of the application of those tools should be maintained.
>
> The philosophy that currently makes hardware development challenging is "cheaper, better, and faster." In order to produce in this environment, the balance of analyses, design, and testing must be constantly scrutinized and adjusted, i.e., if functional performance, reliability, and confidence goals can realistically be met with analyses as opposed to testing, and the analysis approach is cheaper, it should be used. The analytical tools at hand are truly amazing but they have limitations.

The WIRE failure is an example of this. Although there were other contributing factors, it is doubtful that analyses could have predicted the failure due to its transient nature. This also resulted in inadequate testing at the breadboard, subsystem, and system levels. There were indications in the literature and similar problems with other spacecraft developments that there could be a problem, but that information was not widely disseminated. Certain test results were not understood, or [were] rationalized to be test equipment deficiencies or limitations. [The "WIRE failure" refers to the Pegasus launch, which had control problems at transonic speeds. The mishap investigation board later examined this incident as past of efforts to understand the loss of the HXLV.]

I feel that we can now perform more realistic analyses, and produce more robust designs in order to minimize testing, but due to high-speed operations, transient conditions, and the unpredictable nature of functional performances when subsystems are integrated into a system, a certain level of well-thought-out testing is and will continue to be required. The issue as always, is how much.[5]

Testing was critical at all points in the fabrication, assembly, and preflight preparations for the Hyper-X. The qualification, acceptance, verification and/or validation testing required should, ideally, be specified beforehand. However, with the Hyper-X project, the compressed schedule meant that initial tests had to be designed concurrent with the production of the systems to be tested.

One of the roles that such testing fulfills is determining the reliability of the vehicle systems. With production systems and software, quantifying their reliability is easily done. In contrast, unique research systems, involving a handful of modified and/or completely new designs, are much harder to assess in terms of reliability. The prime example is the fin actuation system. Recall that the three HXLV launches were each made with a different FAS design.

The testing of the vehicle systems and software must be as thorough as possible, given its importance to the success of the mission. This requirement was not only a reflection of the Hyper-X project's nature, but also of larger changes in flight test and research. The introduction of computer fly-by-wire systems, which began in the 1970s, required extensive validation and debugging before the first flight could be made. This added a whole new level of testing that did not exist before.

Based on past experience, a number of basic rules for preflight testing have been established. The most basic of these was to carefully follow the project checklists, test rules, general practices, and procedures. There also were the ever-present issues of schedule and available time. The Flight 2 and 3 vehicles were checked out in the long stand-down during the mishap-investigation-board investigation and the return-to-flight effort. By the time Flight 2 was made, the components for the Flight 3 stack were nearly ready to fly.

Only with the Flight 3 final preparations did schedule pressures begin to have an effect on vehicle testing. The first impact came in the decision to eliminate certain planned tests, such as aircraft-in-the-loop and X-43A compliance testing, which had been successfully passed with predictable results. This alteration to the test plan was not carried out; the checkout of X-43A #3 went so quickly that the tests which were to be deleted were rescheduled and successfully completed. This was only possible because the core team was highly experienced and had remained together.

A separate issue was the decision to not incorporate Flight 2 data into the Flight 3 models. The original plan called for using the Flight 2 results, but the compressed schedule created by the delays prevented this option. The only direct use of the Flight 2 data was as a guide for Flight 3 updates and stress cases. Flight 3 was a success, but in retrospect this was largely because of the skill of the team in a situation where the lack of thorough analysis could have been detrimental. Additionally, there was the potential that the results from Flight 3 could have been better had the original plan been followed and Flight 2 data incorporated.[6]

Although these decisions did not seriously affect the project results, they did represent actions counter to established practice. First, relaxing a test plan to meet a schedule was done only at great peril. The other truism is that schedule acceleration and/or budget cuts might mean increased risk. In this case, the actions were the result of shifting NASA priorities—there was pressure to complete the Hyper-X project before the end of 2004. The reality inevitably faced by managers and team members alike is that ideal engineering practices must continuously adapt to a less-than-ideal world.

The most serious incident to occur during the testing sequence was the X-43A #3 left rudder-wing contact. This resulted from a personnel and procedural error in conducting a test, rather than from scheduling pressures. The wing trim test was done a day earlier than originally scheduled at the request of management. The incident was attributed to performing a test in a nonstandard way and without benefit of a written procedure. As the rudder had to be moved to perform the test, and there was a risk that it would come in contact with the wing, a written procedure should have been established and used to conduct the test.[7]

A project team can do all of the testing it wants, but unless the ground-test hardware and software match the flight hardware and software, the entire effort is wasted. It is an old but still-true engineering adage that "you test what you fly and fly what you test." Given the complexity of aerospace vehicles, there is great potential for errors in the configuration control between the ground-test articles and actual flight hardware.[8]

On the Hyper-X, configuration control was among the positive lessons learned. The mishap investigation board completed examination of configuration control at Dryden in the first week they were at the site and was complimentary as to the quality of the records. Documentation regarding open issues was kept in the work area. When an issue was closed, the documentation was filed. A copy of the Hyper-X vehicle maintenance log book was even kept on file. Every decision was documented, and every change made was recorded. As a result, errors in configuration control, investigators determined, did not enter into the mishap.[9]

Once testing activities were complete, the project team had to be prepared for the flight itself. This was accomplished through emergency procedures training. These simulations were critical, as controllers needed to know how to identify and deal with whatever situation might develop, with reporting procedures, and with such mundane but critical issues as the proper phrases to use in addressing a given issue.

The emergency procedures training improved considerably between Flight 1 and Flights 2 and 3. Fewer displays were used in Flight 1 simulations, and those that were used lacked many of the features of a real flight. In the three-year downtime following the loss of the first vehicle, these capabilities were expanded. To give one example, no recordings or postflight data could be generated from the Flight 1 simulations. This capability was subsequently included in the later training sessions.

The simulations were designed to accomplish several goals. They were to test controllers' knowledge of emergency procedures and the go/no-go rules, to give them an understanding of the difference between an actual abort situation and a condition caused by a single bad sensor, where a launch could still be made.

Another goal was to train controllers to remain aware of the overall situation. The hour-long flight to the launch point saw little activity, and controllers would need to remain attentive to the nearly static instrument readings during this period. In contrast, the period from L-9 minutes to the launch was frenetic. Controllers were trained through the simulations to not become so focused on a minor problem that they missed a major, but subtler issue.

One change made in the course of the training was to eliminate the distinction between nominal mission simulations and emergency procedures training. Controllers were showing signs of complacency during a nominal mission simulation, to the extent that some were not bringing their flight cards with them to the exercise. When a problem was sprung on them during the nominal simulation, they regarded it as a computer anomaly rather than a "real" malfunction and ignored it. Their responses indicated to mission managers that the controllers did not expect such a problem to occur and so did not prepare for it. To correct this, future simulations were never identified as nominal or emergency procedures, keeping the controllers alert.

An important lesson learned from the emergency procedures training was the value of identifying problems with go/no-go rules and flight cards. On several occasions a simulation would be followed by lengthy discussion about how an ambiguous problem should be handled during a real launch. The simulations also contributed to improvements in controllers' responses and communications and control-room displays, and verified operational equipment and calibration coefficients. Finally, the simulations were a timely way of training controllers, without interfering with their normal day-to-day duties with the Hyper-X project.[10]

The emergency procedures training proved its worth during the B-52B fuel-transfer problems on the second flight. The solution was identified by controllers, as well as by the flight crew, and the launch was successful. None of the serious failures simulated in the emergency procedure training came to pass. The stack never had to be jettisoned, nor did a fire ever break out in the vehicle. But the harder one trains, the easier the task becomes.

With the Hyper-X project, however, the role of the ground controllers was far more limited than in either manned space missions or missions with unmanned satellites or deep-space probes. This was because, unlike previous unmanned research vehicles, the HXLV and X-43A had no manual backup system. Once the hooks were released, controllers had no control over the vehicle or its systems, and there was no human pilot on the ground who could take over if the electronics failed. This was akin to a rocket carrying a satellite, in which the only option was to send the destruct command in the event of a failure. The X-43A was an *autonomous* aerial vehicle, not a remotely piloted one. The onboard systems and software had to perform autonomously in any foreseeable contingency, without external intervention. In the future, such autonomous vehicles—both air and space—might become more common.[11]

This requirement of autonomous operation for the Hyper-X project was accomplished by reliance on off-the-shelf equipment, such as Pegasus in its role as the HXLV booster. As a satellite launch vehicle, the Pegasus followed preprogrammed guidance instructions. From a practical point of view, the Pegasus was also the only logical choice as HXLV. It met the performance requirements, whereas an air-launch capability eliminated technical problems with the ground-launched booster options. The tight schedule and budget of the Hyper-X project precluded development of an all-new booster. Yet this use of off-the-shelf equipment, and more important, the Pegasus design models, also were the origins of problems leading to the loss of Flight 1.

In deciding how to accomplish the Mach 7 flights, Hyper-X engineers faced two options—off-load propellant from the Hyper-X launch vehicle or launch at the lower altitude. Each option violated one or the other of two well-established principles. Off-loading the HXLV booster violated the principle that engineers should avoid a situation where one developmental item (the X-43A) was dependent on another developmental item or system (the off-loaded booster). A reduced launch altitude, on the other hand, violated the caution that even proven systems might not work as expected when used in a new application or different operating environment.

In evaluating the choice between an off-the-shelf booster in a new operating environment or a "new" booster in standard Pegasus launch conditions, engineers had to use the information available. There wee little hard engineering data on how an off-loaded Pegasus might meet the launch requirements. But there *were* the Pegasus design models which showed that the different conditions of a 20,000-foot launch altitude could be met successfully. There was also the policy to consider the Pegasus as proved hardware. Given these assumptions and policies, it was not surprising which of the two options engineers selected.

But the mishap investigation board found the assumption that Pegasus design models were valid for the new profile to be in error. The tests with the new wind-tunnel model, with the fins that could be positioned at 2.5-degree increments, showed that there was a nonlinearity in the roll moment of the fins. This started the sequence of events that led to the loss of the first HXLV. The original wind-tunnel tests, with the five-degree increment model, had failed to indicate this nonlinearity existed. There were also errors in the Pegasus compliance model and other design tools that contributed to the accident. In retrospect, the change in launch altitude should have also led to a reexamination of the forces and moments that the HXLV would have experienced during the new profile. This was not done, however.

This situation illustrates the often-difficult process through which decisions are reached in aerospace engineering. Decisions must be made based on the best-available data, then options must be weighed, and the final actions carried out by engineers to the best of their abilities. If enough analysis and care goes into the effort, the best option will emerge. But even then, some factor might be overlooked in the process, and a mistake might be made unwittingly. There are no magic methods to be used in reaching a decision—only hard work.

Project engineers' treatment of the fin-actuation-system problem illustrates another side of the decision-making process. The addition of a second actuator seemingly provided an easy means of increasing fin torque margin, yet led to delays that nearly scuttled the project, meant endless testing and modifications, and was the source of uncertainty right up to separation about whether the entire effort would be in vain.

Yet the remedy had been rooted in good intentions. Flight 1 had failed because the dynamic pressure had been higher than predicted, causing the fin actuators to stall because they did not have enough torque to move the fins against the increased dynamic pressure and maintain control. The MIB's role was not just to identify why a failure occurred but to take a fresh look at all aspects of the project, to identify other flaws that might lead to the loss of another vehicle. Even with the 40,000-foot launch altitude, the possibility of an actuator fin stall remained.

In retrospect, the dynamic pressure on Flights 2 and 3 never approached a level that would have required this additional torque. The HXLV could have flown with the original fin actuation system and been successful. But having lost the first flight because the dynamic pressure had been underestimated, any possibility that a similar situation could reoccur had to be eliminated.[12]

The cause of the FAS latch-ups eventually was determined to be excessive electronic noise, and a solution, using electronic filters, was found for the second flight. The FAS passed the ground testing, while the fin sweep test was modified as a final check of the FAS. An accelerated schedule for the third flight was approved based on the assumption that the FAS problem had been solved. But engineers soon discovered that the issue had not, in fact, been resolved. Lot differences between components meant that the fix used for Flight 2 had to be changed for Flight 3.

Then, a new problem with the field-effect-transistor (FET) timing error indicated that the risk of failure was actually higher than had been suspected. A failure, engineers realized, could not only occur during large fin movements, but at any time once the fin actuation system were activated.

Scrapping the existing system was not an option—the Hyper-X project was operating under a finite schedule and with limited funding. A new FAS design would require time and money that was not available. And even if they had been, there was no guarantee that a new system would not have its own, entirely new, problems. Although proper procedures dictate that mission success must take priority over cost/schedule issues, the reality is that a balancing act is almost always required.

An intensive effort was launched to analyze the fin-actuation-system problems. The electronic filter was modified to accommodate the varying sensitivities of the different components, and extensive stress testing was done, but the exact cause of the latch-up was never really understood. In the end, the problem with the FAS was not so much solved as beaten into submission.

Yet despite the assessment that a FAS latch-up or field-effect-transistor timing error would occur only during the stress cases, and not in normal operation, there were doubts. The team had endured the loss of Flight 1. There was the realization as they watched the Flight 3 ascent that the next second could bring a repeat. If the FAS operated through separation, a failure after that did not matter, but if a failure occurred before separation, then all would have been in vain. Those were the two possibilities, and there would be absolutely nothing ground controllers could do to change the outcome.

As mentioned earlier, the unusual nature of the Hyper-X project also entered into the risk equation. It was an unmanned system flying over open water in a restricted test range. The probability that the stack would collide with the B-52B if an Hyper-X launch-vehicle control failure occurred at ignition was minimal. The stack would roll over into a dive and head toward an ocean impact. If a failure occurred, the mission would fail, but no loss of life would likely result.

The risk assessment would have been far different had the Hyper-X been a manned research vehicle, a second-generation shuttle, an airliner, or an operational hypersonic bomber. In these cases, single-string systems would have been unacceptable from the start. By keeping the X-43A a simple research vehicle, small in size and with limited goals, a higher level of risk would be acceptable. No pilot would be lost in the event of a failure.[13]

A subtle aspect of the fin-actuation-system problem was that it illustrated the need for an adequate supply of spare parts. The original HXLV FAS was that of a standard Pegasus unit. When the FAS was modified with a second actuator, digital drive system, and power supply, it then featured one-of-a-kind parts. When failures began to occur during preflight qualification and troubleshooting efforts, spare parts became an issue, for there was not a supply immediately on hand.

After this experience, a recommendation was made that the number of spare parts should be carefully considered in planning stages for a research vehicle, particularly in instances where existing systems would undergo major modifications. When failures begin to occur during a testing phase, it was critical that the part-supply situation be reassessed as soon as possible. If the supply of components required long lead times to produce runs short, significant schedule and cost impacts would be the inevitable result.[14]

In the Hyper-X project, this was not the only example demonstrating the need for adequate spare parts. When the delaminated carbon-carbon chine was discovered, only the availability of a spare billet that already had been through some of the heat treatment cycles allowed Flight 3 to proceed as scheduled. Had the billet not been available, the replacement chine would have had to be fabricated from scratch, causing significant schedule delays and cost increases that might may have been fatal to the project.

This incident also pointed out the importance of in-process inspections. The delamination could have been discovered early on had noninvasive tap tests or thermographic inspections been made. These tests would have raised costs, but in retrospect the long-duration manufacturing process requires that any defective parts be identified early, to prevent last-minute schedule changes.[15]

Whereas the machine gets the attention, engineering is a human activity. CNN carried video of the X-43A flights, but not of an engineer sitting at a computer terminal for eight hours analyzing the vehicle's stability at Mach 7.112. How the project turns out depends on how well that engineer does that analysis. The same is true of all of those who worked on the Hyper-X. Success depends on the management procedures, the working environment, and the skill, drive, and dedication of each individual, no matter how major or minor their role. Just as there are no unimportant parts in a single-string research vehicle, there are no unimportant people working on an aerospace project.

Some aspects of building and maintaining a team derive simply from common sense and basic good behavior among coworkers. These include recognizing accomplishments, helping team members do a good job, having dedicated communications link among all participants, co-locating people if possible, holding regular meetings, letting everyone know what is going on and why, and having the vendors of critical hardware/software on site for the testing process. Finally, and perhaps most important, finger pointing is not allowed. In the event of failure, the goal was simple: fix the problems, and then go fly.[16]

Several examples of these basic tenets are illustrated by the Hyper-X project. The configuration control board and engineering review board meetings were held in a large conference room at Dryden. These often did not have the formality one might expect. Grindle recalled that she ran the weekly configuration control board meetings from a seat on the side of the conference-room table, rather than the head of the table. There was not a seat reserved for Joel Sitz. Instead, people sat where they wanted to, either at the table or along the walls. It was a cohesive team that got along well together. On one wall of the conference room was the complete fault tree for the loss of the first flight. This sheet of paper stretched from the ceiling to the floor, and across much of the length of the room. During meetings, project status was updated, problems were discussed, individuals were assigned tasks to complete, and open items were dealt with. As a result, communications among participants was ensured, and all were kept abreast of developments.[17]

Both NASA and contractor personnel attended these meetings, just as they worked side by side on the project. Dryden's history has been marked by this partnership between civil service personnel and contractors working together. During the past two or three decades, however, the balance between civil service and contractor employees had shifted, with contractors outnumbering civil servants. The Hyper-X project was able to achieve a true integration of the work force. This was achieved through decisions large and small, from who would undertake analyses of design issues on down to the checkout of the vehicles before launch.[18]

In terms of avoiding finger pointing, the clearest example was Orbital Science's Phil Joyce, project manager for the contractor that built the HXLV, who stood up at the meeting immediately following the loss of the first flight and accepting responsibility for the failure.

In today's risk-averse America, the idea that failure is inevitable and a key element in achieving success finds little favor. To say "failure is good" is to risk being branded as a heretic. But the history of technology is replete with examples of failure as a path to success. Before the Wright brothers, many had attempted to fly a heavier-than-air craft, yet all had failed. Otto Lilienthal and Percy Pilcher had died in their quest to fly. What the Wrights did was to learn from their failures and to separate a few solid facts from the mass of suppositions and dead ends. From this small seed, they began to build a series of gliders. Each of these glider tests was marked by repeated failures, but each new glider built on the knowledge gained from the previous aircraft. By early 1903, from both the glider flights and wind-tunnel research, they had the data on lift, drag, stability, and control needed to build an aircraft large enough to carry a pilot and engine. They had accomplished in four years a task that had eluded humanity for centuries.

In contrast, the early scramjet efforts kept making the same mistakes over and over again. These included taking small-scale experiments and projecting huge vehicles able to fly directly into orbit, that used engines that did not exist, which were built from materials that had yet to be developed, and depended on systems that existed only as ideas. Again and again, the promoters' optimism and the potential of their ideas exceeded the existing technology, virtually repeating the early heavier-than-air attempts at flight, ironically.

What the Hyper-X project did was to take the data that this dysfunctional process had produced and to apply it to the basic question that had yet to be answered—will a scramjet work in flight? It did not attempt to build an operational vehicle. Instead, it was to serve as a technological demonstrator. More important, it showed the lessons from the previous, failed attempts, had finally been learned. Yet even when a practical, well-thought-out approach was finally taken, the Hyper-X still suffered delays, failures, and difficulties.

Rocketry in the 1960s gave an example of how failure played a role in the development of a new and emerging technology. The Scout rocket was a small four-stage solid-fuel booster developed to launch small satellite payloads at low cost. The project had a very high early failure rate, which was traced to numerous failures in quality control, standardization, and the speed at which the project was undertaken. A 14-month reliability program was undertaken to correct the shortcomings. Following this effort, the Scout became a highly successful booster.

Eugene Schult, looking back on his difficult experiences with the Scout's guidance and control systems, observed,

> We wouldn't learn anything if we didn't have problems; that's basic in engineering training. Success doesn't tell us anything. It doesn't tell us where the limits are, or what the limiting aspects of the envelope are. But when you hit a mistake, you dig into it and you find out there's a weakness. And by curing weaknesses you get success.[19]

Schult's comments are something no engineering student should leave school without both learning and understanding. It is equally important that the public at large understand the difficulties of research and development efforts. In any project there will be problems and setbacks—even deaths.

If a project is terminated at the first sign of trouble, then technological advancement will halt, and human society will stagnate and decay.[20]

Another aspect of engineering is that it is rarely a nine-to-five job. Although it is good to remember that people (and their families) have a life away from work, there are times when 12-hour shifts are part and parcel of the job, and weeks or even months at a time away from home at a temporary duty station are the norm. On the Hyper-X project, personnel were working weekends and holidays beginning in the spring of 2004 to get Flight 3 ready. In this case, life had to be put on hold. The issue was not taking time off, or the real possibility of the third flight never being made.[21]

This is the balancing act between the responsibilities to one's family, the responsibilities to one's coworkers, and one's own well-being. The engineer's spouse and children can find themselves unwilling participants in a project. Perhaps the best approach for an engineer is to make them part of the project from the start, to show them what he or she will be working on and to let them understand the engineer's interest and excitement in the project. That way, they will understand the inevitable missed birthdays, school graduations, and wedding anniversaries.[22]

The Hyper-X project served as a training ground for a new generation of scramjet and hypersonic researchers, many of them right out of school. This new crop included civil service as well as contractor personnel, providing them with experience in ground testing and component development; vehicle design, construction, integration, and system checkout; and, ultimately, flight testing and data analysis. Additionally, researchers learned the practical details of managing a project within finite budget and time limits, about the ambiguousness of risk assessment, and about the need to spend a significant amount of time and effort dealing with engineering problems, such as those with the fin actuation system, that ostensibly have little to do with the project's research goals.

Finally, all of those who worked on the X-43A project now know what it is like to spend years transforming an idea into a functional vehicle, only for it to be lost in a matter of seconds—and then to undergo years of work correcting problems, to face the possibility that still more might exist, and finally to savor the triumph of two successful flights. For those who were part of the Hyper-X effort, these experiences might prove to be the most valuable lesson learned.[23]

TO THE FAR HORIZON

In the years after the Hyper-X's successful demonstration of a scramjet, there has been a resurgence of interest in hypersonic research and high-speed airbreathing propulsion systems. Unlike in the overly ambitious National

Aerospace Plane project, this new interest has taken the form of either tests of different aspects of scramjet technology or small-scale air- or ground-launched vehicle tests. These efforts are extensions of the work begun in the X-43A project.

Although the X-43A was groundbreaking in that it demonstrated a scramjet in flight, there remains much to be done. Burn times must be extended from seconds to minutes and then to hours. The size and thrust of the scramjet must be increased from those of a subscale demonstrator to engines capable of propelling an operational vehicle. There are also the challenges of materials, heat protection, life support, control systems, human factors, and the rest of an operational vehicle's myriad requirements. At present, scramjet technology requires extensive testing and checkout, and a large work force to prepare a vehicle for flight. It is still a young technology, despite the decades spent reaching this point. Much remains to be discovered. And the dragons still await mistakes or flaws.

But the same was true 101 years before the X-43A made its successful flights. We can see that moment—when the dream was realized, when history changed, and when the future took another form—preserved in a single glass photographic plate.

There, in that photo, it is always 10:35 a.m. on December 17, 1903, at Kitty Hawk, North Carolina. The footprints in the sand are still there in the foreground, along with the small bench used to steady the wing, and a shovel, can, and battery. There too is the launch rail and the cart that is about to roll off the end of the rail. Wilbur Wright, in a dark suit and cap, is frozen in place, as he witnesses the impossible. Orville Wright, also in dark clothing, is stretched out on the lower wing, his right hand pulling back on the control stick. The Wright Flyer's forward elevator is pitched up, while the twin rudder at the aft end is centered. The aircraft is rolling slightly to the left. The two propellers are a blur. The fabric-covered wings are bright white against the colorless sand and sky. The skids are about three feet above the sand. The Wright Flyer is under control, it is stable, and it is *flying*.

The four flights the Wright brothers made that morning did not go very far, were not very fast, and not very high. But without question, they were flights. And there is something else in that picture. The eye is drawn to it. In the far distance, ground and sky meet at the horizon. That far horizon is the Wright's destination.

Throughout the 20th century, generations of engineers and pilots continued their quest. They faced many challenges in that century and endured countless, wrenching setbacks and failures. But the successes were greater and greater. Wood and fabric gave way to metal and then to composites. Piston engines were replaced by jet engines, while speeds went from tens of miles per hour to hundreds, and then to thousands. Altitudes increased from a few feet to space itself. Within three decades or so of the Wrights' first flights, the atmosphere became permanently occupied by humans; by the close of heavier-than-air flight's first century, space was, as well.

Just as the Wright Flyer introduced the first century of flight, the X-43A ushered in its second. Soon, you will become the latest in that long line of aerospace engineers, stretching back across more than a century to the Wright brothers. Soon, it will be you who will turn dreams into reality. Like those earlier engineers, you do not yet know the challenges you will face, the failures you will suffer, and the triumphs you will achieve.

The far horizon waits.

NOTES

[1]Grindle, Laurie, history interview, tape no. 4, Jan. 20, 2005, NASA Dryden Flight Research Center History Office, pp. 4–8.

[2]"Air Force Rocket Laboratory X-43A Data Briefing," p. 38, and X-43A "Flight #3 Fact Sheet," p. 4.

[3]Personal observations by the author while an astronomy major at San Diego State University, 1976–1978.

[4]The Hypersonic Revolution Case Studies in the History of Hypersonic Technology, Vol. III, edited by Larry Schweikart, Air Force History and Museum Program, Bolling AFB, Washington, DC, 1998, pp. 234, 235.

[5]Sherrill, R. T., "Thoughts on the Development of Flight Test Equipment," Oct. 14, 1999.

[6]Marshall, Laurie, Catherine Bahm, and Griff Corpening, "Overview with Results and Lessons Learned of the X-43A Mach 10 Flight," AIAA Paper 2005-3336, p. 22.

[7]Ibid, p. 22, and Yohan Lin interview, Dec. 12, 2006.

[8]"Flight Testing Lessons" summary from a JANNAF Workshop in Oct. 1999. This is the complete list:

General

- Avoid too many firsts on a flight test.
- Need a simple system design.
- If in doubt, pick up the phone and call. Don't rely on e-mail or faxes.
- Use e-mail only for information exchange, not to debate issues.
- The time to change a plan is not in the heat of battle.
- Be careful who you listen to—"People who ain't paying don't care about the cost."
- Recognize accomplishments.
- People have a life away from work.
- Help people do a good job.
- Hold people accountable.
- Off-the-shelf rarely is.
- Everyone must be a systems engineer.
- Arrogance is the enemy.
- There are no magic solutions, only diligence.
- Be careful of lists, rules, and general practices and procedures.
- No finger-pointing allowed—learn from all issues.
- Avoid flight testing where one developmental item is dependent on another developmental item or system.

Program Management

- Need one person in charge—program manager.
- Define a chain of command.
- Establish and maintain a risk-reduction process.
- Budget cuts or schedule acceleration means increased risk.
- Mission success must be priority over cost/schedule.
- Relax a test plan to meet a schedule only at great peril.
- Establish dedicated communications link between all participants.
- Co-locate people if possible.
- Hold regular meetings.
- Make everything available electronically.
- Make everyone use the same software.
- Manage by walking around.
- Set up a rigorous method to capture lessons learned.
- Let everyone know what's going on and why.
- Document key decisions.
- Get vendors of critical hardware/software on site for testing.

System Engineering

- Need one person in charge of technical details—system engineer.
- Safety must be involved early on in the design.
- Focus the risk on the technologies to be proven.
- Even proven, production hardware might not provide what you expect in a new application or environment.
- Quantify reliability of components and controlling software.
- Ensure software changes are thoroughly tested.
- Pretest hardware and software to extremes.
- Pay attention to all areas of system, even if not changed.
- You cannot overtest software or electronics.
- Maintain configuration control between ground and flight tests.
- Assume things will go wrong in the field. Know how to recover.
- Update documents regularly.
- Maintain a good paper trail—log books, engineering workbooks, etc.
- Specify the required qualification, acceptance, verification, and/or validation testing required.
- Simulation is critical.
- Use a step-wise approach to performance testing.
- Do a thorough integration of subsystems into the test vehicle.
- Never use HWIL as a tool for debugging, only for verification.
- Use logic flow diagrams for scheduling.
- Plan a heavy concentration of up-front work.
- Account for all critical components under a major subsystem.
- Avoid wearing out hardware prior to flight tests.
- Ground-test hardware and software must replicate flight-test articles.
- Review all of the data, even from the tests that look good.

Test Preparation/Readiness

- Clearly lay out test requirements—be specific.
- Get test range involved early—get them requirements ASAP.
- Visit test range early.

- "Improve" on what range wants to provide.
- Develop instrumentation and measurement techniques early.
- The debris field might be larger than you think. If the test is terminated or if parts are released at high altitude, parts, especially those that are lightweight, can drift quite a ways. Also need to be wary of aircraft flying through the area.
- Use a check list—don't skip steps.
- Have dress rehearsals

[9]Soden, Linda, telephone interview, Dec. 18, 2006.

[10]Lux-Baumann, Jessica, Ray Dees, and David Fratello, "Control Room Training for the Hyper-X Project Utilizing Aircraft Simulation," NASA/TM-2006-213685, Nov. 2006, pp. 11–17.

[11]This potential use of autonomous vehicles could apply to hypersonic aircraft, where events are happening too fast for a traditional ground pilot, or for space probes where the round-trip time delay for a signal is too long for manual control from Earth to be effective.

[12]Reukauf, Paul, history interview, Feb. 17, 2005, NASA Dryden History Office, p. 73, and "Flight Testing Lessons."

[13]"Flight Testing Lessons."

[14]Brown, Jonathan, "Lessons Learned Entry 1602, Subject Fin Actuator (FAS) Redesign Implementation/Spares," NASA Lessons Learned Knowledge Network.

[15]Marshall et al., "Overview with Results and Lessons Learned of the X-43A Mach 10 Flight," AIAA Paper 2005-3336, p. 22.

[16]"Flight Testing Lessons."

[17]Grindle, Laurie, chapter comments, and Curtis Peebles X-43A notes.

[18]Peebles, Curtis, X-43A notes. To give some examples of the divisions of authority, only a NASA employee could issue the order to destroy a vehicle should a malfunction occur. However, technically a NASA employee cannot give an order to a contractor, as the latter is under the authority of his company supervisor, not of NASA. A critical aspect of creating an integrated team is not letting such issues get in the way, while still following procedures.

[19]Hansen, James R., "Learning Through Failure," National Form (Winter 2001), http://www.findarticles.com/p/ search?tb=art&qt=%22Hansen%2C+James+R%22.

[20]Gelzer, Christian, review notes to Chapter 4 and discussions.

[21]Grindle, Laurie, history interview, tape no. 3, Jan. 20, 2006, NASA Dryden Flight Research Center History Office, pp. 19, 20.

[22]Involving family members in the details of the Hyper-X project was not a problem, as only a limited amount of information was classified. For an engineer working on a "black" project, however, this is not an option.

[23]Peebles X-43A notes, p. 1.

INDEX

SUPPORTING MATERIALS

Many of the topics introduced in this book are discussed in more detail in other AIAA publications. For a complete listing of titles in the AIAA Library of Flight series, as well as other AIAA publications, please visit http://www.aiaa.org.

The Disc accompanying this book contains the following supporting materials.

X-43A RELATED PAPERS AND REPORTS

The following papers and reports are included on the disc; file names are listed in bold type.

Bahm, C. et al., "The X-43A Hyper-X Mach 7 Flight 2 Guidance, Navigation, and Control Overview and Flight Test Results" (**AIAA 2005-3275**).

Bakos, R. J. et al., "The Mach 10 Component of NASA's Hyper-X Ground Test Program" (**NASA-99-M-10 ground tests**).

Blocker, W. D. and Reubush, D. E., "X-43A Stage Separation System— A Flight Data Evaluation" (**AIAA 2005-3335**).

Bui, T. T. et al., "New Air-Launched Small Missile (ALSM) Flight Testbed for Hypersonic Systems" (**Phoenix scramjet**).

Buning, P. G. et al., "Prediction of Hyper-X Stage Separation Aerodynamics Using CFD" (**AIAA 2000-4009**).

Cockrell, C. E., Jr. et al., "Integrated Aero-Propulsive CFD Methodology for the Hyper-X Flight Experiment" (**AIAA 2000-4010**).

Davidson, J. et al., "Flight Control Laws for NASA's Hyper-X Research Vehicle" (**AIAA 99-4124**).

Ferlemann, P. G., "Comparison of Hyper-X Mach 10 Scramjet Preflight Predictions and Flight Data" (**AIAA 2005-3352**).

Ferlemann, S. M. et al., "Hyper-X Mach 7 Scramjet Design, Ground Test and Flight Results" (**AIAA 2005-3322**).

Freeman, D. C., Jr. et al., "The NASA Hyper-X Program" (**NASA-97-HX overview**).

Harsha, P. T. et al., "X-43A Vehicle Design and Manufacture" (**AIAA 2005-3334**).

Huebner, L. D. et al., "Hyper-X Engine Testing in the NASA Langley 8-Foot High Temperature Tunnel" (**AIAA 2000-3605**).

Huebner, L. D. et al., "Hyper-X Flight Engine Ground Testing for X-43 Flight Risk Reduction" (**AIAA 2001-1809**).

Hunt, J. L. and McClinton, C. R., "Scramjet Engine/Airframe Integration Methodology" (NASA-97-engine integration).

Joyce, P. J. et al., "The Hyper-X Launch Vehicle: Challenges and Design Considerations for Hypersonic Flight Testing" (AIAA 2005-3333).

Ko, W. L. and Gong, L., "Thermostructural Analysis of Unconventional Wing Structures of a Hyper-X Hypersonic Flight Research Vehicle for the Mach 7 Mission" (NASA/TP-2001-210398).

Leonard, C. P. et al., "Hyper-X Hot Structures Design and Comparison with Flight Data" (AIAA 2005-3438).

Marshall, L. A. et al., "A Chief Engineer's View of the NASA X-43A Scramjet Flight Test" (AIAA 2005-3332).

Marshall, L. A. et al., "Overview with Results and Lessons Learned of the X-43A Mach 10 Flight" (AIAA 2005-3336).

McClinton, C. R. et al., "Hyper-X Wind Tunnel Program" (AIAA 98-0553).

Rausch, V. L. et al., "Hyper-X: Flight Validation of Hypersonic Airbreathing Technology" (NASA-97-HX validation).

Reubush, D. E. et al., "Hyper-X Stage Separation—Simulation Development and Results" (AIAA 2001-1802).

Reubush, D. E. et al., "Review of X-43A Return to Flight Activities and Current Status" (NASA-2003-RTF).

Reubush, D. E., "Hyper-X Stage Separation—Background and Status" (AIAA 99-4818).

Rogers, R. C. et al., "Scramjet Development Tests Supporting the Mach 10 Flight of the X-43" (AIAA 2005-3351).

Vachon, M. J. et al., "X-43A Fluid and Environmental Systems: Ground and Flight Operation and Lessons Learned" (AIAA 2005-3337).

Voland, R. T. et al., "Hyper-X Engine Design and Ground Test Program" (AIAA 98-1532).

"X-43A—Emergency Procedures" (EP-Rev T).

X-43A Mishap Investigation Board, "Report of Findings: X-43A Mishap," Vol. 1 (X-43A Mishap).

X-43A/HYPER-X FLIGHTS I AND II

A split screen video of the flights is included on the disc.

X-43A MACH 10 FINAL FLIGHT

Video highlights of the final flight mission, including preparation stages, animated scenes, and a tribute to project team members, also are on the disc.